WONDERS
OF THE
WORLD

WONDERS OF THE WORLD

Simon Goldhill,
Richard Barber, Theodore K. Rabb
and Jonathan Glancey

LONDON *The Folio Society* MMVI

Front endpaper: aerial view of the Pyramids of Khufu and Khafre,
Giza, built twenty-sixth century BC. (© *Reza; Webistan/CORBIS*)

Rear endpaper: particle tracks from proton–anti-proton collision,
1985. (*Cavendish Laboratory UA5 Experiment, CERN/
David Parker/Science Photo Library*)

Slipcase: the Great Sphinx and the pyramid of Khafre,
Giza, built twenty-sixth century BC.
(*Dagli Orti/The Art Archive*)

TYPESET AT THE FOLIO SOCIETY IN JANSON.
COLOUR REPRODUCTION BY DOT GRADATIONS LTD, UK
PRINTED AT CPI BATH, GLASGOW, ON LUMIMATT PAPER.
BOUND BY THE BATH PRESS, BATH, IN FULL BUCKRAM
BLOCKED WITH A DESIGN BY NEIL GOWER

CONTENTS

INTRODUCTION

Simon Goldhill

THIS BOOK is motivated by two of the most basic human responses to the world. The first is *wonder*. 'Wonder is the beginning of philosophy,' said Socrates, a man who died for his philosophical principles. And Plato and Aristotle agreed. For the great philosophers, philosophy is the crowning triumph of human achievement, and it finds its origin in the moment of bafflement and awe a human feels when faced by the amazing sights of nature. Wonder is the beginning of asking how and why. For nearly 2,500 years this idea has been repeated. So Francis Bacon, the greatest of English Renaissance scientific minds, called wonder 'the seed of knowledge', and Ralph Waldo Emerson, in the newly emergent society of nineteenth-century America, gave his own twist to the thought when he wrote, 'All men love to wonder and that is the seed of our science.' Amazement at the world is the motor of human curiosity and progress.

Wonder not only prompts science and philosophy, but also the emotions of religion. Thomas Carlyle, one of the most influential of Victorian thinkers, writes: 'Worship is transcendent wonder.' As the book of Exodus sums up the Israelites' escape from Egypt, 'When Israel saw the wondrous power which the Lord had wielded against the Egyptians, the people feared the Lord and had faith in the Lord.' The wonders of the Lord demand fear and faith. The Gospels and the Lives of the Saints repeatedly record the response of the disciples and the crowd to the miracles of Jesus and the calm suffering of the saints: 'and they were amazed'. The fear, awe and confusion of ordinary people at the extraordinary events before them are a fundamental sign of the recognition of the divine. When the world is seen as God's creation, then amazement at the world is itself a feeling of religious wonder. That is why Carlyle can write: 'The man who cannot wonder, and does not habitually wonder (and worship) . . . is but a pair of spectacles, behind which there is no Eye.' For Carlyle, if you do not look at the world with wonder, you do not have eyes to see, and (with a common enough pun) you cannot be a real 'I', a truly living and feeling person.

Carlyle thought that the worship of great men – heroes – was and should be a driving force of history (no surprise that it was Carlyle that was still being read to Hitler in his last days in the bunker). But a different, more enchanting kind of wonder at other people motivates the

Centuries of wonder: astronomers at the top of Mount Athos, in the *Picturebook of Sir John Mandeville's Travels, c.*1410

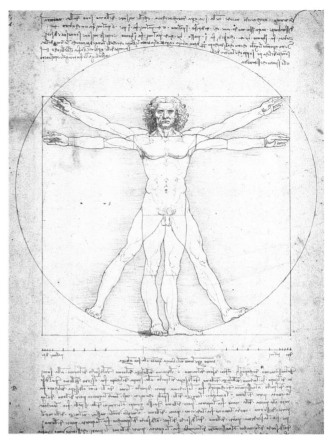

Girl with a Pearl Earring, by Vermeer, *c.*1665

'Vitruvian Man', by Leonardo da Vinci, 1490

glorious and infinitely long tradition of love poetry: wonder runs through every love story ('I wonder by my troth, what you and I did till we loved' is John Donne's marvellous opening to a lyric to his lover; ''Swonderful, 'smarvellous...' is Gershwin's). In visual art, too, the desire to capture the wonders of the physical world, and to see beyond them, has led to Vermeer's attempt to catch the flicker of light in the pearl in a girl's earring, or to Leonardo da Vinci's obsessive anatomising of the human body, or Turner's swirling seascapes. Art, too, begins with the transfixed stare of wonder.

Behind science, philosophy, worship, art, poetry, sits human wonder, and with it the human need not just to stand in awe but also to ask why and how, to record, to explore. This book is an invitation to participate in the history of wonder in more than one way. It is, first, to look at and explore with us some of the most amazing human achievements over the centuries of civilisation. From the ancient and huge Pyramids to the modern and tiny silicon chip, humans have created objects that are simply amazing. This book takes us on a tour around this truly wonderful panoply of artistic, literary, architectural and scientific achievement. Second, however, every one of these wonders is itself a response to the world that stems from human wonder. The Pyramids are grand, religious and political responses to the crisis of death, and the pharaohs' monumental hope for immortality – a human attempt to come to terms with fearful wonder at the mystery of mortality. The silicon chip is one result of the extraordinary new understanding of the physical world which modern science has provided, from quantum physics to the genetic code. Einstein's wonder at the behaviour of light led to his foundational contribution to modern physics, just as Watson and Crick's amazement at the molecular order of the world gave rise to the discovery of DNA. Our tour of the wonders of the world is not just an opportunity for some touristy gawping, but an attempt to understand the how and why of these monuments.

The second basic human response to the world that motivates this book is the list. This may sound frivolous or facetious, especially when almost every Sunday newspaper these days has an article called 'Ten Things to Do on a Wet Thursday', or 'Fifty Best Kitchen Gadgets'. But it is a striking fact that as soon as writing is invented, humans do three things. They write their names on things, they write rude graffiti and they write lists. Lists are a primary means of ordering the world, of recording property in a systematic way, of maintaining the genealogies which give family history. That is, without lists society would lack its own history as well as its principle of organisation. If wonder is an awestruck feeling of amazement, a list is a much calmer way of putting some order into a response to the world.

Each of the scholars who has contributed to this book was asked to produce a list of the seven great wonders of the world for his own period – the ancient world, the medieval world, the Renaissance world and the modern world. The only restrictions were that each wonder should be man-made and still exist. Each of us has found this task daunting in that there are some impossible choices to be made, but it has also been surprisingly good fun and a surprisingly provocative and reflective project. Just as choosing eight favourite pieces of music for a desert island involves a revealing process of self-representation, a biography through music rather than just a question of individual taste, so each chapter here also presents a history of the period in question, and each selection reveals a personal take on what counts in culture. And just as when you hear someone else's choice of music for a desert island, so, too, here there are some surprises, a few challenges and the opportunity to think what your different list would include.

The idea of a list of the seven wonders of the world is, of course, an ancient one. The lists varied slightly, but settled eventually on the Great Pyramid of Egypt, the Hanging Gardens of Babylon, the Statue of Zeus at Olympia, the Temple of Artemis at Ephesus, the Mausoleum of Halicarnassus, the Colossus of Rhodes and the Lighthouse of Alexandria. Only the Great Pyramid survives standing today, and there was barely any moment when all these wonders could have been viewed by one

The Hanging Gardens of Babylon, as imagined by Athanasius Kircher, *Turris Babel*, 1679

Ruins of the Temple of Artemis, Ephesus, in modern-day Turkey

person: the Colossus only stood for fifty-six years, before an earthquake tumbled it. The Temple of Artemis was actually three different buildings, rebuilt each time after destruction. But the words 'mausoleum', 'colossus' and 'pyramid' have entered the English language, and Pharos, the name of the Alexandrian Lighthouse, is used in most Mediterranean languages for 'lighthouse'. Each one of these wonders has a long and continuing life in the human imagination.

The Great Pyramid of Egypt is discussed in the first chapter: it is the oldest of all these wonders and part of its awesomeness comes from its combination of huge size, immense age and powerful religious aura. The Hanging Gardens of Babylon were built by Nebuchadnezzar II, the king who destroyed the Temple in Jerusalem and founded the Babylonian empire. The gardens were built, the story goes, to cheer up his queen Anyitis, who was pining on the parched plain of Babylon for her mountainous and wooded homeland. The gardens were a series of vaulted terraces, planted with overhanging trees and bushes, which rose perhaps to 320 feet (98 m) (that's the figure given by Herodotus, the earliest of the Greek historians) – a mountain of green in the sun-baked capital. They were watered by a remarkable series of water pumps, and it was the irrigation system as much as anything that impressed Greek visitors over the centuries.

The Temple of Artemis in Ephesus was the central building of the Greek-speaking eastern Mediterranean. It acted as a bank as well as a religious temple. The first large-scale temple on this site was built by Croesus, the famously rich king of Lydia, to a design of Theodorus in the sixth century BC. It was already one of the largest buildings of the world. It was destroyed by a man called Herostratus in 356 BC, who burnt the building down so that his name should be remembered for ever. The Ephesians made it illegal to mention his name, but his terrorism worked, and he is still remembered for this one act of barbaric vandalism. The temple was rebuilt to a design by Scopas. It was said to be the first temple solely in marble, and was huge – four times the size of the Parthenon. It was here that St Paul preached to the Ephesians, though stories in the Acts that the temple was destroyed by his Christian mission are no more than wishful Christian thinking. The temple stood in its impressive splendour until it was destroyed by the Goths in AD 262.

The most celebrated ancient temple statue was that of Zeus at Olympia, designed by the great sculptor Pheidias, who also was responsible for the sculptures for the Parthenon (including the so-called Elgin Marbles). Zeus sat on a throne, with a winged Victory on one outstretched hand, a spear in the other. The statue was more than 40 feet (12 m) high. 'If he stood up,' wrote one ancient Greek author, 'he would lift the roof.' The statue was made from ivory and gold. But for the Greek viewers it was not the lavishness of the sculpture that impressed, but its dignity and sense of supreme authority. It was an icon of the power of the

The statue of Zeus at Olympia, a fanciful depiction based on descriptions by Pausanias, 1792

The Colossus of Rhodes, as imagined by Johann Bernhard Fischer von Erlach, *c.*1700

gods, here in a temple, at the centre of Greek competitive athletics. This statue stood in Olympia until the fifth century AD, when the Christian emperor banned the Olympics. It was taken to Constantinople where it was destroyed in a fire.

The Colossus at Rhodes was also a huge statue, but unlike the Statue of Zeus which lasted a millennium, this work survived for only fifty-six years. This bronze statue of the god Helios, the Sun god, stood at the entrance to the harbour of the island of Rhodes. It was designed by Chares of Lindos (who was said to have killed himself when a flaw in the design was revealed to him) and was built to celebrate the freedom of the island, after it managed to repel invaders: it was built out of the melted-down metal from the enemies' siege engines. The statue was 110 feet (34 m) high (a few feet shorter than the Statue of Liberty in New York) and had a pedestal of another 50 feet (15 m). (The Statue of Liberty, with its raised arm and huge pedestal, would in fact dwarf the Colossus.) There is no evidence at all that the Colossus had open legs through which ships could sail – a late Romantic fantasy. It fell in an earthquake. There it lay in pieces along the harbour front where it was still marvelled at by Roman visitors for centuries to come – but finally the pieces were broken up and sold as scrap metal by Arabs when they conquered Rhodes in the seventh century.

Pharos of Alexandria was designed in the third century BC by Sostrates of Knidos, and it stood at least until the twelfth century AD. Its ruins were rediscovered by divers in the late 1990s, and it is hoped that at

least a museum will arise from the ashes of this wonder. Sostrates' story offers a nice twist on the common desire for immortality through monumentality that runs through these wonders. He wanted as the designer to put his name on the lighthouse. The ruler Ptolemy refused permission. So Sostrates carved an inscription on the foundation announcing that he made this work as a dedication to the gods on behalf of sailors, and then plastered over the inscription, on top of which was recorded Ptolemy's name. As the years passed, the plaster crumbled, leaving Sostrates' name shining forth. The Lighthouse rose in three stages, a large base of marble blocks (as high as 200 feet (61 m)), then an eight-sided tower, and on top of the tower a cylinder with an open cupola on top. When it was built, the only taller building in the world was the Great Pyramid, and it served as a working – and essential – lighthouse for the new city of Alexandria for many centuries.

The final wonder on the ancient list is the most personal, a tomb for King Mausolus, built by his wife Artemisia. It was designed by Scopas, who also built the Temple of Artemis, to be the grandest tomb in the world. It stood on a hill above the city of Halicarnassus. Enclosed in a courtyard and approached by a monumental ramp, the tomb was built on three levels. A square tomb, nearly 50 feet (15 m) high, was covered in beautiful sculptures on mythic themes (many of the greatest sculptures had been brought in from Greece along with Scopas, as well as hundreds

The Pharos Lighthouse, Alexandria, built under Ptolemy II 280/279 BC, as imagined by Johann Bernhard Fischer von Erlach, c.1700

Colossal statue of a man traditionally identified as Mausolus, from the Mausoleum at Halicarnassus. Marble, by a Greek sculptor, c.350 BC

Imaginary reconstruction of the tomb of King Mausolus at Halicarnassus, by Johann Bernhard Fischer von Erlach, c.1700

of local workmen). On top of this were thirty-six columns concealing the tomb's roof, and between each column stood a sculpture. Above these columns rose a stepped pyramid (again around 50 feet (15 m) in height) on top of which was a monumental sculpture of Artemisia and Mausolus himself in a chariot pulled by four horses. This was a stunning work of art, which stood proudly for nearly seventeen centuries. It was first partially destroyed by earthquakes, then it was plundered by the Crusaders, who continued to grind down its marble sculptures for lime and take away marble blocks for the fortress at Bodrun (where they can still be seen). But amazingly Charles Newton, a Victorian archaeologist, rediscovered the site nearly five hundred years later, and found not only the foundations of the buildings and fragments of its construction, but also the two statues of Mausolus and Artemisia from the crowning sculpture, which can still be seen in the British Museum in London.

These seven wonders embody many of the themes that will return throughout this book. First, a certain grandeur and majesty of scale link several of these monuments. The Great Pyramid is the largest building in the world for centuries, and continues to dominate its landscape in an awe-inspiring fashion. The Colossus becomes a byword for sheer size, the largest sculpture of its age. The Mausoleum is the grandest tomb ever, the Temple of Artemis the largest temple, the Pharos of Alexandria the tallest tower in the world. Size does matter. But, second, there is also in these monuments a desire for immortality, for preserving the name and reputation of great men and women. The Great Pyramid originally held the mortal remains of the pharaoh Khufu, whose soul travelled via the Pyramid's complex of ritual and buildings to the other world, and the whole stands as a monument to the preservation of his memory. The Mausoleum preserves and celebrates the rule of Mausolus and Artemisia, as king and queen, husband and wife, figures who helped spread Greek culture in Asia Minor. The names of Scopas, Pheidias and the other artists associated with such projects are recorded because of the beauty of their work, and the work stands as a memorial for them. These works defy the transience and fragility of human life. Third, these are also icons of human scientific ingenuity and skill. The Hanging Gardens of Babylon made a mountainous green garden in a desert plain, to soothe a queen's longing for her homeland. The romantic image depends on water engineers of real expertise and daring ambition. The Pharos was a working lighthouse that was central to the economic and mercantile strength of the fastest-growing urban space in the ancient world. These works embody man's ambition to control nature and the world around him. Fourth, these works are also touched not just by man's ambition but by a relation to the divine: the Temple of Artemis may have functioned as a bank, but it was primarily a centre of religious worship. The Statue of Zeus inspired worshippers from across Greece with the authority of Zeus the king. Each expresses the sense of something grander than man. Fifth, these are works that deserve to be called 'works of art'. The Mausoleum, the Statue of Zeus and the Temple of Artemis were made by famous artists and architects, whose names we know. But all the works in question impressed their viewers with a profound sense of beauty. They all produced reactions of amazement, and also of deep pleasure. None was in an art gallery or set up just as an aesthetic object: even the Colossus was there as a political symbol to celebrate freedom. But for each, beauty is a fundamental aspect of their status as wonders.

Yet what makes these works wonders of the ancient world is not any one of these qualities, but the combination of scale, function, beauty with a numinous power that overwhelms the spectator with a sense of awe at human achievement and ambition. Even when these works celebrate the divine or act as testimony to the fragility of human capabilities, there is a sense that, when we observe these marvels, we can say with Sophocles, the Greek tragic playwright, 'There are many awesome things, but none more awesome than man.'

The four sections of this book are as varied as the wonders they depict, but they do follow some of these general categories. We see huge and staggeringly beautiful buildings dedicated to the divine, from the Parthenon in ancient Athens, to Hagia Sophia in medieval Istanbul, to the Piazza di San Pietro in Renaissance Rome. We see secular buildings of similar grandeur from a Renaissance palace like Versailles to the modern glory of the New York City skyline. We discuss scientific inventions that changed the world, from the alphabet in the ancient world to the particle accelerator at CERN near Berne and the model of the DNA double helix – and more practical objects like the Forth Railway Bridge as well as objects whose beauty is as impressive as its practicality, such as Concorde. Memorial finds a place with a gravestone sculpture from ancient Greece, which stands for the wonder of Greek sculpture; the Bayeux Tapestry records a political event of considerable importance for England and the rest of Europe. El Escorial was built to memorialise its royal patron (and to challenge the dominance of Muslim architecture in Spain at the time). There are works of art in the narrow sense, from sculptures to an illuminated book like the Book of Kells to some of the world's most beautiful architecture. But every item has some claim to impress with its beauty as well as its grandeur or importance.

But there is here also a fascinating history of world culture, as the chapters shift in focus and direction. In the chapters on the ancient world, we find first of all a range of cultures, stretching over thousands of years. The Great Pyramid is from ancient Egypt, before it had had any significant contact with the northern Mediterranean. The Parthenon comes from the glorious days of classical Athens, the height of ancient Greek culture. The Colosseum is still the prime icon of the ancient Roman empire with its gladiatorial games. The Great Wall of China begins under the first emperor of China, in the Far East, in a culture far removed from the West's classical past of Greece and Rome. The Temple Mount in Jerusalem is a Jewish site, built in its current form by a Jewish ruler under the Roman empire, though now covered with the beautiful buildings of its later Muslim conquerors. The Rosetta Stone takes us back to Egypt, but an Egypt now fully integrated into the Roman empire, a culture that has changed unrecognisably from the days of Khufu. Here we see the privileged past of the West, as the ideas, monuments and images which have dominated the imagination of later generations are put in place. The rediscovery of Greece and Rome goes on to fuel the Renaissance; the tradition of Judaeo-Christian culture runs through medieval culture up to the present; the image of Egypt and the East, as the mysterious or threatening other, has been a fundamental element of the West's self-definition. This first section is, then, truly foundational for what follows.

The medieval section stretches from Istanbul's Hagia Sophia in the East to Edward's castles on the Welsh border in the West. It includes a variety of media, from the stone of the border castles to the wool of the Bayeux Tapestry to the parchment of the Book of Kells. But at the same time, there is also a remarkable continuity of focus. The medieval wonders chosen in this section fall into two basic categories, Christianity and war. There are the magnificent buildings into which medieval wealth flowed for the greater glory of God: Hagia Sophia, which begins as a Christian church, before being turned into an even more extraordinary

Muslim mosque; the chapel in the imperial palace at Aachen; the monastery of Batalha. These are monuments of the public face of a Christian world. The Book of Kells, whose beauty epitomises a more intimate luxury and a more personal act of piety, turns us to the act of worship central to this community. This focus on Christianity as the defining frame of wonder is an inevitable product of the medieval world picture, where the ultimate wonder is precisely God's creation, the world itself and man in it, and to suggest that anything made by man could be spoken of in the same breath would be a challenging blasphemy. Medieval Europe lacked the wealth and the productivity of either the Roman empire or the Renaissance kingdoms, and consequently their monuments lack the conspicuous splendour of those eras. But the intensity of feeling and boldness of expression, especially in relation to a powerful sense of spirituality, are uniquely impressive.

War is the other grand narrative of the era. The Bayeux Tapestry celebrates the Norman victory over England; the Welsh border castles evidence the strength of Edward's military policy and the danger to his kingdom; the Castel del Monte is Frederick II's attempt to impose himself on the Italian landscape as a military presence, a sign of his secular power and authority. It is not by chance that the chapel at Aachen is the *imperial* chapel. With these wonders, we trace also a history of great men who dominate the narrative of the medieval history of Europe: William the Conqueror, Charlemagne, Edward, Frederick II. They remind us that Christendom was a military and imperial realm, whose piety was never far from a chain-mailed fist.

The wonders of the Renaissance world take a quite different route. Where in the medieval period we were treated to a range of media, in the Renaissance we tour only great buildings. It is with more than a sigh of regret that Shakespeare's plays are left behind (and we might add Diderot and d'Alembert's *Encylopédie* or Milton's *Paradise Lost* or Newton's *Principia* and many others). These are books that changed the way we look at the world, and books that still have a major impact on today. Nor are any of the scientific wonders of the age included: double-entry bookkeeping, the printing press, navigational instruments – all of which affect us all every day. The Renaissance rediscovery of the classical models of ancient Greece resulted in an extraordinary efflorescence of new art. Our image of the body is formed through this Renaissance rediscovery of the Greek male form: Michelangelo's *David*, along with the great painting and sculpture of this period, has changed how we see and know the human form. Yet what emerges in this chapter is not a personal predilection for architectural history, but a vivid map of the spread of Renaissance ideals across the world, changing the landscape of modern Europe. From the earliest Renaissance in Italy, travelling slowly across

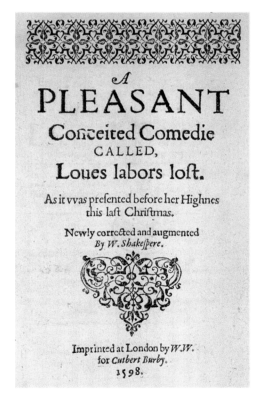

Title-page of *Love's Labour's Lost*, by William Shakespeare, 1598

Michelangelo's *David*, 1501–4

the Low Countries towards Greenwich in England, we are treated to the spread of what we now call European culture. We meet the great kings and princes who dominated the history of the period and whose patronage (and imperial wealth) made the art possible; we meet the architects and artisans, artists and thinkers, who created spaces which at first captivate the eye with splendour, symmetry and mastery of form, but which also provide a deep contentment that remains in the mind and satisfies the deepest aesthetic feelings. These are wonders to inhabit, to contemplate, to enjoy. Through these marvellous palaces, piazzas, churches and building complexes, we discover the ideals and achievements of the culture which formed modern Europe.

The modern world is the period where there is likely to be most argument about what a wonder is: none – by definition – has yet stood the test of time; none has the stamp of approval of generations of viewers. Yet this is a period which stretches the boundaries of human awe, and amazes with its technical achievement. The image of the earth from space, a picture produced by a staggering array of technology from the camera that took the picture to the rocket which propelled the men into space, is an image which changes the perception of the whole world for all of us: for the first time, a sight of the planet revolving in the darkness of the universe. This humbling change of perspective is equally mind-boggling with the discovery of the DNA molecule, the tiny building-block of all life. The advances in genetics, and in the understanding of matter itself, as represented by the particle accelerator at CERN, a machine which uses as much electricity as the whole city of Berne, have fundamentally altered how we understand our selves and the world; in a way undreamt of by the poet Blake, they have fulfilled his hope to 'see a world in a grain of sand'.

All of the wonders in this chapter on modernity are wonders of technological achievement. Two involve transport. The Pacific 4-8-8-4 Freight Locomotive looks back to the nineteenth century, a period of intense belief in progress and intense anxiety about the past. The railways opened up the world to new forms of imperialism, new forms of commerce and new forms of tourism and travel. This engine is the culmination of a long development, which more than any technological advance changed society. And you do not have to be a railway buff to enjoy the beauty of this machine, and to feel a twinge of the romance of the long journey towards the west coast, land of hope and dreams. Concorde is a machine that looks forward to the continuing marvel of air travel. As anyone who has seen Concorde in the air will recall, it is a remarkably awe-inspiring sight – sleek lines, elegant and sharp form, the very epitome of modernity in motion. The final two wonders are constructions – but neither involves the church or war. (The change of focus from the earlier periods is marked and fascinating to reflect on.) Instead, we have the Forth Railway Bridge, a triumph of engineering and sign of British technological power (which, through the empire, was so influential in shaping the modern geo-political map), and the New York skyline, an instantly recognisable (and recently so scarred) silhouette – the perfect icon of the new wealth and power of the new empire of the United States of America, and also an image full of the wonder of the modern city, with all its bustle, excitement and alienation. The modern world emerges here in striking contrast with earlier periods: no more religious architecture, grand patrons, art to change our understanding. Instead, science and technology, collective achievements, state patronage. Will this be how our current era is viewed hundreds of years from now?

We hope this introduction will whet the appetite for what follows, and set the scene for our four personal guided tours of the wonders of the world. But now it is time to start those tours. As T. S. Eliot wrote:

> Do not ask 'What is it?',
> Let us go and make our visit.

SEVEN WONDERS OF THE ANCIENT WORLD

Simon Goldhill

WHEN WE STAND in front of some ancient buildings or artefacts, wonder is an overwhelming feeling. The sheer expanse of time over which these objects have survived is awe-inspiring in itself. Our imagination struggles to reach back to a past so distant and foreign. In the face of such history, wonder can be provoked by even the most humble of sites. Take Skara Brae in Orkney. A storm in 1850 blew back the sand on the bleak shore of the island to reveal eight buildings and the connecting streets of a neolithic village from four thousand years ago. The small, painfully constructed stone huts in so forbidding a landscape give us a powerful image of man on the edge, struggling against a harsh natural world to construct a community. The village was continually inhabited for perhaps six hundred years, never growing any bigger than these eight houses. For generations, men and women used the furniture (the best-preserved examples of any Stone Age site), threw their rubbish in the midden and made a life together in this harsh environment. What is so uncanny here is not just the dizzying sense of a lost world from four thousand years ago, so different from today's material comforts and expectations. It is also the strange closeness one feels, standing on the worn streets where these distant ancestors walked and talked. It is not only the wind that makes the visitor shiver at Skara Brae.

This sense of uncanny closeness to a lost past is even more striking in another group of buildings which have been preserved over many centuries by a freak of nature. As an image of the ancient world, Pompeii could not be further from Skara Brae. Here we enter a society of imperial luxury, with its beautiful villas by the warm Italian coast under the volcano Etna. There are art objects of stunning beauty, set in gardens inside housing complexes that would grace Malibu. The walls are painted with beautiful images of myth, the bath-houses with shockingly graphic sexual scenes, the streets adorned with political and scurrilous graffiti, advertisements for prostitutes and for gladiator fights. Yet what grips the visitor to Pompeii is not just the luxurious urban delights of the Roman elite. It is the fact that the whole town, as with Skara Brae, is held in a

Skara Brae settlement, Orkneys, inhabited between 3200 and 2200 BC. View of the neolithic shoreline huts and the interior

21

Frozen in time: a mother and child from
Pompeii

time capsule of preservation. In Pompeii, our gaze is fascinated by the
bodies of men and women with their children and pets, captured by the
ash in poses of fear and flight. What makes us wonder is that frozen
moment of the past, displayed in its moment of disaster, an everyday life
on the very point of its total destruction.

Western writers and painters have repeatedly been moved to wonder
by the vivid immediacy of the archaeological record of the last days of
Pompeii. But a quite different sense of awe and mystery is evoked by
another monument of a lost empire, one far from Europe, in a country
destined to come into all too close and bloody contact with the West.
The so-called Pyramid of the Sun at Teotihuacan in Mexico is the
largest pyramid in America, the third-largest anywhere in the world, and
it was built probably sometime between the second and third centuries
AD without the use of iron or the wheel. It stands over 100 feet (31 m) high,
and is the central building in a massive religious complex that was surrounded by a city which grew by the sixth century AD to have perhaps as
many as two hundred thousand inhabitants. Yet for all their monumental
scale, we know next to nothing about the religious use of these buildings.
Indeed, we do not even know what ethnic group built them, nor have we
found any writing to help decipher what must have been a hugely important urban centre, with all the trade and social form necessary for such a
development. In Teotihuacan, both the monumentality and the intractable archaeological silence of the site distances us: yet in a different way
from the tiny and precious remains of Skara Brae, or the rich humanness
of Pompeii, to look over the ruins of the city from the top of the Pyramid
of the Sun provokes wonder, a perhaps melancholy wonder at the contrast between the massive scale of the building, and the total loss of the
civilisation that built them.

Neither Skara Brae, nor Pompeii, nor Teotihuacan is in my list of
seven wonders from the ancient world, though each could clearly have

been included. But each of them does tell us something about how wonder can grip us in different ways, and about how the ancient world can inspire a special wonder. Wonder can come from the vastness of time and culture separating us from our furthest forefathers and foremothers. Wonder can grip us in the face of beauty, the beauty that makes us stop and stare in amazement. Wonder can seize us from the sudden recognition of ourselves in the past, or from a glimpse of a frozen moment in time, that seems to stop the flow of history. Wonder can swell in response to man's attempt to make a monument for himself and of himself, and from both the loss and the survival of previous generations' hopes and dreams.

So how have I chosen my seven wonders of the ancient world? I have selected human achievements that are, first of all, instantly recognisable. This is not because there are not beautiful, hidden surprises from the ancient world. I could happily have chosen an exquisite painting from a Greek vase, my favourite masterpiece of calligraphy from China, a carved jewel or glass from a Roman table. There are innumerable ancient works of precision, elegance and profound beauty, many of which are largely unknown, and I would have enjoyed providing a guide to them.

Monumentality and intractable silence: the Pyramid of the Sun, Teotihuacan, Mexico, built between the second and third centuries AD

23

I could equally easily have turned away from traditional canons of beauty, and chosen seven items of iconic value: a totem pole from Native American culture, an Egyptian mummy, bandaged in its painted coffin, a silver drachma from Athens, embossed with an owl, Athena's bird. These are objects that express something essential about the cultures which produced them, and each is capable of transfixing our attention, with their strange mix of familiarity and oddness. These items may be instantly recognisable in a general way, but the very number of examples makes them eventually less amazing than individual and specific objects.

My choice of instantly recognisable monuments from the ancient world is to make a different point. I want to stress that these great monuments are also inside all of us – inside the Western imagination, images that evoke associations that go far beyond any simple artistic or archaeological history. When we look at the Parthenon, we cannot see just a building on a rocky outcrop in the Mediterranean: it inevitably invokes the myths of the glorious Greek past – just as the Pyramids summon up a host of ideas about Egyptian mysteries and the magic of the pharaohs. The ancient world provides the models through which we view the modern world. It is not by chance that the ancient Greeks provided the first list of the seven wonders of the world, and that we still enjoy making our own versions! The wonders of the ancient world are the examples that still help us to formulate our understanding of things. Our imagination is structured by this longest inheritance.

So when we look at the wonders of the ancient world, I shall be interested not merely in the physical appearance of the monuments nor just in their use. We will need to look also at how these monuments have been viewed over the centuries, and how they continue to have an effect today. This heritage is part of what makes these buildings true wonders.

THE GREAT PYRAMID
AT GIZA

The Great Pyramid at Giza is the only one of the seven original wonders of the ancient world to survive today, and it is a sobering thought that when this monument totally amazed Herodotus, the fifth-century BC historian of wonders, it had already been standing for over two millennia. What makes the Great Pyramid such a wonder? At one level, it is the simple, geometric shape and its sheer size. As you approach the Pyramid, it rises out of the shifting sands of the desert as an abstract, dominant form – hard lines, made by man, against the natural world around it. Its massive bulk gradually becomes apparent as you reach closer to it. At its foot, it seems overwhelming, impenetrable, soaring. It has such a power-ful effect even if you come through the tatty tourist junk on the road from Cairo. This impression of scale, however, is also intricately bound up with its age. The Great Pyramid was built as a tomb for Khufu who ruled as pharaoh in Egypt for twenty-three years around 2500 BC. It is hard to grasp such antiquity: that more than two thousand years before Pericles an edifice like this could have come into being. It changes our sense of what historical time is. We wonder how at such a time and in such a place so large and impressive a building could have been made.

But the Pyramids have other lures for us too. The discovery of the treasure of Tutankhamun was a great media event of the twentieth cen-tury, as well as an archaeological triumph. It fulfilled one of the great collective fantasies of the Western imagination. Since at least the time of Herodotus, tourists have visited the Pyramids and entered the tunnels made by graverobbers and seen the empty tombs. The hope of discover-ing an undisturbed burial chamber, and of being the first to roll back the rock to reveal the treasures of the pharaohs had haunted many a novel along with every history of Egyptian antiquity. The Pyramids are fasci-nating also because we know that they have secret tunnels, chambers and treasures within their forbidding exteriors. They appeal to the ex-plorer and archaeologist inside each of us.

This notion of the secrets of the Pyramids has also fuelled more extreme and uncontrolled speculation. Already in the Bible, Pharaoh is said to have had magicians who managed to match Moses, miracle for miracle, at least in the early stages of the ten plagues. Ancient Egypt has been associated with mysterious knowledge since antiquity, when Greek travellers came into contact with a culture so much older than their own. Spells, occult wisdom, the curse of the Mummy – these are the spe-cial province of the mystery of Egypt, at least in the minds of Western

Howard Carter (holding a crowbar) open-ing the sealed doorway to the sepulchral chamber of King Tutankhamun's tomb, with Arthur Mace of the Metropolitan Museum standing to his right, 1922

writers. The Pyramids have been the object of centuries of feverish mathematical and occult imagination. It is this, too, that gives the Great Pyramid its special aura.

Khufu was the founder of the fourth dynasty, and evidently a great king, a figure who appears in mythic tales many centuries later; but actually we know very little about his reign. His name appears on monuments over a wide area, and there are many officials, priests and family members buried in their own tombs around Giza. But this all reveals very little about the man or his rule. Herodotus, who claims to have visited the Pyramid, and to have gained his information from the priests there, tells us that Cheops, as he calls Khufu – it was one of his official names – was an arrogant and corrupt tyrant. He closed down the temples and forbade the Egyptians from worshipping their gods. He forced them into slave labour to build the Pyramids, and even compelled his own daughter to work in a brothel, and set the price of her hire. She added a surcharge of one block of stone from each customer, however, and with those stones built the middle of the three small pyramids in front of the Great Pyramid. Now, even if we did not know that this small pyramid was in fact the tomb of one of the wives of the pharaoh, this lurid (and fun) story should put us on our guard about believing Herodotus' evidence too fervently. He was fascinated by the otherness of the Egyptians. He delighted in reporting weird stories about them, including such anthropological curiosities as the fact that Egyptian men urinate sitting down while Egyptian women urinate standing up – a detail whose main interest for him is that it reverses normal Greek expectations. Herodotus gives us the longest ancient account of the Pyramids, but he can tell us little reliable about Khufu himself.

Remarkably, we do have one small portrait statue of the man who built the Great Pyramid. This tiny figurine, barely 3 inches (8 cm) tall, was discovered by Flinders Petrie, one of the founding fathers of statistical archaeology and a leading Egyptologist, at his dig at Abydos, several hundred miles south of Giza. When he found the body, he realised that the head had only recently been broken from it. He had his whole team sift through the surrounding rubble for three weeks, until the head was discovered and rejoined to the torso. It is a rare image of an Egyptian king, because it does not seem to be idealised, at least as in the standard forms of honorific statue. Egyptologists have been thrilled to see here a portrait of what Rappoport, in his *History of Egypt*, described as 'the energy, the commanding air, the indomitable will, and the firm ability, of the man who stamped for ever the character of the Egyptian monarchy'. Whatever personality emerges from the face, this is a precious and unique testimony.

The Great Pyramid is the centrepiece of a huge, monumental complex

Satellite image of the three Pyramids at Giza in northern Egypt, built twenty-sixth century BC

Ivory figurine of Khufu, discovered by Flinders Petrie at Abydos

The Pyramid of Sneferu, Giza, with the *mastaba* of the prince in the foreground

at Giza, a raised plateau 25 miles (40 km) north of Dahshur, where Khufu's father, Sneferu, had built his pyramid: new monumental geography for the new dynasty. Khufu's brother and successor Khafre [Chephren] built his pyramid at Giza, and added the huge statue of the Sphinx. Menkaura [Mycerinus], Khufu's grandson and eventually pharaoh himself, added a third grand pyramid. Each of these pyramids is itself part of its own elaborate ritual site. In front of the pyramid stood a mortuary temple, used for the funeral rites of the pharaoh. The Mortuary Temple of the Great Pyramid is now largely destroyed but there is a black basalt pavement of an open court, with sockets for granite pillars of a colonnade, and the walls were of fine limestone carved in relief. From the mortuary temple a wall stretched right round the pyramid (sometimes called the *temenos* wall). Away from the mortuary temple and down towards the river stretched the causeway. Herodotus thought the causeway of the Great Pyramid as much of a marvel as the pyramid itself: '5 furlongs (1 km) in length, 60 feet (18 m) wide, 48 feet (15 m) high at its highest point, and constructed of polished stone blocks decorated with the carvings of animals'. A few stones of this have been recovered, including one which shows beautifully carved long-horned cattle and a cartouche which spells out the name of Khufu (with two chicks, a viper and a shaded circle). Where the causeway reached the water, a valley temple stood, to receive the boats of the funeral cortege. The Sphinx sits beside the Valley Temple

28

of Khafre, with a further temple, the Sphinx Temple, next to the Valley Temple.

The Pyramids of Khufu and Khafre, Giza

In front of the main pyramid, next to the mortuary temple, stood the pyramids of the pharaoh's queens. There are three in front of the Great Pyramid (as well as a small, satellite pyramid only recently discovered and of uncertain use). Behind the Great Pyramid, there is a huge grave-yard of monumental tombs (*mastabas*) of the officials, priests and family of the royal court. The most remarkable modern archaeological discoveries have taken place in the area in front of the Great Pyramid. In 1925, one of the photographers of George Reisner's dig put the leg of his tripod on the ground and it disappeared into a hole. This revealed an 89-foot (27-m) shaft undisturbed for over four thousand years, which led to the discovery of the burial chamber of Hetepheres, the mother of Khufu. In the chamber, folded up, was the furniture of the queen's boudoir, a canopy, chairs and table of breathtaking elegance. In 1954, an equally remarkable find was made. Below the *temenos* wall on the south side of the Great Pyramid a 102-foot (31-m) pit was found, sealed with forty-one limestone blocks, each weighing about 16 tons, and cemented

29

Gilded-wood sedan chair of Queen Hetepheres, from her tomb at Giza

together with plaster. Inside this watertight container was found a boat, more than 141 feet (43 m) long, dismantled into hundreds of pieces, now painstakingly reconstructed and in a special museum next to the Pyramid. This royal boat of Giza was probably intended for the use of the king's spirit in the afterlife, perhaps to ascend heavenwards. A second boat pit was discovered in 1985, with a further boat in it. When such extraordinary discoveries are still being made, for anyone lured by the promise of buried treasure the Pyramids exert a particular fascination.

The Great Pyramid itself is made out of approximately 2,300,000 blocks of stone, each weighing on average 2.5 tons. It is traditional among writers on the Pyramids to try to capture its size by more homely comparisons: so, it is said, it would be possible to fit inside it the Houses of Parliament and St Paul's (or, for Italians, the cathedrals of Florence, Milan and St Peter's basilica) with plenty of room to spare. It is probably the most measured and remeasured building in the world. This is in part because of a desire to show the extreme care with which the building was constructed, and in part because of the modern theories of hidden meanings to be found in the dimensions and angles of the building, which has led to much paranoid recalculation. The most accurate measurements show that the four sides are not quite equal in length, but each is around 755 feet (230 m), and the difference between longest and shortest is under 8 inches (20 cm). (This gives its base an area of 13.1 acres (5.3 hectares).) Similarly, it is aligned so that each side faces one of the cardinal points of the compass. The orientation here is also very accurate. The four corners are almost perfect right-angles. This does indicate that the Great Pyramid was constructed with the utmost attention to detail, and, considering

The reconstructed royal boat, from the tomb of Khufu

the technology available, it must have been an obsessive effort of diligence and will to bring the plan to completion.

The Great Pyramid looks in good condition from a distance, but it has suffered from robbers and despoilers. The top dozen courses of stones are missing, as is the capstone. Originally, the whole pyramid was faced with tufa limestone. With the exception of a few pieces at the base, this has been completely stripped from the building. We are told by Abd-al-Latif, an Arab writer of the twelfth century, when the facing was evidently still there, that the building was covered with inscriptions (and graffiti). Herodotus tells us that there was one inscription in hieroglyphic writing which he had interpreted for him. It detailed, he says, the cost of the radishes, onions and leeks for the workers, and it came to 1,600 talents of silver – a massive sum. It's hard not to suspect that Herodotus might have been gulled by his interpreter, but for him it still indicates the immensity of the project in terms his Greek audience would revel in. There is also a significant hole cut into the north face, an opening made in the ninth century by Caliph Ma'mun, son of Harun-al-Rashid of *Arabian Nights* fame. He was looking for buried treasure (though the chambers had been robbed centuries before). Between treasure hunters and builders looking for cheap and easy stone, the Great

Pyramid has suffered – but still stands with a monumental grandeur.

The entrance of the Great Pyramid leads into a descending corridor only about 3 feet (1 m) in width and slightly larger in height. This descends beneath the bedrock, and then flattens out before turning into a chamber, with a further unfinished tunnel beyond. This is generally believed to have been a plan for a royal burial chamber that was abandoned (for whatever reason). Instead, an ascending corridor of the same dimensions as the descending corridor rises from near the bedrock. This flattens out and leads to a burial chamber, known misleadingly as the Queen's Chamber. It may have been intended to hold a statue of the pharaoh, but there are good signs that this chamber too was unfinished: the floor, for example, is extremely rough. The abandonment of the so-called Queen's Chamber led, however, to the construction of two of the most celebrated architectural works of Egyptian antiquity, the Grand Gallery and the King's Chamber.

The Grand Gallery is 153 feet (47 m) long and 28 feet (8.5 m) in height. It has walls of polished limestone that rise for over 7 feet (2 m), and then seven courses of blocks, each projecting in over the one below, creating a vault of magnificent but eerie proportions. (It is the sort of tunnel down which many a Hollywood adventurer has fled from monsters within.) There are holes for wooden struts and space for a wooden platform, but it is not clear for what part of the burial ritual such a platform would have been used. The Great Gallery leads into the King's Chamber. This central room is built entirely of granite, and against one wall sits a granite sarcophagus, without a lid, in which the body of the king once lay. The sarcophagus is wider than the ascending corridor. So it must have been put in place while the chamber was being built. The roof of the King's Chamber is made of nine huge slabs (total weight about 400 tons), but above them are five compartments. These seem to be to lessen the weight on the roof of the chamber itself and guarantee that nothing fell in on the king's corpse. This has worked: every stone of the roof of the King's Chamber has been cracked by earthquakes, but so far there has been no rock-fall.

The Great Pyramid, like all such monuments, was not just a memorial to a monarch. It was a machine for transporting the king to the afterlife. It was through the full theatre of rituals and architecture of the Pyramid complex that the king's 'soul [*ba*]' could rise into the celestial sphere. The corpse arrived by boat, and was unloaded into the Valley Temple. The body needed purification and embalming – mummification. This could take many days. The body was finally ready for its journey to the tomb, a journey accompanied by the possessions the ruler would need in the next world. (It is unclear exactly what role the Mortuary Temple played here.) The burial, however, constituted a process of rebirth and transformation

onto another level of existence, crucial for the king and for the continuing order of the state. The beautiful Books of the Dead, along with images of the funeral, and inscribed hymns and spells, evoke an elaborate and astonishingly rich theological world, now quite lost, all of which made sense of the massive labour of the Pyramid-building projects.

The mathematical care with which the Pyramids have been built, the profusion of hieroglyphic texts with which they are surrounded, and their placement all along the Nile, have often prompted those that are prone to such things into fantasies of a huge, occult system. Some have insisted that the Pyramids are a huge astronomical device; some think this astronomical device predicts the arrival of a new race; others the second coming of Jesus; for others still, the end of the world is always nigh. These are all responses that begin with wonder at the Pyramids. But for me, what still stirs amazement about the Great Pyramid, however familiar the image may seem, is not just the impressive scale and dizzying antiquity of the building. It is also the melancholy and awe-inspiring attempt of a great king to transcend the limits of his own mortality and nature itself. The Great Pyramid, soaring out of the desert sands, sets a human monument, a monument of humanity, against time itself.

The Great Sphinx and Pyramids of Khafre and Menkaura (to the left), Giza

THE WESTERN WALL
OF THE TEMPLE MOUNT
IN JERUSALEM

There is no building that epitomises the long-lasting effect of ancient monuments on the imagination of the West more fully than the Temple of Jerusalem. The Temple itself no longer exists, but the site where once it stood has been fought over by generations of Muslims, Christians and Jews, from the Crusaders and the armies of Saladin, to the modern Israelis and the PLO. It has been a symbol of the longing for a better, more spiritual life for poets, painters and religious mystics. It motivates the grandest art and the most popular of novels, it inspires music from the great Church masters of the Renaissance to Bob Marley. For any community that has felt itself to be in exile and which longs for rebuilding, the Temple has been an inspirational ideal.

The Western Wall is the most familiar image of the holy city of Jerusalem. It is the central icon of current political turmoil in the Middle East, as much as it is the symbol of religious hope for the three Abrahamic religions of Judaism, Christianity and Islam. How this wall came to have such special power over so many humans is a quite remarkable and little understood story.

We need to begin back with King David, one of the most passionately drawn characters in the Bible, a figure whose political shenanigans, sexual escapades and wonderful songs have made him a favourite of subsequent artists and writers. According to the Second Book of Samuel, David was the first great king of the Holy Land, who created an empire whose capital was the city of Jerusalem. He brought the Ark, the most sacred object of the Israelite religion, to the city, and made Jerusalem the political and religious centre of the kingdom. To cement this reorganisation, he wanted to build a huge temple for worshipping the Lord, but although he raised the funds and drew up a design, he was prevented by the prophet Nathan, who informed him it was against God's will. (The First Book of Chronicles adds the detail that it was because he was a man of blood that he was debarred from this foundational role.) It was therefore left to his son, Solomon, to complete his father's design.

Solomon's Temple, according to the Bible, was remarkable, both physically and conceptually. It was not huge: the building itself was roughly 98 feet (30 m) long, 33 feet (10 m) wide and 49 feet (15 m) high, though with its outer porches the whole structure stretched to about 164 feet (50 m) long and 82 feet (25 m) wide – about two-thirds of the size of

the Parthenon. But it was designed and built with an unparalleled lavishness. Cypress wood and cedar was brought from Lebanon. Thirty thousand Israelites were forced to work on the project, in a three-month rota in shifts of ten thousand. At the same time, seventy thousand porters and eighty thousand quarriers prepared the stone – under the guidance of 3,300 officials. The carved doors of olive wood were inlaid with gold,

Jewish women praying at the Western (Wailing) Wall

35

and the entire building was overlaid with gold, inside and out. By the door stood two pillars, called Jachin and Boaz, and in the large, stone-walled courtyard there were an altar of bronze, tables for offerings and a bowl of bronze, resting on twelve bronze oxen, known as 'the sea', which held up to 15,400 gallons (70,000 l) of water, and around it there were ten bronze stands for ritual washing.

The Bible's description of the Temple is designed to emphasise its monumental scale and its splendour and wealth – a sign of the great empire and status of Solomon, as well as the glory of God. But more remarkable still was the way the building was conceptualised. First of all, it was a temple for God's name. In the Ten Commandments it is specified that 'thou shalt make no graven image', and there was indeed no image of God in the Temple. Unlike all the other temples around the Mediterranean, there were no cult statues here. The Holy of Holies was the innermost sanctum of the Temple, but in it there was only space for God's presence. When the Romans first captured Jerusalem and entered the Temple, they were simply amazed that when they got to the very heart of the building, there was nothing there: no treasure, no objects to plunder.

Second, this was the *only* temple for the Israelites. It was the only place where the religion's central rituals could take place. All Israelite men were required to come to Jerusalem three times a year for the so-called Pilgrim Festivals, and to pay a yearly tax to the Temple. It was the single properly authorised site of worship. This is an amazing act of religious centralisation, quite unlike anything attempted by any other ancient kingdom. It made the Temple the one and only centre of Israelite worship.

The Temple of Solomon is the first temple and is often called just The Temple. Over the centuries it has been invested with many myths and legends, and, in fact, our only record of it is from the Bible itself, and that account was itself written many years after the destruction of the building, with a longing gaze back towards former glories. For Solomon's Temple was destroyed by Nebuchadnezzar, who captured and sacked Jerusalem in 587 BC. The Jews were sent into exile in Babylon ('By the rivers of Babylon, I lay down and wept as I remembered thee, O Zion'). Yet Nebuchadnezzar himself was overthrown by the rise of the Persian empire, and in an act of political generosity typical of the media-savvy new rulers, the Jews were allowed to return to Jerusalem in 538 BC. Not all now wished to return, but many made the journey, led by Zerubbabel. They found nothing of the old temple left, and they set about rebuilding. The project was slow, dogged by dissent, and clearly had little of the splendour of the First Book of Kings' description of Solomon's building. Jerusalem was now a backwater of empire, without the financial or political clout for monumental building programmes. The book of Haggai, although the prophet has high hopes for this Temple's future glory, gives a rather depressing account of its foundation: 'Who is there left among you who saw this House in its former splendour? How does it look to you now? It must seem like nothing to you.'

Zerubbabel's Temple is called the Second Temple, and it stood for five hundred years. During this time, Judaism developed as a religion and a national identity, and when we pick up the story in the first century BC, Judaea, the country of the Jews, is now a Roman province, ruled on behalf of Rome by Herod, a vain, cruel and tyrannical king, familiar today for his massacre of the innocents, as recounted in the Gospels. Herod embarked on a massive building programme, designed not merely to fortify his kingdom, but also to glorify himself in monuments. Central to this was his plan to rebuild the Temple.

Herod found it hard to persuade the Jews to destroy the Temple, which had stood for five hundred years. He pointed out that it did not match the dimensions or the splendour of Solomon's Temple; but it was only when he promised to collect all the building materials for the new project before touching the old building that he was allowed to proceed. His plan, however, was of an extraordinary magnificence, and it has changed the very topography of Jerusalem for ever.

Herod decided to build a huge platform over the site of the Temple, and to place his new temple on the top of this platform. The platform is 1,550,000 square feet (144,000 m²) – the equivalent of twelve football pitches – and 105 feet (32 m) high. This was one of the greatest engineering projects of the ancient world. The solid rock of the hillside was cut back and four huge walls were built, retaining walls, which supported the weight of the platform and the buildings on it. These walls were built out of huge blocks of Jerusalem limestone, quarried near by. The blocks are dressed on their outside face, and around the edges they have a chiselled border between 2 and 4.7 inches (5 and 12 cm) wide and about 0.4 inch (1 cm) deep. They were fitted together without mortars or bolts. Despite the pressure of retaining the Temple Mount, and the buffeting of wars, these walls are still standing and doing their job two thousand years later. As the historian Josephus wrote at the time, these walls are 'the greatest ever heard of by man'. We will see one challenge to this claim shortly in the Great Wall of China. But even to the Romans, great builders, this was a site of wonder. As a disciple said to Jesus, when he came out of the Temple, 'Look teacher! What wonderful stones!'

Part of the reason for the remarkable strength and durability of the walls is the fact that the foundations were always dug to bedrock, even when bedrock was several metres beneath the surface. Partly it is because of the stones' huge size. The smallest blocks weigh between 2 and 5 tons.

Arch of Titus, west façade, built AD 81

Triumphal procession with the seven-armed candlestick from the Temple of Solomon, from the left internal wall of the Arch of Titus

But there are several that weigh around 50 tons each, and the bigger blocks weigh more than 400 tons and are over 39 feet (12 m) long.

The Temple itself was one of the richest and most splendid buildings in the Roman empire, with lavish decorations of gold. It was set amid courts with towering porticoes on the top of the platform. But Herod's Temple was destroyed in the year AD 70 by the Romans, led by Titus, as they put down a revolt of the Jews against the empire. It had stood for less than ninety years. The Romans, with characteristic thoroughness, left not a brick standing, and they took the ritual objects from the Temple back to Rome, as is memorialised on the Arch of Titus. They even cast down the top courses of the great walls (and the fallen blocks can still be seen in their ruined form at the foot of the Temple Mount). With the loss of the Temple, Judaism changed for ever.

The Western Wall (or the Wailing Wall), is one of the four retaining walls, and it was at the time of Herod an engineering marvel. But it had no religious significance at all. It was a big wall, with a street alongside it that led round to the entrance to the Temple Mount and the steps up to the religious centre. How, then, did it become so invested with religious awe? It is not any part of the Temple: so why is it treated with such longing and respect?

The Romans eventually banned the Jews from Jerusalem, and apart from pointedly building a small temple to Jupiter, left the Temple Mount undeveloped. When the Christians came to power, they used the deserted Temple Mount to make an even stronger ideological point. Although Jesus had worshipped at the Temple as a Jew, and taught there, this site was turned into a sort of negative memorial of the failures of Judaism, a visible symbol of the punishment of the Jews for their refusal to accept Jesus as the Messiah. The Christians took away the Roman buildings and deliberately left the site empty, unused and derelict. When the disciple asked Jesus to admire the wonderful stones and buildings of the Temple Mount, Jesus had replied: 'Do you see these great buildings? There will not be left here one stone upon another that will not be thrown down.' This prophecy echoed with its readers who saw in the destroyed Temple confirmation of the triumph of the Christian message.

Jews, banned by the Romans from Jerusalem, were not allowed to come back to Jerusalem by the Christians – except on one day of the year. On this occasion, they were allowed to come and mourn the loss of the Temple, and the one place they were allowed to stand was by the Western Wall. Their lamentations for the lost Temple are the beginnings of why this place is also called 'the Wailing Wall'. St Jerome, at the end of the fourth century, describes how a few Jewish pilgrims struggled to lament the destruction: 'You see a sad people coming, decrepit little women and old men encumbered with rags and years, exhibiting in their bodies and their dress the wrath of the Lord ... they are not worthy of pity.' It may seem disturbing to see a Christian saint denying pity to the old and weak, but it certainly stresses the strength of the Christian need to distinguish themselves from the Jews and to express their triumph in symbolic form. The Christians emphasised that they had no place for animal sacrifice, that the rules of purity applied to each individual, not to a building ('my body is a temple'), and that their worship could be practised anywhere. Hence they made a show of leaving the Temple Mount as a ruin, and letting the decrepit Jews for one day a year wail outside by a wall.

When the Muslims rose to power in the Middle East in the seventh century, there are yet more twists in the story of the Western Wall. Caliph Omar captured Jerusalem in AD 638. He entered the city on foot, dressed only in a camel-hair tunic, and was shocked to discover the state

Aerial view of Jerusalem, with the Temple Mount and Dome of the Rock and the Western (Wailing) Wall visible

of the Temple Mount. He forced the Christian patriarch to crawl through the rubbish and to start to clear it up himself. In Islamic thought, starting from the Koran, it was from the Temple Mount that Muhammad rose to heaven on the steed Burak, where he met the prophets and received the fundamental principles of Islamic prayer and abstinence from alcohol. The site is the third most holy place in Islam. The rock at one end of the Temple Mount was believed to be the original altar of Solomon's Temple and also the spot where Abraham had bound Isaac for sacrifice and where David had begged for God's forgiveness. It was over this rock that Abd-al-Malik in 691 built the Dome of the Rock, a shrine for pilgrims, which is still the most beautiful landmark of the Jerusalem skyline. Once again, the Temple Mount became a central site of a world religion for worship and for pilgrimage. And the Wall became the only place where Jews could pray close to where the Temple once had been.

Omar allowed Jews and Christians free access to Jerusalem, though not to build or worship on the Temple Mount. He made the city what it

40

is today, a polyglot and fervent mixture of beliefs and nations. But the Crusaders, when they captured Jerusalem in the eleventh century, massacred Jews and Muslims alike and again banned all but Christians from the city. For a century, Jerusalem was once more only an object of longing. With the return of Muslim rule, Jews and Christians were again allowed into the city, though with the growth of nationalism and anti-Semitism in the nineteenth century, increasing restrictions were put in place. Under the British Mandate in the twentieth century, a heated case of international law broke out over who had the right to control prayer at the Western Wall. Could chairs be brought to it for the elderly to sit on, or was this an infringement of the Arabs' rights of passage? In 1948, the Wall was again banned for Jews, as it was in Arab-controlled Jerusalem after the war of Israel's independence. In 1967, the recapturing of the Wall was the most emotional moment in the capture of Jerusalem by the Israelis. Today the Wall is one of the most visited sites in the Holy Land, a spot where countless people have felt the urge to pray, or to wonder at the deep history of the place.

I have chosen the Western Wall of the Temple Mount as a wonder of the ancient world partly because it is a stunning piece of monumental architecture: a memorial to the grandiose ambitions of Herod, and also, more importantly, to man's reaching towards God. Religious art inevitably has a large role to play in such a book as this. It is often where humans have expressed their most profound sense of wonder. This wall has played an integral role in the greatest religious upheavals of our civilisation. But I have also chosen it because it shows how a sense of wonder can be constructed over the strange twists of history. This was once just a wall: a remarkable wall, but a wall nonetheless. Because of the religious wars that have raged over this site, and because of the prayers which have been directed towards it over the generations, it has become invested with a unique religious awe. Years of lamentation have filled the stones with their own significance.

A Roman aqueduct is a great piece of engineering, and has had a long-lasting impact on the Western world. The Great Temple at Petra is a masterpiece of religious and royal architecture – but because the ruins of this city were only rediscovered in the nineteenth century, it remains largely a tourist site. The Western Wall is a wonder of the ancient world because it has come to inspire the imagination of generations of men and women, longing to reach out through prayer and lamentation to a better world.

THE PARTHENON

The Parthenon is probably the most familiar and celebrated building from the ancient world, a ready-made symbol of our ancient heritage, and the backdrop to a thousand advertisements. Yet fewer people are aware that for most of its life, this building was used either as a church or as a mosque, or that the famous view of the columns against the blue Mediterranean sky was created for us in the nineteenth century by a newly appointed German king, who cleared the accretion of medieval and more modern buildings from the Acropolis. Fewer still could confidently describe the original use of the building or the programme of its sculptures. The Parthenon would certainly feature on most people's lists of the wonders of the ancient world, but it is a wonder which more than any other needs a careful intellectual archaeology to appreciate it as more than an easy icon of the glory that was Greece.

The Parthenon was built between 447 and 432 BC in Periclean Athens, the Athens of the fifth-century enlightenment, when science, medicine, rhetoric, political theory and the great theatre of tragedy and comedy were being invented in what is still one of the most remarkable periods of human development. The building was designed and built as a coherent programme by three of the greatest artistic figures of the period, by the architects Ictinus (who wrote a book about the architecture of the building) and Callicrates, and by Pheidias, the greatest sculptor of his generation, who was said to be the general overseer of the project and to have designed the series of sculptures on what was the most heavily decorated temple ever built in Greece up to that point. Pheidias in particular designed and made the cult statue of Athena Parthenos (Athena the Virgin) to whom the building is dedicated, and from whom the building takes its name. Pheidias also went on to make the Statue of Zeus at Olympia which was one of the original seven wonders of the world: the Parthenon through Pheidias thus gives us a link back to that list.

There was no event in the fifth century more significant for the history of Greece than the two invasions by the massive forces of the Persian empire, both of which were repelled finally and with great military victories by the Greeks. John Stuart Mill called the battle of Marathon the most important battle in *British* history, since it was by this stunning triumph of the hardy, few Greeks over the massed ranks of the Persians that the values of liberty and the intellectual heritage of Greece were saved for the West. When Xerxes led the second invasion, the Athenians received an oracle from Delphi to 'trust in the wooden walls'. Their general Themistocles interpreted this to mean to leave the city and

rely on their naval strength. The Athenians surprisingly agreed to this extraordinarily bold plan. The women and children were transported to Euboea, and the men took to the seas – to win the famous victory at Salamis. One result of this was that the Persians took Athens unopposed, which they proceeded to sack and burn partly in revenge for their earlier defeat at Marathon. The Parthenon was part of Pericles' post-war building programme, the most grandiloquent symbol of Athens's new optimism and military strength.

Immediately after the war, the Athenians had established a league of Greek states against the Persian threat. This rapidly turned into the Athenian empire: the treasury of the league was transferred to Athens, and every member state was required to pay tribute to Athens, a policy backed up by often brutal military force. The Parthenon housed this treasury, and was built with money from the empire. The Parthenon is also a symbol of Athenian imperial power over the other states of Greece (something often silenced in current arguments about the return of the Elgin Marbles).

The Acropolis hill and its temples, including the Parthenon

The project had a major impact on Athens. Armies of specialist craftsmen – not just sculptors, but carpenters, metal workers, painters, gilders – were employed. Raw materials were imported from all across the Mediterranean. Most remarkably, the whole work was completed in under fifteen years. As the historian Plutarch, writing some five hundred years later, commented: 'The most wondrous thing of all was the speed of their work.' A monument to last for all time appeared to have been constructed in so little time, and, he continued with self-conscious paradox, appeared to have the awesomeness of age from the moment it was built, and yet appeared 'untouched by time' even half a millennium later. The Parthenon was built to be a monument of the glorious days of Periclean Athens from the beginning and was recognised as such throughout the ancient world.

The Parthenon is a temple and its basic outline follows a recognisable form of other temples in Greece – only with an unmatched balance of proportion and unmatched splendour of decoration and, of course, perfect location. Its plan will help us orientate ourselves, but gives little sense of the effect of the building *in situ*. There is a line of columns surrounding two rectangular rooms, traditionally called the East and West Chambers. (This is in fact different from traditional temples, which usually had only one central room.) The main entrance led into the East Chamber. Around this room on three sides ran a two-storey colonnade, one tier of columns supporting another.

In this room stood the cult statue of Athena. This does not survive, but there is a full-size replica recently built in the Parthenon in Nashville, Tennessee, which has been much praised for its archaeological accuracy. Pheidias' statue was made of gold and ivory (the Tennessee model is only fibreglass and gypsum cement). The figure standing by the right of the statue (actually, its maker, Alan LeQuire) gives a good sense of its scale. The power of the goddess, Athens's goddess, is expressed in the statue's overwhelming size and splendour. She holds in her hand a statue of winged Victory, and carries her usual accoutrements of spear, shield and helmet: Athena is both a warrior goddess as well as the goddess of wisdom, and has a special link to Athens's self-portrayal as a city that links the arts and war in its unique culture. The snake by her shield is the mythic figure of Erichthonios, the first Athenian. Hephaestus tried to rape Athena: she easily fended him off, but he ejaculated onto her thigh. She wiped off the semen onto the ground, and from the soil there was born Erichthonios, in snake form, according to the version Pheidias is following. Erichthonios grew up to become the first Athenian. His image here links the temple to the history of the city's foundation.

There was no way through from the East Chamber to the West Chamber, which had to be entered from the other end of the building. We

Alan LeQuire and his replica of the cult statue of Athena, built 1982–2002, in the Parthenon, Nashville, Tennessee

should not think of these rooms as austerely elegant or empty, however, as some fantasies of the classical aesthetic would encourage us to do. Both chambers, and especially the dark, windowless, western room, were absolutely full of sacred property of all kinds. There were dedications from individuals – both splendid and humble – the treasury of the city itself, war booty and heirlooms of various sorts. The inventories from the Parthenon survive in fragmented form and give a vivid snapshot of the sheer profusion and confusion that must have greeted the visitor. The western room's treasures included, for example: six Persian daggers, one gilt lyre, three lyres in ivory, four in wood, an ivory inlaid table, a silver-gilt mask, ten couches from Miletus, six thrones, two large silver-gilt nails and more than seventy shields. We know the names of many who made dedications to the goddess (including Roxane, the wife of Alexander the Great, who gave a golden drinking horn). The walls of the chambers were covered with cupboards or shelf stacks, which, the inventories suggest, must have been carefully numbered. Some treasures were

45

The west pediment of the Parthenon, with its fluted Doric columns

kept in the porches, and to protect them metal grilles or barriers were erected between the inner rows of columns at both the east and the west end of the building. There must have been guards at all times to preserve such a valuable storehouse of treasure, and access to the building must have been carefully restricted.

This immediately suggests that the Parthenon was not used as a modern-day cathedral is. Animal sacrifice, the central cultic activity in Greek religion, took place on outside altars. There were not even any priests or cults attached to the Parthenon. There were no prayers, no congregants, no hymns sung here. The temple housed the statue of the goddess which was visited as a great work of art and as a powerful symbol of the city's power and hopes for itself. Otherwise, the Parthenon acted as treasury and storeroom.

The outside of the building, however, was seen by all who visited the

46

Acropolis for religious or other purposes, and this offers not only a very beautiful sight, but also one with a message to the citizens. The columns are Doric, the most austere of the orders, and famously the Parthenon's columns bulge towards the top so that they appear quite straight when viewed from below. This design feature is nowhere mentioned in ancient sources, and may have been an on-site adaptation as much as a brilliant mathematical calculation. But undoubtedly the impression of soaring straight lines adds to the building's impact. The columns stand on a platform of three steps, further raising the building from the surrounding terrain. The eight columns at either end lead also to a porch made by six further columns, which lead the visitor's eye inwards towards the statue at the centre of the building.

Where the Parthenon is quite remarkable, however, is in the profusion of its statuary. Many temples have pedimental groups – that is, collections of usually divine figures fitted into the triangular space above the door. The Parthenon does not only have these spaces filled, but also two complete sets of sculptures running round the whole building. Between the tops of the columns there is a series of square framed panels called metopes, each of one of which houses a sculpted scene. Round the outer wall of the central building, at a similar height, ran a frieze. At each corner of the roof there were probably monumental statues of Victory. No other temple before had tried to put all these elements on a single building – and yet the Parthenon achieves this with remarkable success.

The sculptures together make a significant expression of what this temple meant to Athens. Over the east main door on the pediment was a large-scale portrayal of the birth of Athena. Like scenes of the nativity of Jesus, this story is central to the goddess's place in the order of things. She sprang, fully armed, from the head of her father Zeus, after the king of the gods had swallowed her mother, Metis, the goddess of guile and

The sacred robe of Athena held up by cult officials, and Athena and Hephaestus. Central frieze section from the east pediment of the Parthenon

47

A fight between a Lapith and a Centaur, from the south metope of the Parthenon

cunning. Athena is constantly associated with the usually male attributes of intellectual activity and war. As she says in Aeschylus' *Oresteia*, 'I am wholly of the father.' Springing from the head of her father, even at her birth she is separate from the female sphere.

Over the west door, the pediment shows the competition between Athena and Poseidon to see who would be the patron divinity of the city of Athens. This myth tells how Athens became the city of Athena. Poseidon offered the city the horse as his gift. Athena offered them the olive tree, source of food, and oil for cooking, bathing and lighting. In those days, the myth goes, women as well as men had the vote. All the women voted for Athena, all the men for Poseidon. There was one more woman than man, and hence Athena won. In rage, Poseidon flooded the land. After this, women no longer had the vote. The story explains why the fiercely patriarchal state of Athens had a female patron, and in the process justifies the subordinate position of women in the country's political system. The west pediment links Athens and its goddess inextricably.

The metopes enter us into a different mythic world. There are thirty-two metopes on each side, and fourteen at each end. They make up four sequences, and each depicts a battle. At the east end there is the battle between the gods and the giants. This is the war by which the gods became established as the powers of the world, the war which established the order of things. Along the south side, there is the battle of the Centaurs and Lapiths. This is a fight between humans and the half-horse,

half-men monsters, who wished to steal the bride of the Lapith king – a
fight between men and monsters over the cornerstone of social order,
marriage. These metopes take relief carving to an extreme of brilliance.
For example, one shows a Centaur wounded in the back and trying to
escape as the heroic Lapith prepares the death blow. The Lapith is
almost a fully three-dimensional figure, and the energy of the design is
superbly created not only by the twisted body of the Centaur and the
leverage of the Lapith's legs, but also by the swirls of the cloak which
holds the composition together.

On the west end, the metopes show a battle of the Greeks and the
Amazons. The Amazons are everything that good, Athenian citizens are
not: they are female but military, nomadic not householders, pillagers
not crop-growers, resistant to marriage. They are defeated by the Athenians led by Theseus, the king who brought the state of Athens together
into a single political entity. Again, we see the triumph of the forces of
order over the violence of disorder.

The north side shows the battle of Greeks and Trojans, the epic founding war of East versus West, which was the model for the war between
the Greeks and the Persians, which gave rise to the Parthenon. It shows a
further account of 'us' versus 'them'. Together these four sets of images
create a system of analogies: the Athenians are encouraged to see themselves as forces of order ranged against the forces of disorder, to see
their enemies as figures like the Trojans, the Amazons, the Centaurs, the
Giants, enemies of all that makes civilisation civilised. The Parthenon's
metopes offer an ideological image of self-definition for the Athenians.

Chariot group, detail from the south frieze
of the Parthenon

49

The frieze that runs around the inner building further supports this. It shows a religious procession of men riding, animals for sacrifice, water carriers, chariots, all converging on the east end of the building above the entrance to the Parthenon. It is a stunning piece of relief carving. Although it is never more than 2.4 inches (6 cm) deep, it manages to portray teams of horses four deep, and create a bustling, exciting flow of figures. Scholars have argued fiercely over what the frieze represents, however. Most these days agree that it shows the Panathenaic procession, the greatest religious occasion in the Athenian calendar when representatives of the whole state processed to the Acropolis to make a huge sacrifice. That is, it shows the Athenians an idealised vision of themselves. The religious procession constructs an image to set alongside the mythic tales of the destruction of the forces of disorder. The Athenians are to see themselves as active players in the long history of the triumph of civilisation.

Most of the sculptures of the Parthenon have been destroyed over time. Most of the frieze and some of the metopes from the south side are in the British Museum (taken there by Lord Elgin in the early nineteenth century). There are also tantalising fragments of the pedimental sculptures. Much of the building, including statuary that had survived the centuries, was destroyed when a Turkish gunpowder store, placed in the Parthenon, was hit by a Venetian shell in 1687. Twenty-eight columns were smashed, and the structures inside the Parthenon devastated. The Venetian commander tried to take down the west pediment to bring back to Venice, and succeeded only in destroying it. What we see now on the Acropolis is the product of painstaking restoration of the fragments, and the result of Prince Otto of Bavaria, the first king of Greece now liberated from Turkish rule, who had all evidence of any building after the classical age removed. He took away all signs that the Parthenon had been used as a mosque by the Turks (complete with a minaret) for several centuries, and as a church by the Christians before that, who had built an apse to augment the classical simplicity of the original.

Yet for all these depredations and violence, and even with a full recognition of how this building fits into the political world of fifth-century Athens, who could stand on the Acropolis and look across the stone-outcrop towards the ruin of the Parthenon and not marvel? Even in our cynical age, who would not wonder not just at the beauty of such a building but also at the burst of intellectual and political and artistic life in those few decades of the fifth century, when Athens became as Pericles says, 'an education for all Greece'? The battered Parthenon stands still as the most fitting symbol of the heritage from ancient Greece in the modern West, a building that embodies a soaring sense of the hopes and ideals of humans.

THE COLOSSEUM

Like the Parthenon, the Colosseum is instantly recognisable, a monument that immediately and powerfully evokes the ancient world. Yet while few tourists know or care what the Parthenon was used for, the glamour and excitement of the Colosseum for its three million visitors each year is to a good degree tied up with the bloodthirsty thrills of the gladiatorial games which took place there.

The Roman empire included most of Europe, and its impact on European culture is immense and continuing. Latin was the language of civilised exchange for many centuries, the Catholic Church is still centred on Rome, the French legal system is based on the Roman code, English schoolchildren travel on Roman roads to visit Hadrian's Wall – and so on. There is a certain continuity between the Roman empire and the modern West which makes the phenomenon of the Roman games all

The Colosseum, Rome, built AD 72–80

51

Engraving by Antonio Lafreri, 1575, of the Colosseum, showing the building's construction as a piece of architecture. The elevation is restored and complete, with a section removed to reveal the interior construction and ground plan

the more amazing. How could the people of Rome, which produced the elegant houses of Pompeii, the masterful epic poetry of Virgil, the wit of Ovid, the rhetoric of Cicero, also have created as the centrepiece of their public pleasures the phenomenon of the gladiator? How could thousands of people in a highly civilised community gather to watch men fight each other to the death, or to cheer as wild animals ripped apart human bodies, or to observe increasingly baroque executions?

Gladiators bring for us a strange double frisson: on the one hand, a horror based firmly in our cultural superiority; on the other, a voyeuristic fascination with the laceration of the flesh and with the baying crowd. It is not as if public executions have not provided a grim fascination for people throughout European history. Nor is the modern world without its horrible spectacles of violence and degradation – as the pornography industry demonstrates all too clearly. Yet the gladiatorial games must nonetheless remain deeply alien to us, a shocking and mesmerising event which gives the Colosseum a special charge. We do not wonder merely at the towering architecture and technical brilliance of its construction: we are inexorably drawn to reflect on the brutal pleasures enacted there, and what it tells us about human behaviour.

The history of the Colosseum is intertwined with the destruction of the Temple, which led to the Western Wall, my second wonder, developing its place in the longing imagination of the pious. In AD 68, the emperor Nero committed suicide. Eighteen months of civil war followed, which resulted finally in a victory for Vespasian, the general who was in charge of the Roman army ordered to suppress the Jewish revolt, which had begun in 66. The Temple itself was sacked by Titus, Vespasian's son (and the future emperor). They both returned to Rome in 71 to celebrate their victory with a traditional triumphal procession. This procession not only marked the end of the war with the Jews but also the re-establishment of peace and order in the empire. To mark the beginning of his dynasty, like many Roman leaders before and after him, Vespasian set about stamping his authority on the physical layout of the city. After the great fire of Rome, Nero had appropriated hundreds of acres to build his notorious Golden House, which included amid its hundreds of rooms a colossal statue of himself as a Sun god over 98 feet (30 m) high, and a lake, which was 'more like a sea', according to the historian Suetonius. With the canny populist gesture of an expert politician, Vespasian gave back to the people what Nero had taken for his private use. He took the land of the infamous private lake, and built over it the Colosseum, a pleasure-palace for the people. As the poet Martial celebrated:

> Rome is restored to herself. Under your rule, Emperor,
> What had been the tyrant's is now the people's pleasure-dome.

Indeed, Martial was explicit that this building took pride of place over more ancient wonders of the world. The Pyramids, the Hanging Gardens of Babylon, the Temple of Artemis at Ephesus, the Mausoleum, he wrote, all must cede place to 'Caesar's amphitheatre', the newest and greatest wonder.

What we can see today in Rome is impressive, but it is still only a shadow of its original form. Two-thirds of the fabric of building is lost, including all the seats, the flooring of the arena, half the outer wall. It would have been covered with marble facings, and brightly coloured paintings and stucco walls. (The ancient world was actually much more garishly coloured than the modern museums with their polished white statues would have us appreciate.) The familiar arches of the steep walls outside would have held statues. It has also been repaired countless times over the centuries (as well as being looted for cheap building material), and was severely damaged by fire in the third century. Nonetheless, the design's complexity and brilliance of execution remains clear enough – as does the emperor's ambition of monumentality.

The Colosseum is designed as a series of concentric circles around the central staging area, the arena. The outside walls rise to fully 158 feet (48 m). There are four arcaded storeys, and each of these corresponds to a floor level inside. The first three storeys are made up of open archways, with half-columns in three different architectural orders. The first floor has Tuscan columns, there are Ionic on the second and Corinthian on the third. This pattern was much admired by later architects in the Renaissance. The fourth storey repeats the Corinthian order, but has windows rather than arches. The ground-level arches were particularly good spots for prostitutes, we are told by the ancient sources – the excitement of the crowd produced a good deal of sexual energy – and the days of the games were no doubt good for all sorts of local traders. Perhaps the most surprising detail, however, on the outside of the Colosseum can just be glimpsed at the very highest level of the walls. There is here a series of sockets. These were used to attach the huge awning that stretched over the audience to keep them out of the sun. The games took place through the day, and in the summer this would have made the heat for the thousands of spectators unbearable. The solution is itself an outstanding engineering feat. The 'sails', as they were known, could be lowered to cover the crowd, and presumably they were held in place by guy-ropes of some sort reaching to the ground. One of the crueller emperors, Domitian, started to roast the crowd by having his troops keep them in their seats while refusing to lower the awning. The technical back-up for days of slaughter was never less than expert.

Moving inwards from the walls, there are four circular corridors for spectators to use and a small service corridor. These walkways give access to the different areas of the building, and in particular to the stairways which lead to the upper tiers. They also lead to water fountains and presumably toilet facilities (though none has been securely identified). These corridors support the construction above which was built out of travertine stone (the local stone used for the walls), other stone and brick. The highest-level seats were probably wood, to help reduce the weight. There were eighty entrances to the Colosseum. The four sited at the main axes are different from the others, and may have been used by elite spectators, or even by performers. These were probably surmounted with large-scale statues of the emperor in his chariot. Since the stadium probably sat around fifty thousand people, the eighty entrances were certainly necessary for crowd movement.

The crowd in this massive stadium was organised as a map of the highly hierarchical Roman social order. Each person's seat was determined by his civic status. The front rows were reserved for the senators,

the leading political figures of the state, whose position also depended on a high financial criterion. (There were no poor senators, as there are poor nobility.) Behind them sat the knights, the equestrian order, which was both a social and financial status. Behind them came soldiers, ordinary citizens and finally, in the highest tiers, slaves, non-citizens and women – apart from the Vestal Virgins who sat with the senators at the front. This meant that the audience for the elite at least was overwhelmingly male, and no respectable woman would have sat in the furthest seats with the riff-raff. Certain blocks of seating (the areas and entrances are carefully numbered) were reserved for groups of priests and perhaps other groups. Each group also had its distinctive clothing: purple borders for the senators' togas, white for the citizens and so forth. The circular banks of seats created a space where all could see and be seen, everyone in his proper place.

The single most important spectator, however, was the emperor, or the sponsor of the games. The emperor had his own box, and, as ever, had to be adept at staging his own appearance. It was an occasion when the ruler of the empire came into contact with the massed populace of

Internal view of the Colosseum, Rome, built AD 72–80, with its interior circular corridors

Rome. The emperor displayed his authority not just in the lavishness of the games, but also by enacting his power of life and death over the gladiators. At the moment of the climax of a fight, when the decision to kill or spare a defeated gladiator might have to be made, the whole crowd and the performers turned to the emperor, who decided the fate of the man by the turn of a thumb. It would be hard to construct a more intense or insistent spectacle of power.

The emperor might demonstrate his benevolence by throwing tokens into the crowd which could be redeemed for cash or other prizes. The crowd might indicate its disapproval of taxes, or, when Tiberius was emperor, demand that a statue taken by him from the public baths was returned. He complied with their wishes. The audience could become vocal and even hostile. (We know that the space allocated per person was only 16 inches (40 cm), and the average legroom was no more than 28 inches (70 cm). This is smaller than an economy-price seat on an aeroplane. The audience at the games was so closely packed together, that this must have added greatly to their volatility.) The emperor might threaten the elite, as Commodus famously did by killing an ostrich, whose head he held up before the senators with a grin – as if to say that their heads were on the line. The historian Dio, who was in the Colosseum on this occasion, tells us he had to chew on laurel leaves to stop himself laughing – with fear and shock, no doubt, as much as at the spectacle of an emperor killing an ostrich. The games were a place where the emperor could appear as the benefactor of the people, but his position always was at risk in the glare of public disapproval: a high-stake competition in public status.

Yet it was on the arena that eyes focused most intently. The floor of the arena is now lost, but it reveals to the modern tourist the complicated machinery and planning necessary for the elaborate charades of death. There is a long underground tunnel leading directly to one of the major training camps for gladiators, with its practice areas. The whole structure is a maze of tunnels and corridors with hoists that would have lifted wild animals to the surface via trapdoors in the wooden floor. Stage scenery could also be hoisted into place in this way. This must have been a fearsome place to work, dark, hot and full of frightened men and animals, as well as sweating slaves and pressured workmen. The noise from the arena could be heard in a horrific mix of thuds and screams and the roar of the crowd. This is the side of the gladiator's life that ancient and modern romantics alike do not care to focus on.

In the arena itself, the floor was covered with sand (Latin *harena*, hence the word 'arena') which was used to soak up the blood and other body fluids of men and animals. The opening festivities of AD 80, when the building was dedicated by Titus, give a strong idea of the pain and

organisation behind so bland a description. The games lasted one hundred days. They were an extravaganza that included the slaughtering of nine thousand animals on a single day, some killed by specially trained female hunters. There were mass gladiator fights. There were pitched battles, and even, according to some ancient sources, though bitterly contested by modern scholars, a sea-battle with fully manned galleys on a specially flooded ring. There were individual contests of pairs of superstar gladiators. As many as three thousand gladiators fought in a single day. The emperor had small wooden balls thrown into the audience which could be exchanged for food, money, even slaves. The emperor Trajan later had ten thousand gladiators fight on the same day: that is the equivalent of every professional footballer, basketball player and

A fight in the amphitheatre, showing a battle between citizens of Pompeii and Nuceria, from Pompeii, AD 59 baseball player in America fighting with lethal weapons in the same arena on the same day. This was a status bloodbath on a truly staggering scale.

The Colosseum was also used for punishment of criminals. Men were forced to fight wild beasts, or to enter the ring as prey for the beasts (although there is actually no securely attested story of any Christians being thrown to the lions in the Colosseum, for all that it was a story later Christians loved to tell). The punishments could be absolutely bizarre to our eyes. Criminals were forced to act out the most horrific deaths of mythic figures: a woman was forced to mate with a bull, like Pasiphae, the mother of the Minotaur; another was burnt to death on a pyre in the costume of Hercules, who in myth had died in just such a way. These scenes were the most visible – and baroque – demonstration of the state asserting its right to punish the criminal.

The gladiators themselves were as fascinating to the Romans as they have proved to modern audiences. They were the lowest members of society, often slaves or criminals, whose bodies were there to be used as machines. They were trained by the harsh realities of the gladiator school in the arts of killing and dying. Therein lies the beginning of their paradoxical interest to the Romans, who privileged hard military values in their long pursuit of empire. Cicero even described gladiators as being turned into examples of Roman virtue through their training: 'Look at the gladiators,' he wrote, 'corrupt men or barbarians, what blows they receive! See how men who have been well trained prefer to receive a blow than basely avoid it! Who of them has disgraced himself?' Consequently, gladiators could become heroes of manliness in the eyes of the Romans, despite their degradation. They became sexual fantasies of women. There are graffiti on the walls at Pompeii that record gladiators' celebrity status, with all the typical mixture of envy and admiration that celebrity brings. There are expensive mosaics of gladiators. Some free men were even drawn towards becoming gladiators in the hope of a successful career and long retirement (which few gladiators ever achieved). Most scandalously of all, even the occasional well-born man was led to pursue such a life, and – beyond scandal in terms of its shocking-ness – the emperor Commodus actually dressed and trained as a gladiator (though his chosen opponents were there only to be fodder for his weapons) and he even killed animals in the ring, as we saw earlier with the story of him beheading an ostrich . The modern world of Hollywood has, of course, repeatedly fallen in love with these fighters, from *Spartacus* to *Gladiator*. But it was the Romans themselves who first made media stars out of these brutal killers.

There is no doubt that the Colosseum was designed, as Martial celebrated, to be a wonder of the world. It was the largest stadium ever built

Bust of Emperor Lucius Verus (Lucius Aelius Aurelius Commodus (d. AD 169) in gladiatorial dress

for gladiatorial games, there at the centre of the capital of the largest empire the world had ever known. As a building, it has a scale and design to impress every visitor with the power and authority of those who built it. To walk underneath those immense and towering walls, towards the central gates, beneath a statue of the emperor in his four-horse chariot, with fifty thousand fellow citizens to see the games, where three thousand men would fight and perhaps die in front of you, was to take part in a spectacle of imperial power like no other. For the modern visitor, it is this history of bloodshed, our bafflement and voyeuristic fascination with the dark side of civilisation, that gives the Colosseum its special lure. We cannot but wonder at what man can do to man in the name of entertainment or power.

THE ALPHABET AND
THE ROSETTA STONE

It is hard to conceive how impoverished and strange the world would appear without writing. It is so basic to Western civilisation that it would take a concerted effort of the imagination to remove it from our world view. It is not just that so much technology would never have been developed, it is also that most of what we value in Western civilisation from political systems to institutions of learning to literature to our ability to communicate across distances, all depend on the written word. It would be a society without history (though it could have oral myth), a society without science (though it might use drugs), a society restricted in perspective to a local and personal knowledge (though it may have wisdom of its own). When we look back at the Stone Age village of Skara Brae, perched on the edge of Orkney, we can actually know very little about it, because all we have is the bare stones. We can try to contemplate the harsh limitations of its world, but without writing it is a place without history. All the monuments in this book could not be discussed, and would not be such wonders, if it were not for what people have written and recorded about them. Only the Great Pyramid survives of the traditional list of seven wonders of the ancient world, but we can see the lost monuments in our mind's eye because of the written word's record. The everyday marvel of literacy – of which reading this book is one sign – defines Western civilisation. There is no invention, no physical object, no intellectual achievement of the ancient world, which comes close to the alphabet in terms of its influence on every person's life today.

The great turning-point in the history of human communication took place in the Greek world probably about 800 BC when the Greek alphabet was invented. This deserves to be called the great turning-point not because it was the first attempt at writing – it certainly was not, neither in Greece, nor elsewhere in the Mediterranean, as even the ancient Greeks themselves knew well – but because it was the first alphabet to combine abstract signs for both consonants and vowels. It was this combination which hugely expanded the expressivity of writing, which could now capture any sound, and increased its potential for mass communication: since there were only twenty-four letters to be mastered, the skill of reading and even writing could be more easily acquired than ever before. By the fifth century BC, democracy as a political system, history as a discipline, medicine as a science, tragedy as an art form, had joined the preservation of Homer's poetry as the legacy of Greece to the West.

It was the invention of the alphabet which was the condition of possibility for these momentous changes.

Alphabets are often invented by individual people. The Armenian script, which can be seen, for example, in the extensive floor inscriptions in the church of the Holy Sepulchre in Jerusalem, was invented by St Mesrob in about AD 400. In the ninth century, St Cyril invented an alphabet to convert the Slavs to Christianity, and the alphabet used still in Russian-speaking lands is called Cyrillic after him. As late as AD 1446, King Sejong of Korea invented the Korean alphabet. Consequently, scholars have often thought that the Greek alphabet too must have been invented by a single man, a 'genius and benefactor of mankind'. The ancient Greeks called this inventor Palamedes, one of the trickiest warriors to have gone to Troy with the Greek expedition to recapture Helen; in some other accounts the inventor was Cadmus, the founder of Thebes. There is no way of knowing if the alphabet had one or many points of origin. But we can see how the invention radically changed the systems of record-keeping that had gone before it.

The earliest writing we have is cuneiform, that is, wedge-shaped marks (the Latin for wedge is *cuneus*), found first in Sumeria around 4000 BC. Our examples of this script are usually incised with a wedge-shaped blade into clay tablets, which are then baked hard. Cuneiform writing developed from pictograms, where the mark for a 'fish' looked like a fish. These signs became more abstract, and gradually were treated as phonographs, that is, marks that indicate sounds, usually syllables. The language and culture which used this form of writing most extensively,

Pictograph record of food supplies, probably from southern Iraq, *c.*3000 BC

was Akkadian, and the use of this Semitic language stretched across a broad area from Mesopotamia to Syria for many centuries. In Akkadian cuneiform there were hundreds of syllabic signs, many of which had multiple pronunciation, and which could change meaning as they are compounded. This makes Akkadian a very difficult system to master. The earliest inscriptions are economic records, and there is little doubt that writing was a tool of power, restricted to the elite as a means of control. The most celebrated text of Akkadian is indeed a law code, the famous Code of Hammurabi, dating from the eighteenth century BC. Hammurabi was king of Babylon, and his law code is remarkable for its defence of the weak against the power of the strong. Akkadian cuneiform has left many texts, indications of a flourishing social order. But all our Western alphabets come from a different line of descent.

The family tree of modern alphabets usually begins with Proto-Semitic or Proto-Canaanite. This too began as a pictographic system, where the sign for 'ox' looked like an ox head. But this early and restricted script was changed and extended by the Phoenicians, who are said by the ancient Greeks to be the inventors of writing itself. Phoenician writing consisted of twenty-two syllabic signs, each of which designates a consonant plus an unspecified vowel (or sometimes no vowel). The pictograph for house ('bet' in Proto-Semitic, as in modern Hebrew) becomes thus the syllable 'b + vowel', and will, in turn, become the letter beta, the second letter of the Greek alphabet. In many places across the Middle East this simple syllabary replaced the far more cumbersome Akkadian cuneiform. Phoenician writing too is associated with the instruments of power and trade, and it is from Phoenician that the Greek alphabet developed.

How this transformation happened is a mystery. We cannot be sure of the precise date or the place, or even whether it was one man who sat down with a Phoenician merchant and sketched out a new set of letters, or whether it was a gradual process of adaptation which slowly reached consensus through repetition and common usage. It is striking that let-

Clay tablets inscribed with records in Linear B script. Minoan, 1450–1400 BC

ters immediately appear to represent sounds in Greek that are absent from Phoenician, in particular 'ph', as in 'philosophy'. Also, where Phoenician is written from right to left, earliest Greek writing was 'boustrophedon', that is, the first line is read from left to right and then, at the end of the line, the eye travels on the second line back from right to left, and so on in alternation till the end of the page. ('Boustrophedon' means 'like an ox ploughing'.) Soon, Greek was written only from left to right. What is more, Greek made signs for the vowels.

This new alphabetic system was very different from earlier systems of record in Greece. Sir Arthur Evans, when he excavated Knossos and other Mycenaean Bronze Age sites, discovered many small tablets with a hitherto unknown and unreadable language. What became known as Linear B was first deciphered by Ventris and Chadwick in Cambridge in 1952. It turned out that this was an early form of Greek, and the tablets, when translated, were records of the palace culture of the Mycenaean kings. Linear B is syllabic, and very restricted in its possible range of sounds: there are many sounds of Greek it cannot say, although there are many later Greek words recognisable in this strange script. Also individual signs are used for particular things, such as sheep, as well as particular syllables. The decipherment of Linear B was a brilliant achievement, and it gives an unparalleled insight into the world of the palace storerooms of a Bronze Age kingdom. But as an alphabet system it was clumsy and inadequately expressive – and seems to have had no impact on later centuries. After the destruction of the Bronze Age palaces, possibly by earthquake, possibly by war, possibly by both, Linear B disappeared from even the memory of Greek culture until the twentieth century.

What is perhaps most surprising about the invention of the new technology of the alphabet is that it was immediately used for a range of purposes that we do not see with the earlier syllabic and cuneiform systems which are so linked with the official record-keeping of the authorities. In the seventh century BC on the island of Thera we are already finding graffiti of a distinctly unofficial type. On one boulder we have what looks like competitive boasting from three guys. 'Laqydidas is great,' says one; 'Eumelos is best at dancing,' adds another. A third tops them both: 'Krimon, best in the "dirty dance", has warmed the heart of Simias.' We should not think that 'warm the heart' is just a sentimental or aesthetic judgement. Other graffiti are far cruder: 'Krimon fucked Amotion here' (and there are several more like this). Amid the current arguments about the state of the modern city, it is bizarre to reflect that one of the first things humans did with alphabetic writing was scratch rude remarks on walls.

It was not the only activity of these first alphabetic writers, however. One of the most fascinating archaeological discoveries of this early

The Dipylon Oinochoe vase, with scratched writing round the neck, *c*.735 BC

period is a vase known as the Dipylon Oinochoe. It was discovered on a road out of Athens in 1871, a modest but attractive wine jug about 9 inches (23 cm) high, decorated with an abstract pattern of black slip on the red clay. It was made in the eighth century BC, probably about 735. There is a graffito scratched onto the vase above the shoulder, which seems to read a hexameter verse: 'Whoever of all the dancers now dances most friskily . . .', as if the wine was to be a reward for the best dancer at some symposium or feast. A cup, found on the island of Pithekousa, dates from the same period, and it has an equally tantalising inscription, which reads: 'I am the cup of Nestor, a joy to drink from. Whoever drinks this cup, straight away the desire of beautiful-crowned Aphrodite will seize him.' The inscription is a double tease. It promises, first of all, that anyone who drinks its wine will fall in love: the goddess of sexual desire, Aphrodite,

64

will get him. But it also declares itself to be the cup of Nestor. Nestor is one of the great heroes of the Homeric poems, and in the *Iliad*, the cup of Nestor is described at length as having gold bosses all round, four handles, golden doves decorating it, and of such a size that only a true hero could lift it. This rather more humble clay cup boasts it is such an epic wonder. This is the first literary joke, scratched on a drinking cup, remarkably vivid testimony to the culture of drinking and elegant fun amid the elite of eighth-century Athens. These are two of the earliest inscriptions in alphabetic writing surviving from Greece, and they reveal immediately a fresh and sly use of writing, and a burgeoning community of writers and readers.

There are inscriptions too in temples – individuals dedicating votives to the gods. In the Boston Museum of Fine Arts now, though once in Thebes, there is a bronze statue of a man with an inscription running up and down both thighs in a horseshoe pattern. It reads 'Mantikos dedicated me to the far-darter, lord of the silver bow, as a tenth part [of his spoils]. So do you, Phoibos, grant to me a pleasing gift in return.' A warrior has dedicated a tithe of his victory spoils to the god Apollo, who is addressed by his cult titles of 'far-darter', 'lord of the silver bow' and 'Phoibos'. Writing becomes a way for an individual man to communicate now with god. So too we have curse tablets. Written words can also embody with a unique power the magical properties of language to have an effect on the world.

Along with the gradual development of the sciences, literature and philosophy, that has made Greece such a crucible of civilisation, what alphabetic writing also makes possible is a full and rich literate culture of a sort barely in evidence in the palace cultures of the great kings of the past, where writing was so much an instrument of economic and legal control, and so much in the hands of a professional class of scribes. Greece too used the alphabet for its systems of power, of course: the democratic state put up inscriptions all over the city recording its laws, honours and victories. But putting reading and writing in the hands of the people was one of the most significant and long-lasting political gestures of democracy.

The single object which has most captured the modern imagination when it comes to the alphabet is, however, the Rosetta Stone. It is one of the most visited exhibits in the British Museum. What makes it so alluring is certainly not the content of the inscriptions on it, which record the confirmation of a royal cult for Ptolemy V by a council of priests in 196 BC, along with some tax breaks for the priests. Nor is it the beauty of the stone itself, which has minimal aesthetic appeal. What excites about the Rosetta Stone is the story of what secrets it unlocked and the power of reading it conferred.

Statuette of Apollo from Thebes, made by Mantikos, bronze, 700–675 BC

The Rosetta Stone was discovered by Napoleon's troops in a small fort in the village of Rashid in 1799. (Rosetta is a Western rendition of Rashid.) It was given to the British under the Treaty of Alexandria, and came to the British Museum in 1801. What makes the Rosetta Stone unique is that it records the same priestly inscription in three different languages, Greek, demotic and hieroglyphic. Greek was the normal official language of the Hellenistic kingdoms, and Ptolemy, as a descendant of one of Alexander's generals, would have spoken Greek as his first language. Demotic is a cursive script used in religious contexts in Egypt since at least the sixth century BC. Hieroglyphic is the language familiar from the ancient inscriptions from the Pyramids, which was at that point unreadable.

The decipherment of the Rosetta Stone was slow and involved more than one scholarly contribution (and how the story has been told has often tended to depend on whether the narrator is French or English). Thomas Young, an English linguist, was the first to make a significant breakthrough when he worked out principles to recognise some of the more significant names on the stone. But it was Jean-François Champollion who made the most important discovery, when he showed the phonographic nature of the hieroglyphs, in a paper delivered in 1822. He had read Young's work, and both corrected and extended it. This led not only to the painstaking translation of the Rosetta Stone but also to the decipherment of Egyptian hieroglyphic inscriptions from across Egypt, and the consequent burgeoning of our knowledge of ancient Egypt.

The Rosetta Stone is a surprising tourist draw. It relies to a degree on this story of decipherment, and the revelation of the mysteries of the Pyramids. But it also bears witness to the power of letters, our desire to read, to decode the signs. The alphabet, which was first developed in Greece in the eighth century BC, is a wonder we tend to take for granted. We see it every day without awe. Yet to sit with a child who is learning to read is to see again the opening of a vista of civilisation that the alphabet makes possible. The alphabet is the wonder which grounds all others in this book.

The Rosetta Stone, 196 BC

THE GREAT WALL OF CHINA

If the Great Pyramid of Giza is one of the most extensively measured buildings from the ancient world, and Giza one of the most extensively analysed archaeological sites, the Great Wall of China is certainly the least comprehensively surveyed great monument of the past, and one of the least well understood, both in China and in the West. It is only by kowtowing to the myths which have grown up about the Great Wall that I can include it at all in this chapter of the book. But how could a book on the Wonders of the World not include the Great Wall of China? It has so often been compared to the Pyramids and other extraordinary human labours, it is one of the most popular tourist destinations in China, and the picture of the fortresses and raised roadway winding across seemingly impassable mountains and ravines into the misty distance is one of the most familiar images of China, both here in the West and in China itself. And by any judgement, the Great Wall is one of the most remarkable engineering feats of any period, an act of man that changes the landscape and our relation to geography.

There is a traditional story which is a great favourite not only of tourist guides but also of many books on China. It says that the Great Wall of China was built by Shih Huang Ti, the great ruler who brought together the warring kingdoms of China into a single, centralised empire, under his rule as first Universal Emperor. Shih Huang Ti ruled between 246 and 210 BC, and although his Ch'in dynasty did not last long, the Wall he established continued to be repaired and extended, and acted as a military barrier that prevented the barbarians of the north coming into contact with the civilisation of China. The Wall we see today is a monument of an unbroken tradition that defines the conceptual and physical boundaries of China over the centuries, stretching back in time as it stretches over the mountains. It is the one man-made object that can be seen from space. Unfortunately, this story is almost wholly untrue.

It is easy, however, to see how and why this traditional account has come about and continues to be maintained. The stories of Shih Huang Ti and the building of his wall are certainly ancient, and they have played a constant role in the popular culture of China up to today. Chinese historians and philosophers over the centuries discoursed on the rule of the first emperor and on the significance of his project. It was perhaps inevitable that the extraordinary wall we can see and the extraordinary stories of the ancient Ch'in dynasty should have come together to create a national heritage. Travellers from Europe, especially in the nineteenth century, romanticised the antiquity, mystery and oriental abundance of

The Great Wall of China, built in the Han and Ming dynasties

69

Almost impassable: the wall passing over the jagged mountain top at Simatai, the highest point of the Great Wall

China, and they too were instrumental in producing the myth of the dragon-like wall, ageless, reaching over the landscape and back in time.

Shih Huang Ti was said to have been the son of a merchant and a courtesan. The courtesan had also been the lover of the heir to the throne of Ch'in, and her child was adopted by one of his barren wives, believing him to be the son of the prince. This scurrilous tale of illegitimacy was no doubt circulated by his enemies, as was his description as having 'a high-pointed nose, slit eyes, pigeon breast, wolf voice, tiger heart; stingy, cringing and graceless', that we find in a historian writing only a hundred years after his death. But Shih Huang Ti was undoubtedly an insatiable military and political imperialist, who changed the shape of China. He came to the throne when he was only thirteen, but by the time he was thirty-five he had conquered all the warring kingdoms of what is now China and developed a centralised system of government based on the emperor and the imperial court, a policy which drastically reduced the power of the aristocrats and destroyed the previous feudal system. He embarked on a huge building programme. He extended and

fortified his capital Hsien-Yang (and ordered 1,200 of the richest and most powerful families to move there); he built broad stone roads, radiating from the capital; he constructed new canals. In his general desire for centralisation, he even standardised weights and measures, and introduced copper coinage.

These changes were viewed with undisguised horror by many traditionalists, as if Shih Huang Ti was tampering with the laws of nature, and since traditionalist scholars write the histories of this period, the emperor from first to last appears as the consummate villain. At a banquet, one disgruntled scholar declared, 'Nothing can endure, except those things in which we follow the example of antiquity.' The response was instant: 'In their preaching, these scholars exalt what *was*, only to discredit what *is*; they build their utopias in order to blacken, by contrast, reality. Whenever a new law appears they carp and cavil.' The emperor consequently instigated a new law that all old history books should be burnt; anyone who does not comply should be branded and sent to hard labour; all who wish to study the past, should be made to study at an

Shih Huang Ti (259–210 BC), the first Ch'in emperor, ordering the burning of books and execution of scholars. Painting on silk by Hung Wu, fourteenth century

official school. (The echoes of the modern Cultural Revolution are unpleasantly acute.) Four hundred and sixty scholars were put to death for continuing to teach the old books – buried alive, according to some versions, but the soil where they were buried became so rich that melons could always grow there. The emperor's epitaph for two thousand years has been: 'He burned the Books and buried the Scholars.'

The Wall, Shih Huang Ti's greatest project, is equally scarred with cruelty and violence, as well as grandiose planning and fearsome organisation. He sent off his leading general Meng Ti'en, with three hundred thousand men (as the historian Ssu-Ma Ch'ien of the second century BC tells us), to beat back their enemies in the north and to build a 'Great Wall, constructing its defiles and passes in accordance with the configurations of the terrain. It started at Lin-t'ao and extended to Liao-tung, reaching a distance of more than 10,000 *li* (a *li* is about a third of a mile (0.5 km)). Hence, the Wall is often known in Chinese as the '10,000-*li* wall'. Thousands of people were press-ganged into building the Wall, prisoners, criminals and recalcitrant scholars were forced to work there – and thousands died, giving it also the name of 'The Longest Cemetery in

the World'. Workers who fell behind were thrown into the section of the Wall where they were working and buried alive. (The white brick-dust is said to be powdered bones.) There is a tribe of wild pygmies, we are told, covered all over with white hair, who live in the mountains, who will ask if the Wall is still being built and will flee screaming if they are told that it is. Such stories – and travellers in the Edwardian period were still told this tale of terrified pygmies – vividly capture the fear and despair of peasants forced into such imperial building projects.

The Wall that Meng Ti'en oversaw was partly new, but also was constructed out of several other, older walls that had been built by the warring kingdoms. It may have been built of earthen ramparts rather

Archer wearing breastplate. One of the Ch'in emperor Shih Huang Ti's terracotta army (discovered 1974), from his tomb in Xian, Shaanxi province, 221–210 BC

than the brick and dressed stone of the current wall. Although as a wall it may not have survived long after the Ch'in dynasty, it nonetheless fuelled the stories and ideals of Chinese culture. For there were other wall-building projects, other attempts to define the boundaries of Chinese civilisation, culminating in the great builders of the Ming dynasty.

Awe at the scale of this undertaking is powerfully felt in the stories which swirl around the wonder of the Wall. Shih Huang Ti had a 'Drive the Mountains' whip, with which he could move an entire mountain range with a single crack, or make the Yellow river stand back while the men worked. He had a magic horse, jet-black but with a red mane and flaming tail, which could travel 300 miles (483 km) in a single day. This horse also indicated the path the Wall was to take, by walking with a saddle tied to its tail, which marked the route in the dust. One day, a dust storm rose, and the builders following the horse lost sight of him. They carried on work, however, in what they thought was the right path. When the storm cleared, they found they had gone 40 *li* in the wrong direction, and the horse was patiently waiting near where they had last seen it. This explains why there is a 12-mile (19-km) abandoned stretch of wall, which goes nowhere and seems unconnected with the main line. The Wall of Shih Huang Ti is surrounded by innumerable stories of fear, horror, romance and awe, like these.

These, then, are the tales that bolster the traditional account of the Great Wall of China. Unfortunately, this familiar story is simply not true in almost all of its significant claims. The assertion that the Wall can be seen from the Moon (or even from Mars) was first made at the beginning of the twentieth century, when it could only have been a hyperbolic claim: and astronauts report that no such sighting is possible (which is hardly surprising, as the wall is no wider than a two-lane highway, and of roughly the same colour as the surrounding landscape). Most of the Wall that can be seen today, including all the most famous sections near Peking (Beijing) where tourists are taken, and the famous line of fortresses, were built in the Ming dynasty (AD 1368–1644) and towards the end of the dynasty at that. Thinking of the Wall as contemporary with the great Renaissance palaces or the cathedrals of Europe does slightly reduce the uniqueness of its magnificence. As a military barrier, it was notably inadequate. At various times, the Mongols (and others) simply crossed it and pillaged around the plain of Peking. Many of the places where the wall is built appear to have minimal strategic purpose. While Shih Huang Ti is a fascinating figure, who did build a massive wall, there are actually several long walls built in different places and at different times, and there is no reason to assume his wall followed exactly the same route as the Ming wall. Marco Polo does not mention any wall, when he visited China, and scholars have suggested that consequently there may

The Xitengkou section of the Great Wall, submerged by the building of a dam on the Luan river in 1975

have been no significant or continuous wall standing at that date. While the archaeological work completed on the Great Wall remains exiguous – we know hugely more about Hadrian's Wall, for instance, where every fort and every mile has been scrupulously examined – the claim that the Ming wall was built on the foundations of the third-century BC wall, using the same basic building techniques, is hard to justify. To see the Great Wall as basically unchanged and merely repaired from the third century BC until today requires considerable archaeological and historical blinkers. It would seem that in the case of the Great Wall of China, as with so many other best-beloved stories, familiar tradition turns out to be an invented myth.

The wall we know today was an attempt of the Ming dynasty to deal with the northern nomads. Chinese civilisation had regularly defined itself over and against the 'barbarians' who lived a nomadic life on the steppes, the Mongols, the Tartars, the Manchu. They saw these tribes as representing everything they were not. The Chinese built cities, with walls around them and walls within them – like Peking, with its city walls and the walls of the Forbidden City within the city. The nomads

The Ming-dynasty fortress at Jiayuguan, at the westernmost limit of the Great Wall of China, Gansu province

wandered across the flat open plains, or climbed the inaccessible mountains – regions without walls. The Chinese valued exquisite food and delicate silks and calligraphy as the privileged signs of civilisation. The nomads ripped silk in a couple of rides on their horses, wore animal skins and consumed such disgusting animal products as milk and cheese (which still play no part in Chinese cuisine). To some degree, all the areas of China spoke related languages: but the nomads spoke a different tongue. A wall between the Chinese and the nomads was both a barrier and a symbol in itself.

Over the centuries, there were different periods of warfare and rapprochement. There were times of trade at the border, and times when the nomads looted and pillaged inside China: and the dynasty immediately before the Ming was the Mongol dynasty of Genghis Khan and Kublai Khan, when the whole of China was again reunited but under the foreign rule of 'the barbarians'. When the Ming dynasty fell, it was replaced by the Manchu – another foreign power from beyond the Wall. The Ming wall was built out of a particular necessity. They did not wish to trade with the barbarians, but they did not have the power to defeat them. When they did lead a large army into the steppes, the story goes that they marched for 1,000 miles without seeing a single enemy. After they had returned, within a year the nomadic raiders were back. The barbarians did not fight like the Chinese, either. The Wall seemed a time-hallowed solution to the problem of self-defence.

Yet it did not work. The Wall did not prevent foreign rulers dominating China for centuries. It is a strange quirk of history that the Wall has had such a changing fortune in the imagination of the Chinese themselves. For many generations the Great Wall was a symbol of a failed policy and the collapse of Chinese authority – much as the impressive

Maginot line in Belgium, so easily bypassed by the advancing Nazis, became an icon of misguided defensive strategy. Yet in the nineteenth century, the Wall became a sign of national unity, pride and greatness. For Mao's Cultural Revolution, however, it was seen as one of the most telling signs of the outmoded and of bourgeois hankering for a corrupt past: hundreds of kilometres were destroyed, and the stones used for new projects. In 1984, Deng Xiaoping launched a new campaign to love the country and rebuild the Wall – because the Wall was again to be a banner of patriotic feeling.

The length of the Wall is given as various figures between 1,500 miles (2,414 km) and 4,000 miles (6,437 km) (a sign not just of the lack of standard archaeological work but also of the difficulty of deciding which parts of which walls will count). But there are long sections of unbroken fortification that remain extraordinarily impressive. The Ming established an astonishing number of fortresses every few hundred metres. There are temples near the Wall at key points with gods to protect the passes. The Wall travels a dizzying route over the tops of jagged mountains where no one could seriously have expected an invading army to traverse. The Wall here offers a powerful symbolic barrier rather than a military necessity (though some Mongols say that it is best conceived as a road rather than a wall – the quickest way to cross those hills). There are fascinating inscriptions along the way which give a tantalising insight into the world of the soldiers who built it. So we are told that General Tsui Ching, along with a list of other officials, contractors and workmen, built 591 feet and 6 inches (180.3 m) of Third Class Wall at the end of military graduate Lung Kuang-hsien's portion of Tower 55 of the Black Letter 'Wu' series, on the sixteenth day of the ninth Moon of the fourth year of Wan Li. There are several such inscriptions recording first-, second- and third-class Wall building, by a host of officials, who lived out by the Wall with their wives, building and guarding the frontier.

There are also votaries along the Wall. One records a useful cure for a cut mouth. The 'magic mortar' should be taken from the bricks and crushed with an unborn mouse, and then applied as an ointment to the cut. The recipe usefully adds that if a mouse is not available, substitute oil. These evocative remnants of a lost and busier world bring a certain pathos to the now largely deserted Wall.

But above all, what makes the Wall still such an object of wonder is the sight of the towers and the walkway disappearing over some of the most precipitous mountainscape in China. Perhaps we do not need to worry too much about the myths and legends, when we have before us such testimony of man's wilful desire to impress himself on the landscape, and to erect a barrier of self-definition across so inhospitable a terrain.

THE WONDER OF GREEK SCULPTURE: A *STELE* FROM PAROS

When the Elgin Marbles, the friezes hacked from the Parthenon by Lord Elgin, were first displayed in Britain in 1807, it was for most British men and women the first time they had seen real ancient Greek statues. Some gentlemen had completed the Grand Tour and would have seen some of the splendid temples that were still standing, including the Parthenon. Many more knew Roman copies of the great masterpieces of the Greek world, from ancient examples or from modern plaster casts. But actual pieces of Greek statuary were extremely rare. Yet throughout Europe, the educated had been well prepared over several generations to be amazed by these carved stones. Since the Renaissance, when the rediscovery of Greek and Latin literature, science and philosophy had fired the imaginations and intellects of the leading scholars of the day, Greek art had been held up as the standard, the yardstick, by which all art should be judged. The perfection, calm and poise of an art that had not really been seen provided the exemplary models for artists and critics alike. So, for many people, seeing the Elgin Marbles was an overwhelming experience. The poet Keats captures the full, emotional romance of the moment:

> My spirit is too weak; mortality
> Weighs heavily on me like unwilling sleep,
> And each imagined pinnacle and steep
> Of godlike hardship tells me I must die
> Like a sick eagle looking at the sky.
> Yet 'tis gentle luxury to weep,
> That I have not the cloudy winds to keep
> Fresh for the opening of the morning's eye.
> Such dim-conceived glories of the brain
> Bring round the heart an indescribable feud;
> So do these wonders a most dizzy pain,
> That mingles Grecian grandeur with the rude
> Wasting of old Time – with a billowy main,
> A sun, a shadow of a magnitude.

This poem, 'On Seeing the Elgin Marbles for the First Time', epitomises the Romantic pursuit of the sublime through ancient Greek art. For the poet to look at these masterpieces is to be like a 'sick eagle looking at the sky', yearning to be able to soar, but conscious more of his own mortality and weakness of spirit. He can only wallow in 'the gentle luxury' of his tears. He experiences dizzying pain, an 'indescribable feud' of feelings, as he contemplates the glories of past art, now worn by age – which he strives to conjure in the famous final phrase, 'a shadow of a magnitude'. Weeping, marvelling, confused – the poet sums up the archetypal response to 'these wonders' of Greek art.

Keats's reaction to Greek art is typical of the eighteenth and nineteenth centuries in particular, when Greece exercised a tyranny over the European imagination. It is still the case, however, that the ideals of Greek art are dominant in the Western representation of the human form. The wonder of Greek sculpture changed how we see the body and how we imagine a human should look. My problematic task is to choose one single work to sum up this amazing artistic and cultural phenomenon. For many viewers, the Elgin Marbles themselves epitomise Greek sculpture, and they are certainly famous. But I have chosen a less familiar work. To appreciate its restrained, sad beauty, we should look first at some grander works of art, which have been instrumental in making the Greek body a modern as well as an ancient ideal.

A statue discovered by a peasant farmer on the Greek island of Melos in 1820 has become one of the most familiar icons in the world, second in popularity only to the Mona Lisa for the tourist groups in the Louvre. It was obtained by the French ambassador – a phrase that conceals a story of skulduggery and flight across the high seas to escape the Turkish authorities – and taken back to Louis XVIII. The next year, it was presented to the Louvre, where it has remained ever since. Originally the statue was associated with a base, which is now lost, but which identified the artist as Alexandros of Antioch on the Maeander. (We know nothing more of this sculptor, and can only imagine his career, moving from one of the larger cities of the Greek-speaking eastern Mediterranean to international recognition.) The statue is of the goddess Aphrodite and was produced probably towards the end of the second century BC for a temple on the island, and it is known most frequently by its Romanised title of the 'Venus de Milo', or the 'Aphrodite of Melos'.

Its discovery in 1820 at the height of European mania for all things ancient and Greek no doubt helped its instant popularity. But it is also a very fine piece of work. Although it was probably sculpted towards the end of the Hellenistic period, it looks back in style to a more classicising era – and both the pose of the goddess and the sculptor's technique make this a very sexy cult statue indeed, which has helped define an ideal of female beauty for the modern world.

The most striking aspect of the pose is the torsion of the body. The left leg is pushed forward, but so is the right shoulder. At the same time,

Aphrodite of Melos (Venus de Milo), by Alexandros of Antioch, 130–100 BC

the torso is twisted sinuously by the raised right hip and left arm. It makes it seem as though the body is moving in two directions at the same time. This is not by chance. Aphrodite is the goddess of sexual desire. She teases and twists her victims – with all the playfulness, misleading and despair of thwarted love. She also stimulates human passion, and leads her human viewers into the lures of her world of passion.

So the viewer here, approaching the statue, finds it hard to catch the goddess's eye. Her head is turned away from the vector of her body, and the slight angle of the head takes her gaze up and away. The undefined emotion of her expression further distances her from any contact with the viewer. We watch the goddess thus as if we are not watched by her. The scenario of a beautiful woman caught unawares by our gaze is one of the classic ruses of erotic art. But with this Aphrodite, the goddess who controls such encounters, things are not quite so straightforwardly voyeuristic. Aphrodite is the mistress of desire, and what is knowingly on display here is the power of the goddess. The robes which are carved with consummate skill, flowing over the raised left leg and around her hips, are part of this game. It seems as if they are about to fall to her feet, revealing the full form of the divine body. The curve of the belly and the right hip shows off the top of the goddess's thigh. The statue seems an invitation to the erotic imagination – to enter into the power of the goddess.

It was a commonplace in the nineteenth century and previous centuries to restore statues by adding the missing parts with freshly carved stone. Many such restorations seem grotesque to modern sensibilities. But although Louis received various suggestions of how the arms of this statue might have been, the statue was left as it was found. This too has become part of the fame or notoriety of the Aphrodite of Melos. Many have noticed – either with pleasure or annoyance – how the fragmented body encourages the play of fantasy, and artists from Salvador Dalí onwards have taken up the challenge of this image. But the slipping robe of the goddess shows how such a challenge to the viewer's erotic self-control was part of this statue's lure, even when it was whole and stood as the religious centrepiece of a temple of the goddess of desire.

The Aphrodite of Melos has become part of our image repertoire. It stands as an icon of how Greek sculpture learnt to represent female flesh in stone, and this artful combination of revelation and concealment of the body in flowing robes has deeply influenced the Western artistic tradition, and its ideals of female beauty. But although this is so familiar an image, it is not my chosen wonder of Greek sculpture.

If the Aphrodite of Melos epitomises Greek sculpture of the female form, the Hermes and Dionysus of Praxiteles is equally representative of the Greek love of the male body. The Greek city was filled with statues

Hermes and the infant Dionysus, from the Temple of Hera, Olympia, by Praxiteles, c.343 BC

of men, often naked. The citizens honoured famous men such as the city founders, heroes of war, athletic victors, with life-size nude statues. Gods, too, and great human figures from epic and myth, decorated temples and other religious shrines. The citizen was surrounded by images of what the perfect body should be.

Greek sculpture's earliest masterpieces remind us of Egyptian monumental art, and the *kouros*, a larger-than-life-size grave marker, is typically a four-square, solid production, with a minimum of movement, a bare indication of anatomical form and the mysterious archaic smile. But within a surprisingly short time, technique and artistic vision had developed to such a degree that our canons of realism remain fully indebted to these masters of plastic form. Praxiteles was one of the most famous and influential of these sculptors.

He flourished in the middle of the fourth century BC, and made some of the most celebrated sculptures in the ancient world, including the Aphrodite of Knidos, the first nude female statue, which was so erotic that a man fell in love with it, and, the story goes, locked himself in the temple at night to consummate his passion. (He was never seen again, adds Lucian, the second-century AD satirist, but you can still see a stain on the inside of her thigh from his transgression.) The statue of Hermes and Dionysus was made to a commission from the Eleans and Arcadians to celebrate a peace treaty in 343 BC. It was finally set up in the Temple of Hera, where it was seen by Pausanias, the travel writer and art critic who describes it for us. And that is where it was discovered amid scenes of extraordinary excitement in 1877. This is the only example of a work of Praxiteles that has survived from the ancient world (except in later copies, as with the Aphrodite of Knidos), and although there have been the usual worries about whether this is the statue itself, there seems little reason to doubt that here is a quite remarkable find: a work described in ancient sources, found in the right place, and from at least the workshop of one of the greatest artists ever. It does not disappoint such expectations.

The pose is one of Praxiteles' trademarks – an elegant curve of the body created by the weight thrust forward on the right leg, with a soft twist of the upper body. (It is evident that the sculptor of the Aphrodite of Melos had learnt from Praxiteles!) The body is also a Praxitelean ideal. Hermes appears as slim-hipped, long-thighed, lightly muscled, with unexaggerated musculature. Hermes is depicted not just as a divine being but as the perfection of young male beauty so worshipped in Greek culture. He has no beard (or any other body hair, except for pubic hair, as all Greek males and no Greek female statues have). His body is carved with a delicacy and softness to express a lack of adult hardness or body weight. There is a certain pathos in the contrast between

Aphrodite of Knidos, a Roman copy after Praxiteles' original of *c.*350 BC

the permanent perfection of a god's body and the fleeting beauty of human life.

Hermes is holding the baby Dionysus in the crook of his left arm, and, in his right, dangles some (lost) object to attract the baby. This creates the dramatic lines of the work: the reaching hand and focused stare of Dionysus, the arm of Hermes and his angled head form a triangle of focus for us. The head of Hermes is carved with particular skill, and it is still extraordinary to reflect how stone could make so soft and luminous an impression. The mouth is about to turn into a smile, the eyes, carefully shadowed, look down with intensity at the baby, and the shadowing on the contours of the face is splendidly nuanced. The full nudity of the god (something that Christianity has traditionally found rather difficult) is emphasised by the tree stump covered with some finely carved and complex drapery. It is as if the god has taken a pause from exercising or bathing to distract his infant brother. This adds a touch of the homely to the divine scene.

The Hermes of Praxiteles was only rediscovered in the late nineteenth century. But the male form of Greek statuary changed the West's idea of how a man should look. In the medieval period, ideals of the male form included the emaciated and hunched monk, poring over his book, or the knight in armour, or the robed and crowned king. The Renaissance's discovery of Greek and Roman art produced instead Michelangelo's David, naked, lightly muscled, standing tall, and with it, a change in how we all think about how we want to look. Greek sculpture has helped form our image of the male body, and this, coupled with the great beauty of the Hermes of Praxiteles and the amazing story of its survival, makes it a prime candidate for a wonder of the ancient world. But it is not the piece I have chosen.

Both the Aphrodite from Melos and the Hermes by Praxiteles are from the grandest tradition of Greek art. Both were on display in temples, and were commissioned by states or by wealthy individuals to celebrate a community. Both are part of the highest echelons of art and art criticism. I have chosen as a wonder of the ancient world, however, a piece that was probably barely looked at except by one family, a small-scale work. But it is a piece of exquisite beauty, pathos and skill.

It is a gravestone, called a *stele*, carved in marble and found on the island of Paros, where the best marble comes from. It was sculpted in about 460 BC, and we know nothing about the sculptor and nothing about the family who bought it and set it up. We do not know if it was sculpted to order, or bought 'off the shelf'. All we can surmise is that it is a gravestone for a beloved young daughter, probably no more than six years old. It is a work which brilliantly captures the restraint and power of classical sculpture.

Marble grave *stele* depicting a girl holding two doves, from Paros, *c.*460 BC

The work is carved in relief, but, like the friezes of the Parthenon, there is a subtle and sophisticated three-dimensional effect. The weight of the girl is on her straight right leg, and the folds of her undertunic are cut like the flutes of a column. Her left leg is lightly bent forward, and her torso leans slightly backwards. There is none of the sinuous torsion of the Hellenistic works we have been looking at, but a gentle monumentality of form: the line of her cloak straightens the whole left edge of the composition. This is in contrast to the stunning central focus of the work, the girl's head and her sorrowing gaze at the doves she holds. The head is turned deeply down, with her mourning lips barely touching the beak of the bird nestled in her left arm. She holds a second dove by the feet, its head turned back towards her.

The memorial is for the young girl, and she is depicted with her two pets. Her sadness is partly at leaving the joys of her life, partly at leaving her pets, whose fragile life stresses the heartbreak of the family's deeper loss. Yet there are no mourning parents here, no crying and bereft family. The deep turn of the head and the girl's mournful gaze at the birds stands for all our grief in a gesture of restraint that is all the more moving for its very control.

This gravestone does not have the exquisite naturalism of the Aphrodite of Melos or the Hermes by Praxiteles. The girl's hair is almost abstract with its curvy grooving, the robes are articulated with a simple formality that have none of the complex brilliance of the Hellenistic masterpieces. But it epitomises what is meant by the classical aesthetic. Its sense of loss, of the fragility but beauty of human life, and the restrained expression of grief is deeply moving across the centuries. And for that reason this *stele* from Paros is my final wonder of the ancient world.

SEVEN WONDERS
OF THE
MEDIEVAL WORLD

Richard Barber

WHAT IS A WONDER? If you had asked someone in the Middle Ages, they would have thought first of miracles in the Bible, and then of natural wonders; as an afterthought they might have mentioned the relics of the Roman past. The idea that something man-made could be a wonder was alien to them. The author of *The History of the Britons* in the ninth century lists the wonders of the island of Britain for his readers, and these are all natural phenomena: lakes and rivers with strange properties, including the Severn bore, places with legends attached to them, particularly tombs which cannot be measured, or revolving hills and wandering stones. Equally, the marvels of the East, best described by Marco Polo among a host of other writers, are almost entirely natural – or perhaps unnatural. The mandrake root, shaped like a man, which screams when it is torn from the ground, or the cotton-producing lamb-bushes, which are both animals and plants and cannot move, are the kind of object which inspires wonder. The ultimate wonder in the Christian thought of the Middle Ages is of course God's creation, and to rank any of the works of men's hands as wonders in the face of this greatest wonder would smack of blasphemy.

So there is no list of seven medieval wonders such as we have for the classical world; indeed, the nearest we come to it is the book on the marvels of the city of Rome, written in the twelfth century, which describes first the saints' relics preserved there, and then presents the classical ruins that were still visible as something which might attract the pilgrims' curiosity. We start, then, with a blank sheet of paper: and at once we are overwhelmed by the possibilities. If we were to range throughout the world in the centuries between the end of the Roman empire in the West and the discovery of America, to take the broadest definition of the Middle Ages, we would have to take into account Aztec temples, the great ruins in Zimbabwe, Angkor Wat in Cambodia and the whole world of China and Japan, a civilisation as great or greater than medieval Christendom. But since this must inevitably be a subjective choice, I have limited my range to medieval Christendom, a world both familiar and unfamiliar.

Despite the attempts of popes and emperors to pretend that the Church and the Holy Roman Empire were powerful and well organised, the sheer organisational drive evident in many of the ancient wonders – the Pyramids, the Great Wall of China and even the Colosseum – is missing. The skills of the Romans in engineering, their roads and aqueducts, had been forgotten, and it was only in the seventeenth century that civil works on a comparable scale reappeared. The greatest achievements of the medieval period belonged either to the Church or to individual rulers. Of the seven wonders I have chosen, all save one owe their existence to the will of a single powerful figure. And here I have to admit that I have passed over the obvious wonders of church architecture, the great Gothic cathedrals that were created from the early thirteenth century onwards, often taking centuries to complete. The extreme example is Cologne, begun in 1248, left unfinished at the end of the Middle Ages, and finally completed after thirty years of work in 1880. The medieval crane on one of the towers dominated the skyline of the city for five centuries, and almost deserves a place in the list of wonders on its own account. The masterpieces of French and English Gothic would provide a list of seven wonders in themselves; but in a sense they are less marvellous simply because there are so many superb buildings among them. Gothic does figure among my choices, in the east end of the palace chapel at Aachen, and in its last and most fantastic form in the Portuguese style of the early sixteenth century.

Similarly, the great artists of the late Middle Ages, creators of the extraordinary miniatures that embellished bibles and above all prayer books in the fourteenth and fifteenth centuries, are not represented here. This is for a different reason: this is a private art form, designed originally for very rich patrons who would not necessarily display these treasures, but would keep them for their private use as an aid to devotion. Even today, the fragile nature of the manuscripts in which they appear, and the lack of accessible facsimiles, make them literally a closed book to most of us. Sometimes such manuscripts could be for public display: in twelfth-century England, a series of bibles on a grand scale were produced, and it was clear that these were intended to be seen by important members of the congregation. Henry II is said to have seen the great bible written by the monks of Winchester for their own use, and to have been so impressed with it that he requested it as a gift; he gave it to St Hugh of Lincoln, who returned it to its original home when he accidentally learnt how the king had obtained it. I have chosen one of the best-known of all medieval manuscripts, which has often been reproduced and is therefore accessible, the Book of Kells.

My list is framed by two masterpieces which look beyond the world of Christendom in different ways. It is difficult to strike the right balance in portraying the degree to which people in the Middle Ages were aware of wider horizons: on the one hand, travel was difficult and dangerous, and many people never ventured more than a few miles from their own home, and yet on the other hand we can point to an extraordinary range of contacts with the Near and Far East, and to travellers who journeyed fast and frequently. The first entry, Hagia Sophia in Byzantium, represents one of the great crossroads and meeting places of the medieval world, a city where the emperor's guard were at one time Norsemen and where the world of Islam was an ever-present concern. At the same time, the emperors claimed authority over the lands to the west and north. Begun by one of the greatest of the later Roman emperors, Justinian, its final fate – to become a mosque – makes it a symbol of the long struggle for the mastery of the Near East. And my concluding choice, the abbey at Batalha, brings another outward-looking image: the caravels of the Knights of Christ sailing down the African coast into the unknown at the end of the fifteenth century, their sails bearing the red cross on a white ground that they had inherited from the Knights Templar.

This was not an age of invention and innovation: writers appealed to authority, the wisdom of their predecessors, and novelties were regarded with suspicion. Hence radical new ideas were imported rather than home-grown. Arabic numerals, based on the Hindu nine-numeral system but with the addition of zero, made possible the beginnings of the Western business world in thirteenth-century Italy. Gunpowder, invented in China around the eleventh century, transformed warfare from the fourteenth century onwards. Printing, even more radical in its effect on society, was another Chinese invention; but it was in the West, where the limited number of letters in the alphabet made mechanisation of writing much easier, that it had its greatest impact. But western Christendom could offer little to compete with such far-reaching ideas.

We have few names to put to the artists and masons who created the seven wonders I have chosen: but we can name all but one of the men who caused them to come into existence. Three emperors, Justinian, Charlemagne and Frederick II; two kings, Edward I of England and João I of Portugal; and a bishop, Odo of Bayeux, were responsible, and, perhaps with the exception of Edward I, the commission was a personal decision rather than a political necessity. The most individual of these creations was Castel del Monte, built by Frederick II, a man who defied contemporary conventions – his attention to personal hygiene was such that he was attacked by clerics for the frequency with which he had baths on Sundays – and who engaged eagerly with new ideas from both West and East. The other works belong to the formal commemoration or celebration of great events, in very different ways: the Bayeux Tapestry has no real surviving parallel, while the great abbey at Batalha is the twin –

even down to the name – of the abbey founded on the battlefield at Hastings by William I three centuries before.

These, then, must stand for the riches, lost and preserved, of the medieval world. There are no specimens of the jeweller's art, such as the extraordinary New Year present given by Isabel of Bavaria to her husband Charles VI of France in 1404, an intricate Virgin and Child in gold, enamel, pearls and jewels before which Charles and Isabel kneel, while below a squire holds a horse of solid gold which has been enamelled white: the Goldenes Rössl is now at Altötting in Bavaria. Nor are there palaces such as that at Sintra in Portugal, which is substantially late medieval, with spectacular rooms perched high above the town. And the riches of Italian medieval painting are another field of miracles, artistic and religious, which must remain unexplored. But the wonders that follow will, I hope, show something of the daring of the medieval mind, the willingness to experiment and explore possibilities despite the essentially conservative nature of medieval society, as well as the ability of medieval rulers, with far smaller resources at their command than those of the Roman empire, to fashion monuments on the boldest scale.

HAGIA SOPHIA

Istanbul spans two continents, Asia and Europe; but it also stands on the great religious fault line that divides Islam and Christianity. In the heart of the city lies Hagia Sophia:

Hagia Sophia, built AD 532–7 by Anthemius of Tralles and Isidore of Miletus

. . . extraordinary to those who behold it and altogether incredible to those who are told of it. In height it rises to the very heavens and overtops the neighbouring houses like a ship anchored among them, appearing above the city which it adorns and of which it forms part. It is set apart by its indescribable beauty, and excels both in its size and the harmony of its proportions . . . Whenever anyone enters to pray, he understands at once that it is not by human power, but by God's will that this work has been so finely finished. His mind is lifted up to God and floats on air, feeling that God cannot be far away, but must especially love to dwell in this place, which He has chosen.

89

The words are those of the Byzantine historian Procopius, writing soon after the present church was built by the emperor Justinian in the early sixth century. It was completed in 537, having taken a mere five years in the making; and both its ambitious scale and the haste with which it was created soon caused problems, compounded by serious earthquakes. It had to be rebuilt in 558, and was rededicated five years later; the dome was twice rebuilt in the succeeding centuries. All this indicates how impressive the building was to its contemporaries; and it remains a wonder of the world for us today.

Hagia Sophia was in many ways the *ne plus ultra* of the engineering skills of the classical world. Before the advent of complex mathematical knowledge and its application to engineering, the only way to discover the limits of a building technique was to go higher and larger than anyone else; the choir at Beauvais cathedral in France, which collapsed in the sixteenth century, marks the ultimate limit of Gothic architecture in terms of height, and Hagia Sophia does the same for the domed designs which were a central theme of Byzantine church building. It is a building without precedent, and its design was the work of architects who possessed both great geometrical skills. Anthemius of Tralles and Isidore of Miletus had written commentaries on mathematics, and were therefore masters of theory; but they must also have had superb confidence in their own judgement of the way in which that geometry would work in practice. The boldness of the design is even more surprising given the circumstances in which the church was begun. The previous church was burned in 532 during a serious riot, together with the most important buildings in the city, and the rebuilding was begun very hastily, about a month after the fire. To conceive such a design so quickly seems so unlikely that it has been suggested that Justinian had already decided on the rebuilding, and events simply accelerated his plans.

But Hagia Sophia is more than a great monument: here we can watch the rise and fall of empires. When Justinian built it, Byzantium was at its most confident; its ruler held sway over much of the Mediterranean, and claimed lordship over the whole of western Christendom as successor to the Roman emperors. Today, the ancient church stands between four minarets, raised in the fifteenth century by the lord of a new empire, Mehmet the Conqueror, who had overthrown the last of the Byzantine emperors and whose victory represented the triumph of Islam over the eastern Orthodox Church and its followers. For the next two centuries, the threat that Europe too might fall to Islam was a very real one.

All of this is reflected in the building as we see it today. The core of Hagia Sophia is still largely Justinian's original church, but it is largely an invisible skeleton. When the church was first completed, it was surprisingly spartan in artistic terms. There were none of the spectacular

images in mosaic like those in contemporary Roman churches, or even in the imperial city of Ravenna. Instead, the surfaces were covered in plain gold mosaic with medallions and borders of flowers or patterns where the arches or windows interrupted this great golden space. The entrance to the church is through two porches, the outer and inner narthex: the latter is almost unchanged since it was built, with nine doors leading into the nave. Its walls are covered in a form of decoration beloved of the Byzantine architects, rich and varied marble veneers, often cut into thin sheets so that one pattern was the mirror of the next. In the nave itself, the marbles become even richer and more exotic; Byzantine writers delight in listing the types of stone and the quarries from which they came: porphyry (purple from Egypt and green from Laconia), onyx and the marbles proper (golden Numidian, pink and white Phrygian, dark red Carian, pale green Carystian, dark green from Thessaly, white and black Celtic from the Pyrenees). The pillars which carry the dome are also of marble; the legend is that they came from the great buildings of the past, such as the Temple of the Sun at Heliopolis, and thus represented the emperor's power over conquered nations. The result is rich in

Interior of Hagia Sophia. A nineteenth-century lithograph by Louis Haghe, after a drawing by Chevalier Caspar Fussati, showing the coloured marble columns

Decorated column capital, Hagia Sophia

Virgin and Child apse mosaic, Hagia Sophia, *c*.867

textures, but to a Western eye the absence of anything pictorial gives it a subdued air for all its splendour.

It is strange that this decor without figures should anticipate the puritan attitude of Islam towards images; but it is because of this that a good deal of the original mosaic has survived to the present day. And Byzantium itself was the home of a Christian sect whose attitude towards images was as unyielding as that of Islam, the Iconoclasts or icon-breakers, who would permit no representation of anything in God's creation. The civil war that stemmed from their militant beliefs dragged on for a century, beginning in 730, and was as vicious as only conflicts based on fanaticism can be. This theological and political turmoil lasted for over a century before the Iconoclasts were defeated. As if to celebrate, the emperors Basil I and Leo VI and the patriarch Ignatius embarked on the elaborate programme of mosaic decoration which we see today. The great image of the Virgin and Child in the apse was one of the first mosaics to be installed, and forms the focal point of what was once

the nave of the church. It is a memorial to the triumph of the orthodox believers over the Iconoclasts, and a Greek inscription tells us that pious emperors have restored what the heretics had once destroyed. Some of the figures in the rest of the nave and the apse have survived: there was originally a medallion of Christ in the middle of the dome, sixteen prophets, the twelve apostles and fourteen bishops, a hieratic army of formal figures marshalled against the heretics. Elsewhere the figure of either Basil or Leo over the imperial door at the entrance to the nave, shown praying before Christ and the Virgin, celebrates the emperor's political victory over his opponents.

It was traditional in Byzantium for women to worship separately from the men; in the twelfth century, when Geoffrey of Monmouth wished to portray Arthur's court as the equal of Byzantium, he made the women go to a separate church at Arthur's coronation. However, it was usually a question of segregation in the same building, and Hagia Sophia is no exception. A spacious ramp – broad enough for a chariot – leads to the galleries where the empress and her entourage looked down on the worshippers. It is an arrangement that found echoes in the most unlikely places, such as a church at Visby on Gotland, in the Baltic; the deeply ceremonial nature of the Byzantine court made a huge impression on visitors from western Europe. Even today, these galleries are impressive in their sheer scale; and the richness of the detail is astonishing, whether in the carving of the stone doors or the patterns of mosaics on the inner face of the arches. Over the centuries the galleries were also decorated with figural mosaics, after the great cycle in the main church had been completed. In the nave and the apse, the immensity of the building overwhelms the mosaics: in the galleries, the mosaics come into their own, and make a much more vivid impression. We can stand at eye level with the group showing the Virgin and John the Baptist interceding with Christ and appreciate the extraordinary shading and subtlety of the technique, a *pointilliste* painting before its time. Here too are portraits of emperors, pious and sinful, of empresses such as the thrice-married Zoe, the portrait beside her altered as she found a new husband. The convoluted history of the later Byzantine empire can be traced on these walls; but the tomb of the man who, more than any other, brought that empire to ruin, lies in the section of the gallery closed off by the richly decorated screen which imitates wooden doors, known as the Gates of Heaven and Hell. Here once lay Enrico Dandolo, doge of Venice, who, although blind and over ninety years old, lured the Fourth Crusade to do his bidding and destroy Venice's greatest commercial rival. (The inscription visible today was probably created during a restoration in the nineteenth century.) The sack of Byzantium in 1204 was one of the great tragedies of Western civilisation: much of the intellectual heritage of the ancient

Gallery with half-dome, in the south-east bay of Hagia Sophia, from which the empress watched the worshippers world was lost, and the empire itself, which should have been a bulwark against the rising power of Islam, was fatally weakened.

Two centuries later, in 1453, the Ottoman sultan Mehmet II overthrew the last emperor and took Byzantium by storm. He was so impressed by the magnificence of his conquest that he halted the looting of the city after one day, instead of allowing his troops the customary three days' rapine. His first act was to order that Hagia Sophia should be converted to a mosque, and it is in this guise that we see it today. There are the furnishings of the mosque, the *mihrab* and the *mimber*, and six huge painted wooden medallions with the sinuous calligraphic inscriptions which are one of the great glories of Islamic art; these hang in the former nave, and remind the worshippers of the six sacred names, of Allah and his prophet and the first four caliphs. In the seventeenth century, the great traveller Evliya Çelebi, who had been a muezzin here, described how the sultan of the day had an enclosure at the southern entrance which he filled with singing birds each Friday, so that he could hear them during prayers: 'Their sweet notes, mingled with those of the muezzin's voices, filled the mosque with a harmony approaching to that of paradise.' Çelebi called Hagia Sophia 'peculiarly the place of God', and described the prayer and studies that were continually celebrated there. Hagia Sophia acquired its own Muslim legends, telling how the collapse of the semi-dome in the 550s occurred on the very night that the Prophet was born, and how Muhammad himself authorised its rebuilding with mortar that was mixed with earth from Mecca, because he knew that it would one day become a mosque. And its architecture, which was too daring to be the model for other Byzantine churches, became the pattern for the first great mosques to be built under the Ottoman sultans.

At the other end of the Mediterranean stands the cathedral of Córdoba, whose Gothic nave stands amid the forest of pillars of the great mosque of that city; Hagia Sophia marks the opposite point of the conflict of Islam and Christianity, the conversion of the most important church of Orthodox Christianity into a Muslim place of worship. Both buildings could easily have been destroyed as infidel creations: instead, the power and aura of these religious masterpieces preserved them for use by the conquerors. Hagia Sophia reminds us both of the rise and fall of empires, and of the opening and closing of the Middle Ages; and it brings to mind as well both the divisions and the common ground between Christianity and Islam.

THE BOOK OF KELLS

Medieval manuscripts are perhaps the most private of all art forms: often commissioned for a single owner, they were jealously guarded as precious objects, and only the most privileged could admire the artistic splendours that lay within their covers. It is perhaps unfair to choose such an object as one of the seven wonders of the medieval world, and yet many of the greatest achievements of medieval craftsmen and painters are to be found only in such volumes. Today, with the advantage of superb reproductions, it is easier for us to appreciate the work of the miniaturists and scribes, and to see how this enclosed world relates to the outside world of architecture and painting. One of the English masters of the twelfth century, Hugh, worked at the abbey of Bury St Edmunds and designed the great bronze doors and the abbey seal as well as the magnificent Bury Bible; he may have worked at Canterbury and in the Crusader kingdom of Cyprus as well. My own favourite among all medieval manuscripts is the Luttrell Psalter, which mixes fantastic imagination with the most down-to-earth portrayals of village life; but the Book of Kells is undoubtedly the greater masterpiece, a true wonder of the world. It has been reproduced many times and has become widely familiar through photography and digital versions; yet it is only fair to say at the outset that these can only give a general idea of the splendour of the original. A manuscript is an object, just as much as a painting or a sculpture is an object, and to photograph it and print it on a modern page can never render the three-dimensional quality of the original. Manuscripts were written on specially prepared parchment, and even the finest parchment wrinkles and moves, and has flaws in it. If we look at the flat gold of a printed facsimile, it gives a totally different impression from the varied reflections of the irregular surface of the parchment, which glints as it catches the light.

However, if the ideal is a visit to the library of Trinity College Dublin, to see the object itself, the facsimiles and CDs which reproduce it still amaze us with the richness of the artistic imagination that created the Book of Kells. Technically, it is a Gospel book, for use in church services, which belonged to the monastery of Kells in County Meath in Ireland, and which was written in the late eighth century or early ninth century. But Gospel books can be plain and practical, and all monasteries possessed one or more of them. The Book of Kells belongs to a group of luxury manuscripts produced in Ireland, Scotland and at Lindisfarne in the north of England, with a very distinctive style. It was famous as early as 1006, when the Chronicle of Ulster recorded that 'The great Gospel of

Columkille, the chief relic of the western world, was wickedly stolen during the night from the western sacristy of the great stone church at Kells because of the rich shrine [in which it was kept].' Two hundred years later, Gerald of Wales wrote a description of Ireland, which had recently been conquered by Norman barons to whom he was related. He describes a book which was miraculously written from drawings shown to a scribe by an angel; the scribe was only able to copy the intricacy of the originals when St Bridget prayed for him. Gerald says of the book:

[It has] almost as many drawings as pages, and all of them in marvellous colours. Here you can look upon the face of the divine majesty drawn in a miraculous way; here too upon the mystical representations of the Evangelists, now having six, now four and now two wings ... And there are innumerable other drawings. If you look at them carelessly and casually and not too closely, you may judge them to be mere daubs rather than careful compositions. You will see nothing subtle where everything is subtle. But if you take the trouble to look very closely, and penetrate with your eyes to the secrets of the artistry, you will notice such intricacies, so delicate and subtle, so close together and well knitted, so involved and bound together, and so fresh still in their colourings that you will not hesitate to declare that all these things must have been the result of the work, not of men, but of angels.

The Book of Kells is a luxury manuscript, but surprisingly there is no gold in it. A brilliant yellow is often used in its place, and the absence of gold might be deliberate, given that the price of the ultramarine blue which is frequently used was equally costly. What is most striking as one looks at the pages for the first time is the extraordinary contrast between the simplicity and regularity of the letters, the bold figures in the minia-tures and the intricacies of the decorative patterns. The most famous page is the great opening to the Gospel of St John, 'In the beginning was the Word' (*In principio erat verbum* in Latin), which was traditionally the place where the artist creating a manuscript pulled out all the stops. Here, the figure of St John is enthroned at the top of the page, with a smaller figure to the right. The rest of the page is a web of patterns, in which the text is scarcely visible: *In p* is rendered as monumental ele-ments of decoration, *rincipio* becomes a line of intertwined Celtic ser-pents, and only the last words are apparently legible – though there are extra letters to fill the requirements of the pattern. Within the architec-ture of the two massive initials, a whole world of detail opens up. Pages such as this are often called carpet pages, because of their resemblance to woven textiles; the lines loop and swerve behind and under and through each other, divided into panels each with their individual style. Even more extreme is the page which begins the genealogy of Christ, showing

Chapter opening to the Gospel of St John, from the Book of Kells, late eighth to early ninth century

98

An otter with a fish, a detail from the Chi-Rho monogram, from the Book of Kells

Incipit or Chi-Rho monogram, from the Book of Kells

his descent from King David. His name is represented by a Greek monogram, the Chi-Rho, so called after the first two letters of his name in Greek. But the monogram takes up the entire page, save for one word at the bottom. The monogram becomes a huge image superimposed on a background of whirling spirals and immensely detailed interlaces, with almost a hundred linked circular panels; and in the spaces are angels, cats and an otter with a fish in its mouth. It is perhaps inspired by the 'tree of Jesse' which the following text describes, but its form is entirely invented: there is nothing so obvious as an imitation of foliage about it.

If the Book of Kells belonged in a library, such an image would make little sense. A volume on this scale belonged in the church, where it would be used for public reading and would be displayed during the services. Interestingly, the text of the Gospels is badly copied and full of errors, as if the scribes knew that this was not the main purpose of their work. The Chi-Rho image or any of the other great pages would give an instant impression of richness and pomp, even if seen from a little way off. The fact that it was stolen from the sacristy in 1006 confirms that its place was in ecclesiastical use. Other medieval manuscripts, notably a series of bibles in twelfth-century England, were even larger, though not more splendid than Kells; they too were intended for the public eye.

How did such a book emerge in an age when secular life knew little of luxuries and when contacts with the rest of the world were few and far between? The monasteries of Ireland and Scotland had become havens of learning in the difficult times following the Roman withdrawal, and in the eighth century scholars from Ireland had played an important part in the foundation of new monasteries in Charlemagne's empire. The Book of Kells was the work of a scriptorium or writing room; most monasteries of any size would have a system for creating the books they needed, by making copies of borrowed originals. But apart from such mechanical tasks, the scriptorium was often the artistic heart of the monastery; and it is clear from an analysis of the Book of Kells that a number of scribes and artists worked on it. How far the scribe also acted as artist is hard to say, though we do know of Irish scribes who tell us that they both painted and wrote their books. It was a generally close collaboration, at all events; the scribe would leave spaces for decoration, though the artist in his exuberance might often overrun them and spread his image into the text and margin (this can be seen on fo. III recto). We do have some clues as to how the scribe worked from the unfinished pages in the Gospel of St Matthew. It was the scribe who planned the page, laid out the text frames with a light ink line and with prickings, very small holes in the parchment which usually served to ensure that the number of lines on the pages was consistent, and the text area was the same. The holes could be made through two or three sheets of parchment at the same time, and

ħgeneratio

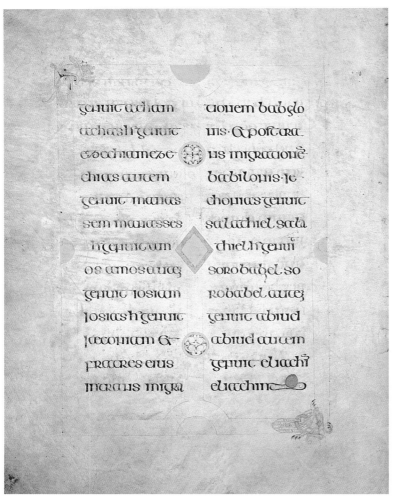

Unfinished page with pricked-out decoration in the Gospel of St Matthew, from the Book of Kells

The Temptation page, from the Book of Kells: in the centre, towards the bottom of the page, is a figure in the 'Osiris' pose

Birds and domestic fowl, from the Book of Kells, fo. IIIr

were the basic template of the book. But it was also the scribe who set out the overall design of the ornament, and he seems to have specified the type of pattern to be used as well as laying in specimen colours to be copied. He may even have sketched the beginnings of the animals which were to enliven the page. The painter was clearly just that: the skilled artisan who actually did the painting, rather than the creator of the grand design. However, where a page had no text at all, but was an illustration, a portrait or the depiction of symbols, the painter was also the designer. There are probably three painters at work on the whole-page miniatures in the Book of Kells, each with a distinctive personality but all drawing on the same general tradition, and clearly working as a team.

The puzzle is where the artistic ideas came from. So far, the best suggestion is that Kells and the other great illuminated manuscripts of the period owe something to a Coptic book which had found its way to England. Many of the figures are in the so-called 'Osiris' pose, with arms crossed and holding croziers or books, which goes back to the traditional pictures of Osiris in Egyptian temples, and the portrait style shows similarities with Coptic art. Such a connection seems almost impossible in an

firmum uel in carcere et non ministraui
mus tibi. Tunc respondebit illis
dicens. Amen dico uobis quam
diu non fecistis uni ex his fratribus
meis minimis ambulantibus in no
mine meo mihi nec fecistis.
Et ibunt hii in supplicium aeternum.
Iusti autem in uitam aeternam.
Et factum est cum consummas
set ihs sermones hos omnes dixit
discipulis suis.
Scitis quia post biduum pascha
fiet et filius hominis trade
tur ut crucifigatur.
Tunc congregati sunt principes
sacerdotum et seniores po
puli in atrium principis sacerdo
tum

age when travel was very difficult, and the Near East was hardly known; but there is good evidence of substantial trade by sea between the Near East and the British Isles. Furthermore, pigments such as ultramarine came from exotic sources; in the case of ultramarine, it was produced in Afghanistan, and brought to the West by a system of trade. Other elements, particularly in the decoration, were home-grown, such as the spirals which ultimately derive from patterns found in early Celtic art, before the Roman invasion of Britain. Interlacing is likewise a theme found on Scottish Christian monuments; but the Book of Kells has a very distinctive extra element in all this, the recurrent animal and human figures and faces which are woven into these patterns. It is these figures which populate even the simpler pages, because they break free from the great formal compositions and become the initial letters throughout the book, often as part of a kind of monstrous animal, but sometimes simply as an interjection between the lines: we find birds, cats, fishes and weird monsters at large in the text, and even a cock and hens and a man on horseback. And then we turn the page and find an image which echoes a manuscript from the court of Charlemagne or an icon from Byzantium. There are many other medieval manuscripts with an immensely rich programme of miniatures and ornamentation, but few which show the range of contacts which went into the making of the Book of Kells. Its origins are the subject of continuing debate, but the most attractive suggestion to my mind – made by Françoise Henry in her 1974 study of the Book of Kells – is that it was made on Iona around 797 to celebrate the second centenary of the death of St Columba: a great work of art in honour of one of the greatest saints of the Celtic Church.

THE IMPERIAL PALACE
AT AACHEN

Hagia Sophia, the first of our medieval wonders, marks the heart of the Byzantine empire, once subservient to Rome as the junior partner in the Roman imperial system. The empire in the West, however, declined steadily in the face of barbarian attacks, and on the death of Romulus Augustulus in 476 the remaining imperial territories acknowledged the Byzantine emperors as their sole rulers. But the memory of the ancient glories of the Roman empire lingered in men's memories in the West as a kind of golden age, and when Charlemagne, ruler of the Franks, succeeded in creating a state which stretched from the Atlantic deep into the heart of Europe, the idea of reviving the western empire was an obvious way of proclaiming his authority.

So it was that the culmination of Charlemagne's career came on Christmas Day, 800, when before the mass in St Peter's at Rome at which Charlemagne's eldest son was to be anointed as king, the pope approached Charlemagne as he knelt before the shrine of St Peter and crowned him with a diadem, while the nobles around him hailed him as emperor in the traditional manner and the pope saluted him in the manner reserved for the Byzantine emperors. This moment marks the revival of the Roman empire in the West as an ideological force, the 'Holy Roman Empire' which was to survive in varying forms until 1792 and was to be imitated by both Napoleon and Wilhelm I of Prussia. But the particular character of this new empire, absent from both its predecessors and successors, is precisely its religious connotation: it is the Christian empire foretold in St Augustine's *City of God*, in which Charlemagne was to be the protector not merely of the papacy but of the whole of Christianity. The Byzantine throne was conveniently empty in 800, when Charlemagne made his claim, and so the nominal claim of Byzantium to fill this very role could be easily ignored.

This new and ambitious political structure is reflected in the art and architecture of the Carolingian court. Little more than traces of the imperial buildings of Charlemagne's day have survived, with one important exception: the chapel of the palace which Charlemagne built at Aachen. Charlemagne may have been born at his father's palace here, built on the site of a Roman town. If it was indeed his birthplace, this would have been one reason why he chose to build a new and magnificent palace here between 789 and 796; another, more compelling, reason for creating a 'second Rome' here was that it lay at the heart of his imperial lands, while serving as a base for the wars against Saxony. In 794,

Charlemagne's imperial chapel, Aachen, built 789–96

having previously led a more or less nomadic existence as his endless military campaigns took him from Denmark to Spain, from Bavaria to Brittany, his court was settled here on a more or less permanent basis.

Much of the great imperial palace complex survives, but it is now the town hall and has been heavily rebuilt, so that the chapel is set amid buildings which have more in common with the nineteenth century than the ninth. Originally, it would have been one element in a group of buildings which included formal state rooms, baths on the Roman model and private quarters. Such a group of buildings would have been an impressive statement of power and authority in an age when most royal courts – like Charlemagne's before the palace was built – lacked any settled base.

The entrance to the chapel lies across a great courtyard, and it requires a feat of the imagination to people it with Charlemagne's courtiers and followers – it could hold up to seven thousand of them – looking up at the emperor in the gallery on the west front of the chapel where he used to make ceremonial appearances. The invisible crowd which we must picture would have been a cosmopolitan affair. The court of Charlemagne was in contact with the whole of the known world: his teachers were Saxon and Irish monks, his vassals ranged from newly converted heathens to the men of Rome itself, his embassies went to Byzantium and on one occasion to the fabled court of Harun-al-Rashid at Baghdad, returning with presents the like of which had never been seen in the West – gold plate, ivory chessmen and an elephant named Abul Abbas which became Charlemagne's favourite pet. The elephant died in Saxony ten years later, but oriental fabrics decorated with elephants which may have been part of Harun-al-Rashid's gifts survive in the treasury at Aachen.

The design of the chapel was said by Charlemagne's biographer Notker to be his own: in fact it is closely based on the church of San Vitale at Ravenna, the imperial church of the last emperors of the West, whose heir Charlemagne claimed to be. Mosaics from Ravenna were sent to Aachen for use in the palace, so the link between the two cities was close and deliberate. In 812, ambassadors from the Byzantine emperor, who also claimed to rule in the West, recognised Charlemagne as emperor in a ceremony in the chapel.

Like San Vitale, the chapel at Aachen is basically octagonal; in the West this plan is almost unknown, but it is not uncommon in Byzantine architecture. In many details, the design recalls the rituals of the Byzantine court, notably in the emperor's isolation from the courtiers by seating him in the upper gallery behind the congregation, making him invisible yet at the same time a presence powerfully felt.

The outside of the church has a Gothic and later cladding which conceals most of the Carolingian work, except on the south side. The two great bronze doors of the west porch are Carolingian, the earliest such bronze doors to survive from the Middle Ages. Two lions' heads and restrained chasing round the panels are the only decoration, a sober contrast to the riches within. For this is one of those rare places where all the high history attached to a site is fully matched by what we see there. The immediate impression is of great richness and great age, of stepping into an unfamiliar world, where both forms and decoration are strange. The inner octagon has two tiers of great square marble-clad pillars; the spaces which they frame are taken up by arcades of columns on the upper storey and chapels around the lower level. It is a space redolent of power and ritual, its striped marble keystones and rich facings evoking the wealth

Lion's-head door decoration from the west porch, imperial chapel, Aachen

and power of empire; yet both the centre of power, Charlemagne's throne, and the centre of ritual, the altar, are at first half-hidden, sensed rather than seen. The golden splendour of the altar is gradually revealed as we walk round the perimeter of the octagon, reading the inscription recording the building of the chapel which runs round the inside and is said to have been written by the great English scholar Alcuin. There are other treasures within: a huge circular bronze chandelier presented by Frederick Barbarossa, with an elaborate Latin inscription which proclaims it to be an image of the heavenly Jerusalem, its octagonal towers echoing the form of the chapel. As a tribute from the greatest German emperor to his even greater forebear, it is a fitting image: the rulers of the earthly kingdom looking forward to the celestial realms. Below, the massive golden altar front, which once shimmered in the flickering light of the forty-eight candles, is nowadays harshly but effectively lit. This 'cape of gold', or *pala d'oro*, completed early in the eleventh century, perhaps at the abbey of Fulda, is another masterpiece in metalwork. Christ sits in imperial majesty in the central mandorla, surrounded by the symbols of the Evangelists, while the outer panels show scenes from the last days of his life, in a bold and unexpectedly lively style. Before this altar, thirty

Tiered interior, imperial chapel, Aachen

Interior of the imperial chapel, Aachen, looking towards the Golden Altar

Scenes from the Life of Christ, from the
Golden Altar, 1020

emperors, from Louis the Pious in 813 to Ferdinand I in 1531, were
crowned.

The most impressive of the imperial relics, and one which was vener-
ated by centuries of pilgrims, is Charlemagne's throne, in the gallery,
looking directly down on to the altar. Its simplicity is in sharp contrast to
the opulence below: white marble slabs without a trace of decoration, set
above a plain flight of six steps. At this level the openings between the
main pillars are filled by marble columns and a bronze railing, contemporary with the main doors and equally restrained and elegant in design.
(The mosaics, as elsewhere in the chapel, are early twentieth century.) In
a chapel off the upper storey is the sarcophagus used for Charlemagne's
remains until his relics were enshrined in 1165; it was made in Rome in
the second century AD and shows the rape of Proserpina. The recycling
of Roman materials also accounts for much of the fabric of the chapel.
Charlemagne brought this from Trier and Cologne to supplement what
could be found in Aachen itself; and some of the columns and marble
work were obtained from as far afield as Italy, from Ravenna, once the
capital of the western empire.

At the eastern side of the original chapel there opens out the Gothic choir, which turned the palace chapel into a miniature medieval cathedral. It is a daring piece of engineering, its walls more glass than stone. The glass has been replaced following war damage, but the colours and tones are suitably medieval. The soaring lines of its vaults are so completely different at first sight from the eighth-century building that it would seem difficult to find a common factor; but both have the same strong vertical emphasis, the striving heavenwards, that is typical of medieval architecture in the West. The east end houses two more great treasures. To the right is the 'golden ambo' or pulpit given by Henry II before 1014. For sheer profusion of wealth, it is unsurpassed. A formal framework divides it into panels, but within each panel order gives way to a riot of jewellery, ivory and even an antique glass tazza, the cup and cover being mounted separately as though they were huge precious stones like those in the central panels. It originally stood in the centre of the octagon, but was moved when the new choir was built.

Beyond, at the east end itself, is the shrine of Charlemagne, commissioned by Frederick Barbarossa but only completed in 1215, when

Charlemagne's gold-and-marble throne at Aachen

Frederick Barbarossa. A detail of Charlemagne's gilded and jewelled shrine commissioned by Frederick II, before 1215

Frederick II transferred the relics from an earlier shrine to this present one, a masterpiece by the Rhineland goldsmiths. Charlemagne himself appears on the end, while his successors are enthroned in serried ranks along the sides. The refinement of much of the work makes the golden ambo seem barbaric in its crude splendour. Here enamel work, pierced ornamentation and figures in high relief testify to enormous advances in technique. Fittingly, this is one of the most magnificent of the great shrines, matched only by that of the Three Kings of Cologne.

The treasury, in a room off the cloisters, has yet more riches: the cross of Lothar, *c.*1000; an ivory probably carved at the imperial workshop in Aachen in Charlemagne's time; the reliquary head of Charlemagne, crowned with the emperor Charles IV's crown; another major shrine, containing a relic of the Virgin; the arms chest of Richard of Cornwall, resplendent in scarlet and gold heraldry; and the crown of Margaret of York.

Imitation of the antique was a central feature in Carolingian culture: if the Roman empire was to be revived, then the appropriate style was also that of Rome. Roman influence can be seen everywhere – in manuscripts, in coins, in metalwork. Late classical manuscripts were copied at Charlemagne's court, and the ornament and decoration of new manuscripts often includes elements from classical architecture, particularly in the formal opening pages. Charlemagne himself is portrayed in the style of a Roman emperor on his coins. At Mustair in eastern Switzerland, there is a statue of an idealised emperor, almost certainly intended to be Charlemagne, wearing the ceremonial dress of the Roman rulers.

Charlemagne's biographer Einhard presented a reliquary (now destroyed) to his monastery at Maastricht which was in the form of a Roman triumphal arch, the saints depicted on it appearing in classical dress. Other relics of this imperial style are the little statue, probably of Charlemagne, in the Louvre; this equestrian bronze seems a clear imitation of the great equestrian monuments of the later empire, one of which was brought to Aachen and stood outside the palace there: the doors on the chapel at Aachen echo classical bronzework. A piece of more mysterious origins, now thought to be Carolingian, is the so-called 'throne of Dagobert', an imitation of the folding stools used in ancient Rome, now in the Cabinet des Médailles of the Bibliothèque Nationale in Paris.

This deliberate combination of an appeal to the classical past, a massive display of wealth and imposing architecture makes Charlemagne's palace at Aachen a reminder that the emperor was set apart from ordinary men in medieval eyes; this is not private luxury, but a public, political statement of the power and riches of the ruler. Aachen retains a fitting share of the pomp and awe of the Holy Roman Empire.

THE BAYEUX TAPESTRY

Two centuries after Charlemagne's death in 814 his empire had fallen apart. The rulers of Germany had inherited the title of emperor, while his Frankish lands were at the mercy of a new seaborne power from the north, the Norsemen who spent their winters at home and their summers at sea, on raiding or 'viking' expeditions. They settled in Normandy in the tenth century, and quickly established themselves as a major force in Europe and later in the Mediterranean; their formidable qualities as warriors were combined with a remarkable capacity for organisation when a strong leader appeared. It was a Norman who wrote of his own people: 'When under the rule of a strong master the Normans are a most valiant people, excelling all others in the skill with which they meet difficulties and strive to conquer the enemy. But in all other circumstances they rend each other and bring ruin upon themselves.' Soon after the emergence of the Norman dukes in northern France, Knut of Denmark ('King Canute') created a Scandinavian empire, ruling England, Denmark, Norway and parts of Sweden before his death in 1035; but it was a personal domain, defying the logic of geography, and it quickly fell apart after his death. Knut was the first of the Norse kings who became a truly international figure, going on pilgrimage to Rome and winning the favour of the pope; his daughter Gunnhild married the son of the emperor Conrad. His successors held his lands for less than a decade: in 1042, England returned to the old West Saxon dynasty.

The last incursion of the Norsemen into England was in 1066, in that often-forgotten episode when Harald Hardradi of Norway, who had a distant claim to the English throne by his descent from Knut, sailed up the Humber and landed in the heart of Yorkshire, aiming to seize the old Norse capital at York as his base, 'drawn there', in Gwyn Jones's words (in *A History of the Vikings*),

by the never-failing Viking compulsions of land, wealth and fame overseas. His first battle had been at Stiklarstadir back in 1030; next came the great arc of sacks and sieges, sea-fights and land-battles, from Poland through Russia by way of Asia Minor and Bulgaria on to Sicily; then his bid for a kingdom in Norway, wars throughout Uppland and along the Swedish border, and seventeen years of hostilities against the Danes.

But this last of the Norse adventurers was surprised by Harold and the English levies at Stamford Bridge, and his army was annihilated in a hard-fought battle.

The Norsemen won England in the end, all the same: Harald Hard-radi's invasion opened the way for William of Normandy, Norse by descent and claimant to the English throne. For once, a crucial event in medieval history is recorded for us by a spectacular work of art. It was probably made for the bishop of Bayeux, Odo, half-brother of William the Conqueror, who had himself taken an active part in the fighting. As bishop, the climax of his career was the dedication of the new cathedral in 1077, of which only part of the west front and the crypt survives. The dedication ceremony was a splendid one, and the newly built church was decorated for the occasion. The centrepiece of the decorations may well have been a huge wall-hanging, nearly 250 feet (76 m) long, one of the largest such works ever made. Its subject was the recent past, from 1063 to 1066, one of the most dramatic moments in the history of medieval Europe, when the Norman duke and his followers had seized the English kingdom.

Today the Bayeux Tapestry is a household name. It was displayed in the elegant eighteenth-century Bishop's Palace, in a specially constructed room, which became inadequate for the huge numbers of visitors who flock to see it, and has now been replaced. To see the tapestry itself is still a remarkable experience. It is an extraordinary document, vivid, individual and impossible to reproduce adequately even with modern photographic and printing techniques. The word 'tapestry' is a misnomer: it is not woven, but embroidered on a linen base in eight different colours of wool, giving an effect of low relief as in sculpture. Indeed, it must have resembled Romanesque sculpture very closely, for much contemporary stonework would have been coloured; and it is the slightly three-dimensional quality of the tapestry that makes it so vivid today.

Although scholars continue to argue over the standing of the tapestry among early accounts of the Norman conquest of England, there is no doubt that it is a historical record of the first importance. It may indeed have influenced some of the early chronicles of the conquest and is very probably the earliest source of the story that King Harold was struck in the eye by a Norman arrow before he was killed, a story once discredited but now seemingly restored to historical favour. The problem is that, although the tapestry appears to be miraculously well preserved, it has in fact been restored many times; the use of chemically dyed wool in the repairs carried out in 1842 is particularly noticeable, especially at the end. In the course of these restorations, details have inevitably been lost, misread or accidentally altered, and the arrow in Harold's eye might be such a point. But the general aspect of the tapestry has hardly changed in the nine hundred years since it was made, and in many cases it provides us with information unknown elsewhere.

Our first impression of the tapestry is of a marvellous record of how

The Norman fleet under William the Conqueror, duke of Normandy, landing at Pevensey on 26–7 September 1066, from the Bayeux Tapestry, late eleventh century

Head of King Edward the Confessor, from the Bayeux Tapestry

Head of King Harold II, from the Bayeux Tapestry

men lived in mid-eleventh-century England and Normandy. The most striking and clearly represented feature is the dress and armour of the nobles, followed by the ships and details of the military preparations. We watch the preparations for the invasion in detail, from the felling of wood to the shipwrights at work with their adzes shaping the planks, and the teams hauling ropes to launch the ships. Mail shirts and spears are carried onto the ships, as well as barrels of wine which arrive on carts, before William and his men embark with their horses. A procession of boats represents the crossing, and once the fleet reaches the other side, we see the horses disembarking; their riders mount hastily and ride off before they can be surprised on the beach by the enemy. Much of the tapestry is highly naturalistic, unusual at this period; but even stylised features, such as the buildings, tell us something: Edward's palace is contrasted with the hovels of the humble folk in the scenes where the Normans forage for supplies.

Perhaps the most remarkable thing about the Bayeux Tapestry is that we are looking at pictures which tell us how a contemporary viewed the events of 1066. When it was created, many of those who fought at Hastings would still have been alive. This is not an imaginary re-creation of the distant past, but the nearest we get in the Middle Ages to photojournalism. As with photojournalism, the tapestry is not a totally reliable witness to what happened; but the standpoint from which the designer – we cannot really call him the author – looks at events is very interesting. The most striking aspect is the way in which he characterises the main protagonists. Edward the Confessor is an elderly bearded man, shown enthroned with a sceptre until his last illness. Harold has the moustache and small beard fashionable among Anglo-Saxons, while William is clean-shaven and hard-featured. Beyond these physical characteristics, the moods and attitudes of the principal characters are also subtly portrayed. Harold's bearing is frank and noble, as if the designer recognised his good qualities and even admired him, except in two or three scenes where he acts in bad faith or has been humiliated, when his posture becomes hunchbacked and apologetic.

Because nothing else like it survives, it is easy for us to regard the

Bayeux Tapestry as an exceptional work of art made to celebrate an exceptional event. But it would be wrong to do so, because wall-hangings like these were not uncommon in eleventh-century churches and palaces, and fragments of others survive. What is exceptional is the scale of the tapestry, which does seem to have been an ambitious project: some scholars have suggested that as many as six separate teams worked on it. Furthermore, the artist responsible for the overall design was a draughtsman of great skill. The way in which a sense of continuous movement is given, of a kind of inexorable sequence of events leading to the Norman victory, shows that a master is at work. The handling of the battle scene at the end, where the confusion of a real battle would have made no sense within the bounds of the tapestry's linear shape, is masterly: he juxtaposes the two essential elements of the fighting, the English shield wall and the Norman cavalry charge, to encapsulate the action, before showing us detailed episodes from the battle, culminating, of course, in the death of Harold and the flight of the English. The actual figures themselves are much less static than in much medieval art, and have a feeling of vivid urgency which is found in Anglo-Saxon art, particularly in the lightly drawn line drawings which illustrate masterpieces such as the manuscripts produced at St Augustine's, Canterbury in the half-century before the Norman conquest, where the margins of psalters and bibles are filled with lively activity. Notice, too, how the borders, at first decorated with scenes from fables or from rural life, change to become an echo of the slaughter at Hastings, filled with dismembered bodies and the debris of battle.

There is a deeper and more subtle level to the tapestry, beyond its highly attractive visual surface. The borders are a kind of commentary on the action, whose meaning is still hotly argued among scholars. Some of the allusions are obvious, as in the scene where the caption reads 'where a clerk and Aelfgyva' without completing the sentence: the margin below shows an ostentatiously naked man. Elsewhere the links are subtler and more intriguing, if more debatable. In the scene where Harold is captured by Count Guy of Ponthieu there is a chained bear in the margin, threatened by a knight with a sword, which seems to stand for the captive Harold and Guy, who was maltreating him and holding him to ransom. It is an image which has links to a contemporary poem, the famous *Song of Roland*, where the same bear imagery for a captive occurs. Here the plot thickens. Not only was the *Song of Roland* recited at the battle of Hastings, according to William of Malmesbury, who wrote fifty years after the event, but it is attributed in the one surviving copy to Turoldus. In the same scene on the Bayeux Tapestry, we find a dwarf named Turold holding the messengers' horses. Coincidence? Perhaps; but this all shows how the tapestry, like most major medieval works of art, operates on two levels, and that beneath the pictorial surface there is a whole complex

world of allegory and allusion. Another intriguing idea is that the tapestry may have been a kind of aide-memoire for a recital of the story of the Norman invasion, and that a narrator would have used the pictures as a kind of slide-show for his performance. There is still much to be learned about the tapestry, even if its immediate message is clear enough.

If the tapestry was indeed designed and produced in Canterbury for Bishop Odo, as now seems likely, it serves as a reminder that, however dramatic the events of 1066 were, they were not a total revolution. After all England had been under foreign rule only fifty years earlier. It is true that there was a wholesale transfer of property, from Saxon to Norman lords in 1066, and that Norman French quickly became the official language of the kingdom. But the Normans were no strangers to England: Normans had accompanied Emma, wife of King Canute, and there had been a strong Norman faction at the court since 1043, when Edward, recently returned from exile in Normandy, became king; and Harold had been the leader of the opposition to this Norman intrusion, and to the Norman claim that Edward had named William as his successor. So the battle of Hastings was in one sense the resolution of a struggle within the English court itself, and it is appropriate that its greatest memorial should have been made by craftsmen working in the Anglo-Saxon tradition and commissioned by their new Norman masters.

Horses tumbling in a swamp during the battle of Hastings, from the Bayeux Tapestry

CASTEL DEL MONTE

Castel del Monte, Apulia, built 1240–50

Driving inland through Apulia from Bari, on the south-eastern tip of Italy, the traveller is aware of a massive low building on a commanding hilltop, which dominates the countryside for miles around. It looks from a distance like a military installation from the Second World War or even one of the aberrations of the Italian planning system. But as you draw near, the mass resolves itself in an interplay of light and shade into a fortress of startling design. The German historian Fernand Gregorovius came here in 1875, and wrote:

As a symbol which is visible from afar and dominates the endless plain, people call it the belvedere or balcony of Apulia. It would be more appropriate to call it the crown of Apulia; for like a turreted crown this golden castle rests on the hill-top. It seemed to me like the diadem of the Hohenstaufen empire, crowning the beautiful landscape, as the evening Sun made it sparkle with purple and gold.

This is Castel del Monte, the remarkable creation of an even more remarkable man, Frederick II, ruler of the Holy Roman Empire, and king of Sicily and Jerusalem. Although this is a region that today lies off the beaten track, it is an area rich in Norman monuments, for this part of Apulia was a favourite haunt of the Norman lords who conquered southern Italy and Sicily in the early eleventh century, and created the kingdom of Sicily. The Norman rule was relatively brief, but the kings created a brilliant court, where Muslim scholars, Greeks and Westerners mingled and where the ideas of Eastern philosophers and the forgotten learning of the Greek world became common currency. The Norman dynasty ended with Constance, daughter of Roger II, whose marriage to the emperor Henry VI of Germany ensured a dazzling finale to this civilisation. This match united two of the greatest powers in Christendom, and their son, Frederick II, ruled from Sicily to the north of Germany, with only the pope's dominions in central Italy separating the two halves of his empire. Frederick was one of the most remarkable and controversial figures of his time, called *stupor mundi*, 'the wonder of the world', by his contemporaries.

The creation of such a superpower did not go unchallenged, and Frederick had to fight off his opponents before he could secure his inheritance. Once he had done so, he created a realm where the energy of his Norman ancestors, the Arabic civilisation of Sicily and the immense tradition of the Holy Roman Empire, with its roots in Roman ideals, were intertwined. He ordered coins to be struck which showed him as a new Caesar Augustus, directly modelled on their classical Roman counterparts; he called on the services of Arab scholars to create works of geography based on the science of Baghdad; and he built castles in the manner of his Norman forebears. He himself wrote the finest of all medieval treatises on falconry, *On the Art of Hunting with Birds*, and if we are to believe a note in a contemporary manuscript, he was fluent enough in Arabic to correct a translation while engaged in besieging a town in 1240. All this was accomplished against a background of constant warfare and endless travel; and if this was not enough, he secured the return of Jerusalem to the Christians in 1229 without striking a blow.

But when Frederick went to the Holy Land, he was an outcast from the Church. In establishing his empire, he had made an enemy of the papacy, because he effectively controlled the borders of their lands in central Italy to north and south. Not only was he a political threat to the domains ruled by the popes, but his religious beliefs were not always orthodox. The struggle was a bitter one, fought with propaganda of the most vitriolic sort; Frederick was excommunicated, not once but frequently, and in return the emperor denounced the Church's wealth as a source of corruption and proclaimed the ideal of apostolic poverty, perhaps influenced by St Francis, whom he had met at Bari in 1220. This excommunication, and his attempts to impose a Norman-style centralised state on the fractious settlers in Palestine, meant that his triumph there was short-lived. In southern Italy, such a state already existed, and his Norman predecessors, notably his grandfather, were known for their heterodox views. Here Frederick was able to indulge his dream of a full revival of the splendour of ancient Rome, and it is here that we find the finest civil monuments to Frederick's reign. The most passionately reminiscent of imperial Rome of these was the fortified bridge at Capua, a kind of symbolic gateway to the kingdom of Sicily. It was unlike anything else built in the West at the time, and must have made a huge impression on travellers. All that remains of its strongly classical central façade are the figures of the emperor, of justice and of judges which once adorned it and which survive in the museum at Capua. These are so classical in form that they were long believed to be genuine sculpture from antiquity which Frederick had reused. This monumental entrance prefigures the triumphal arches of the Renaissance, with its programme of secular inscriptions: under the figure of justice, 'At the command of Caesar, I stand as protector of the kingdom: how wretched I make those whom I know to be false;' under the busts of the judges, 'Those who seek to lead a pure life may enter safely;' 'I shut out the heretic [or faithless]: let him fear to be put in prison.' Frederick himself directed the composition of this remarkable monument; Richard of San Germano records that he 'signed the plan with his own hand'. The fragments are a vivid reminder of his dream of power and order.

Frederick built a succession of great castles in southern Italy and Sicily: in all, there are more than 200 fortresses, citadels and palaces built or rebuilt during his reign. Most of these are purely practical, and are often built on a simple square plan, with towers at the corners; if the details sometimes reflect Frederick's classical interests, they are traditional medieval fortresses. The best examples are Castel Maniace in Syracuse and the well-preserved Castel Ursino in Catania, a highly symmetrical building with towers in the centre of each wall as well as at the four corners. The towers are plain and cylindrical, and the proportions and layout recall the Arab fortresses or *ribats* found from Syria through North Africa to Spain, and which had their origins in the Roman *castra* of the late empire. But Frederick was also interested in experiment, as the

now vanished keep at Lucera showed, a square building standing on a larger base with sloped sides, and with an extraordinary octagonal central courtyard.

Castel del Monte takes the rigidly accurate geometry of the four-square castles and the experiment at Lucera in a new direction. It is not merely octagonal; it has eight octagonal turrets at the angles, a plan as remarkable as the design for the bridge at Capua, which had cylindrical towers rising from square bases. At both Capua and Castel del Monte, we seem to be face to face with Frederick's own concepts of architecture. This is architecture for display and propaganda: Castel del Monte has limited strategic value, though it would be difficult to besiege, but we at once recognise the way in which it dominates the surrounding country. Its plan works round a central octagon, and this centralised layout, it has been argued, was reserved for architecture symbolic of power: the

Doorway and pediment, Castel del Monte

An early twentieth-century reconstruction of the monumental arch at Capua built by Frederick II

pantheon in Ravenna, Hagia Sophia in Constantinople, the chapel at Aachen and the Dome of the Rock at Jerusalem.

If Castel del Monte has a 'programme', it must surely be that it demonstrated Frederick's power and wealth; if he could afford to build in such style and luxury in the depths of the forests, what could he not accomplish elsewhere? The entrance confirms this idea: it is in the form of a great classical triumphal arch, and is built in red marble; there were probably sculptures or mosaics in the pediment, but this is the gateway to a palace, not to a heavily defended fortress. Inside, the rooms are relatively bare; a ring of spacious chambers, cool in the summer, run round the ground floor. The walls were covered in the same red marble as the great entrance doorway and the columns in many of the rooms, and some have tall Gothic fireplaces, but we can only guess at the furnishings. On the upper floor the rooms were faced with marble. There are few surviving architectural features: a massive doorway in the courtyard, evidently leading into one of the main rooms, has the torso of a horseman above, probably the remains of an imperial statue in the style of the mounted images of Constantine. A room on the upper floor has an elaborate window facing towards the town of Andria, one of Frederick's favoured places, where two of his wives were buried. A few sculptures on the vaulting and some decorative network patterning on the walls survive. Otherwise we know that there was an octagonal fountain in the centre of the courtyard, but that is all. We need to envisage a wealth of ornament, perhaps plants and even carpets spread on the ground in the Arab fashion, to reconstitute the original effect. Again, in the interiors, which are

now reduced to the bare Gothic skeleton of the building itself, we must imagine the richest possible furnishings, particularly in the so-called throne room in the upper storey.

One of the towers bears witness to Frederick's favourite pastime, falconry: above the vaulting, there is a space in the roof designed for use as an artificial eyrie for breeding the young falcons, as described in Frederick's treatise on falconry. It could be accessed by a ladder, and from which there is a way out onto the roof. Another feature of the building is the sanitary arrangements, which appear to have used running water fed from cisterns.

But the real marvel of Castel del Monte is invisible to the visitor. Its geometry is extraordinarily precise, and only a ground plan can reveal this. The variation in measurements on the inner surface of the outer walls is less than 0.8 inches (2 cm) on seven of the eight walls; the last is the portico wall, which has a different plan. Other critical dimensions, such as the distance between towers on opposite sides of the building, are

Interior octagonal courtyard of the Castel del Monte

Interior courtyard with breeding eyrie for falcons, Castel del Monte

even closer. This is quite unlike any other western European castle, and the ultimate source of this very precise geometry and engineering must be Islam, where advanced geometrical treatises were in circulation. In Arab decorative schemes, octagons created from this geometrical knowledge are prominent: fine examples can be seen in the Alhambra at Granada. Frederick was in touch with the greatest mathematician of the age, Leonardo of Pisa, who wrote the first explanation of Arabic numerals to appear in Latin, and the emperor's interest in and knowledge of pure mathematics was evidently considerable. We know less about the means by which the elaborate ground plan of the castle was constructed with such accuracy; the masons of northern Europe worked to much less accurate specifications, and some special equipment or technique must have been involved.

The octagon was also, as we have noted, symbolic: it was the shape of the imperial crown, and of the great chandelier ('light-crown' in Ger-

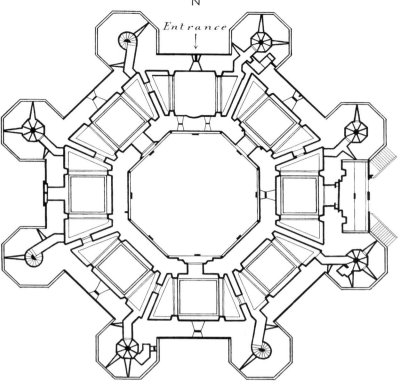

Plan of Castel del Monte

man) presented to the palace chapel at Aachen by Frederick's grandfather, Frederick Barbarossa. It has also been argued that the measurements of Castel del Monte are meant to evoke the divine Jerusalem, and that its plan is linked to Frederick's title as king of Jerusalem. Another suggestion is that the octagonal central courtyard acted as an astronomical observatory, and this is linked with the work of the philosopher Michael Scot, who was Frederick's guide in matters of natural science and particularly of astrology (which was the main reason for studying astronomy at the time). Frederick's interest in the latter is well documented, and we have to remember that astrology was widely accepted, particularly in the cautious form which Michael Scot put forward, until the seventeenth century. Even wilder theories than this have been put forward as to the meaning and purpose of Castel del Monte; even if they are unfounded and imaginative, they are nonetheless testimony to the impact of this extraordinary building and the richness of the cultural heritage from which it sprang.

Castel del Monte's heyday was brief; used by Frederick in the last years of his life, it became the graveyard of the Hohenstaufen dynasty; for, ironically, it was in this jewel-like building, more pleasure-palace than fortress, that the last Hohenstaufen princes lived out most of their lives as prisoners, after Frederick's son Manfred had been defeated and killed at Benevento in 1266 and the dream of a united German and Italian empire had been destroyed.

THE WELSH CASTLES
OF EDWARD I

The Norman rulers of England inherited not only the lands of the Anglo-Saxons, but also the long-standing warfare with the Celts whom the Saxons had driven to the fringes of Britain. The Plantagenet rulers, from Henry II's invasion of Wales in 1157 onwards, had attempted to conquer Wales (and Ireland as well) with varying degrees of success. In both countries they relied on barons who were often little more than freebooters to defend the borders, and when the time was right, attempt to extend their lordship beyond the frontier. In return, these 'marcher' lords enjoyed a large measure of freedom from royal authority until such time as the king decided to undertake a more permanent conquest. In the mid-thirteenth century the English were able to impose direct royal rule on parts of Wales, building castles in the Welsh heartlands to replace those of the marcher lords.

However, the Welsh resisted these efforts, and the Welsh prince Llywelyn, assuming the title of prince of Wales, had reconquered almost the whole of Wales, including much marcher territory. His title was recognised by Henry III in 1267. When Henry's son Edward came to the throne five years later, Llywelyn failed to do homage to him for Wales in the prescribed form, and it became clear that Llywelyn's ambitions were a threat to the English hold on Wales. War broke out in 1277, and Llywelyn's gains in the 1260s were retaken: parts of south Wales which had never previously been occupied now fell to the English barons, and Edward at once ordered fortresses to be repaired or built to act as royal strongholds. Llywelyn's power was restricted to north Wales, and the danger of north and south acting in concert, which had defeated the English on so many previous occasions, was eliminated. Llywelyn now sued for peace, and a treaty was made, leaving Llywelyn with his title and lands which consisted of Anglesey, Snowdonia and little else.

Edward now set out to impose some kind of order on his newly acquired lands; but the replacement of the loose tribal laws of Wales by the formal justice of England led to disturbances, which Llywelyn's brother David used as a rallying-call for a revolt, which broke out in March 1282, and much of Wales was overrun. Edward, who had been on good terms with both Llywelyn and David, was taken by surprise. He was heavily engaged elsewhere, in Gascony and Scotland, and reacted swiftly and sternly to the news from Wales. A summons to the army went out at once, and his forces were ready in August. By October he had reversed the situation, and only the mountains around Snowdon remained outside his control. Efforts were made by the archbishop of Canterbury to get agreement between Llywelyn and Edward, but these came to nothing. A month after the breakdown of talks, Llywelyn was killed in a skirmish in mid-Wales. The following spring, Edward's forces encircled Snowdonia and in June David was captured. He was tried and hanged in October.

The conquest of Wales was complete, but the land had to be made secure against future revolts. Edward's solution was to embark upon the most concentrated campaign of castle-building ever undertaken, an extraordinary feat of organisation which created a chain of seven great fortresses in little more than a decade. The mountains of Snowdonia could not be effectively occupied and garrisoned, but instead Edward created a ring of castles along the coast, stretching from Flint and Rhuddlan to the castle at Aberystwyth in mid-Wales which he already held. Conwy, Caernarfon and Harlech were the intervening sites, with an additional castle at Beaumaris on Anglesey, which was the last to be started, in 1295. Work on all these castles was supervised by one man, the king's 'master of the works in Wales', James of St George, who came from Savoy on the borders of France and Italy. James of St George had an established reputation as a military architect; he had originally been in the service of the counts of Savoy, and had worked on the count of Savoy's castle and town at Yverdon on Lake Neuchâtel. Five of the new castles in north Wales were planned as integral parts of towns, like Yverdon, because the English presence in the area needed more personnel than could be contained in the castles.

A king directs his master mason in the building of fortifications, from a manuscript illustrated at St Albans in about 1250

fic collato: memoria donatorus mdelebr
liter perpetuetur. Et hoc tali largitate op

Willegodum. ĉ incipretaꝝ volens bonu.
Yere em̄ vir bone fuit uoluntatis. et de

Rhuddlan Castle, begun 1277, on the banks of the new canal built for it

The first of the castles, Flint, was started in 1277. Its plan is unusual, consisting of a square enclosure with four corner towers, the largest of which is designed as a separate keep, divided from the rest by a moat. The lower part was for storage, while the upper floor contained accommodation grouped round a central well, an arrangement paralleled only in Castel del Monte. The separation of the tower is perhaps explained by its nearness to the sea: it could be used as a last refuge if the rest of the castle were taken, like any other keep, but with this arrangement it would also be possible to supply it or evacuate the occupants by sea even after the loss of the outer works.

Rhuddlan, on the river Clwyd, was the furthest inland of the new castles, and a new canal had to be dug to the sea to make it accessible to seagoing vessels. This was the first work to be done, from 1277 to 1280. It was largely completed in 1282, when it was attacked by the Welsh during their last great revolt and severely damaged. It was rebuilt without alteration after this, and work ended in 1285. Its plan is concentric and fairly conventional for a thirteenth-century castle: the four-square inner ward, however, has two gatehouses, to east and west, each elaborately equipped with defences. Interestingly, all six towers have identical internal arrangements: symmetry is the hallmark of the design despite an irregular site. There were plans for Rhuddlan to become a cathedral town and centre of the shire, but these never materialised, and the intended town walls never developed beyond a wooden palisade.

Conwy was captured by the English in 1283, and its possibilities were at once realised: commanding the Conwy estuary, the abbey of St Mary stood on a spur of rock which formed a natural stronghold. The additional expense involved in moving the abbey was offset by the fact that it was the burial place of Llywelyn the Great and had enjoyed the patron-

Conwy Castle, north Wales, built by Master James of St George, 1283–7

age of his house: its removal would underline the change of dynasty. A new site was found 7 miles (11 km) away, and the abbey's new buildings were ready in October 1284. Meanwhile work had already started at Conwy itself. The plan of both town and castle was determined by the lie of the land: the castle is almost oblong, following the line of the rock, its long walls strengthened by intermediate towers and the gateway set so that a right-angled turn has to be made before entering. Because the site is so narrow, it has a single massive outer wall, and is divided by a cross-wall into two wards. A water-gate provided direct access to the inner ward, which contained the royal apartments. This royal ward was marked off by four turreted towers, from which royal standards would be flown when the king was in residence. Another impressive feature was the Great Hall, built of stone and 125 feet (38 m) long. Conwy was designed as one of the centres of royal power in Wales, and the associated town is known to have housed royal offices and officials. Its walls, with their twenty-one towers, slope up the hillside to the north and west of the castle, with three gates, one of which is on the quayside. They and the castle were designed as a single unit and were built at the same time. The design is such that each section of wall can be isolated, so that, even if attackers gained a foothold on top of the wall, they could be contained before they overran the whole defences. The whole fortified enclosure is almost 1 mile (1.6 km) in circumference, the most ambitious single project of its kind undertaken in Britain in the Middle Ages, and also one of the best-preserved examples of its kind.

Harlech and Caernarfon were both captured in the summer of 1283, and in both cases work on the castles began very quickly. Harlech, on a beautiful site overlooking the Irish Sea, is perhaps the most 'orthodox' of all the north Welsh castles. Its plan – four-square, with corner towers and

129

Chancel of the chapel, Conwy Castle

a twin-towered central gatehouse on the side – is not dissimilar to that of Pope Clement V's castle at Villandraut in Gascony, also built by James of St George. Just as James drew on recent Continental work, so even from this outlying corner of Europe his achievements were noticed and had their influence elsewhere. But the gatehouse at Harlech is on a more massive scale than either its predecessors or successors, a miniature four-turreted keep. (Two turrets are in fact apses rather than complete towers.) This is largely due to its position: the sheer cliffs on all sides except the east make the line of attack predictable, and James of St George and his associates provided the necessary defence. The moat in front had to be cut through solid rock, which was an expensive operation. The accommodation inside the castle was fairly extensive, but this was not designed as a royal castle, and the apartments are correspondingly less spacious than at Conwy or Caernarfon.

At Caernarfon there was already an earlier castle, founded by Hugh of Chester in 1080 and used by the Welsh princes; but only the site of this was used by Edward. It stands on the mouth of the river Seiont, whose name is a reminder that this is the Roman fort of Segontium. Edward's new castle was also to have Roman and Byzantine echoes. In 1283, what

Harlech Castle, north Wales, built by Master James of St George, 1283–9

was believed to be the body of Magnus Maximus, the emperor from Britain who in Welsh legend was father of the emperor Constantine, was discovered in the town. Perhaps inspired by this, Edward and his architects chose as a model for the new castle the sixth-century town walls of Constantinople, with their patterned masonry of bands of different-coloured stone and their polygonal towers. They were also perhaps influenced by a description of a great Welsh city in the Welsh romance *The Dream of Macsen Wledig* (i.e. Magnus Maximus):

He saw how he came to an island, the fairest in the whole world, and after he had traversed the island from sea to answering sea, even to the uttermost bound of the island, he could see valleys and steeps and towering rocks, and a harsh rugged terrain whose like he had never seen. And from there he saw in the sea, facing that rugged land, an island. And between him and that island he saw a country whose plain was the length of its sea, its mountain the length of its woodland. And from that mountain he saw a river flow through the land, making towards the sea. And at the river mouth he could see a great castle, the fairest that mortal had ever seen, and the gate of the castle he saw open, and he came to the castle. Inside the castle he saw a fair hall. The roof of the hall he thought to be all of gold; the side of the hall he thought to be of glittering stones, each as costly as its neighbour; the hall doors he thought to be all gold. Golden couches he saw in the hall, and tables of silver.

Looking inside the oblong keep, from the Eagle Tower, Caernarfon, north Wales, built *c.*1284

Edward of Caernarfon (later Edward II) is created prince of Wales and earl of Chester by his father, Edward I, at the Lincoln Parliament, 7 February 1301. From *Chronica Roffense*, early fourteenth century

The castle is later named in the romance as 'Aber Seint' or Segontium, and a great fortress is built there for Macsen, with earth brought especially from Rome. So the design of Caernarfon could be a conscious attempt to recreate Magnus Maximus' fortress, appealing to the Welsh traditions in the same way as the fact that Edward's first son was to be born in Wales and become the first of the princes of Wales. Because the circumstances which dictated the design were exceptional, Caernarfon has no close medieval parallels, and once again Edward's architects created something new and remarkable.

The plan of Caernarfon is not unlike that of Conwy: the castle has an oblong shape, with two separate wards inside, and forms the angle of the town walls nearest to the water. The accommodation, except for the great hall, was largely in the seven towers and two gatehouses; but the buildings in the inner ward were never completed. The towers are linked by massive walls equipped with elaborate wall-walks and galleries. The huge scale of operations meant that the work was only partly completed when the Welsh rebelled again in 1294, and much damage was done; however, building began again in 1295 and continued into the early part of the fourteenth century. Yet, despite its intended role as a kind of Welsh equivalent of Windsor, it was never visited again by a king of England until the twentieth century, and only in the investiture ceremonies of 1911 and 1974 has it been used in the way that Edward I seems to have intended seven centuries ago.

The last of the castles, Beaumaris, dates from after a revolt by the Welsh in 1294. James of St George was commissioned to begin work early

Beaumaris Castle, built close to the shore's edge at Anglesey, 1295–1330

in 1295 on a castle which would secure Anglesey against future revolts. Once again a shore site was chosen, on level ground to the north-east of the island. It is the only castle where the site imposed no restrictions, and the symmetry evident at Rhuddlan appears again. The site has no natural defences and St George's answer to this is a forest of towers: the outer wall has eight bastions, four towers and two twin-towered gatehouses, the inner ward six towers and two apses and towered gatehouses nearly on the scale of that at Harlech, giving a huge inner defensive unit containing what are virtually two keeps. The dock, essential to the castle's survival, has its own carefully worked-out defensive system. The accommodation was on a fairly lavish scale, and the lovely vaulted chapel still survives, as a reminder that castle interiors could be elegant as well as practical. But as building progressed, so the threat of Welsh rebellion receded, and by 1330 work had ceased. The original plans were remarkably ambitious: the actual cost of over £14,000 for the castle, which was only half-finished when work stopped, was equal to that of the whole of the walls and castle at Conwy.

The Edwardian castles in north Wales were the results of a remarkable effort; royal accounts indicate the vast reserves of men and money that Edward poured into their building. Even though they were never completely finished, they are a fitting memorial to an architect of genius and an energetic king.

133

THE MONASTERIES
OF BATALHA, TOMAR
AND BELÉM

If the Bayeux Tapestry had continued beyond the flight of the Anglo-Saxon army, it could well have shown William I founding Battle abbey, which still stands on the slope above the battlefield of Hastings. An equally momentous battle in Portugal's history led to the foundation of another Battle abbey, the monastery of Batalha.

When Fernando I of Portugal died in 1383, one of the claimants to the Portuguese throne was Juan I, king of Castile. Eager to gain a second kingdom, he invaded Portugal in 1385 with what should have been an overwhelmingly superior force. But in this case it was the native army that was victorious, against all the odds, under the leadership of one of Fernando's bastard sons, who was master of the military Order of Avis. He met the invading forces at Aljubarrota in central Portugal, and the lack of discipline in the Castilian army, whose knights attacked contrary to Juan I's orders, gave the day to the defenders: the action, late on an August evening, seems to have lasted little more than an hour. When the Castilian attack failed and Juan I withdrew, leaving a large part of his army dead on the field, Portugal's independence was assured.

In gratitude for his victory, the new king, João I, vowed to found a monastery in honour of the Virgin, since the battle had been fought on the eve of the feast of the Assumption of the Virgin. The site of the battle was not suitable for the new monastery, and a site 3 miles (4.8 km) away was chosen. The building was begun some three years later, and Dominican monks were brought in to form the community. The church became the national pantheon of Portugal, symbol of the new dynasty's victory and resting place of its founder and his wife, Philippa, daughter of John of Gaunt. It is their arms which we see on the portal, at the point of the arch of the massive central doorway. The church is in the latest English Gothic style, though the chief architect, Affonso Domingues, was Portuguese. It is built in a warm golden sandstone which tempers the severity of the interior and lends light and grace to the intricate whirling patterns of the windows on the façade. The scale of the west front tells us that this is a place of especial importance, and its insistent vertical emphasis – a pattern of ribbing on the stone panels of the exterior and the high and narrow nave inside – gives it a striking and unexpected power. By contrast, the roofline is fanciful and delicate, a perforated tracery parapet which runs round the whole of the church, with richly

ornamented buttresses linking the walls with the roof of the central nave.

When João I made his will in 1426, he had evidently ordered the construction of the chapel which lies to the right of the nave. He specified that his successors as 'king or queen of these kingdoms' should not permit anyone to be buried in this chapel other than the sovereigns, their children and grandchildren. The chapel itself is by the successor of Domingues, Huguet, and is based on French rather than English Gothic; it is an octagon within a square, with a magnificent stone vault in the central lantern in the shape of an eight-pointed star, with eight further eight-pointed stars on the intersection of each projection, a hugely elegant and satisfying design which is at once simple and highly ornate. The tombs are mostly those of the princes of Portugal, because João's successor, Duarte, decided to build a new pantheon. The chapel is dominated, however, by the spectacular tomb of João and Philippa of Lancaster, who lie in state under Gothic canopies; the effigies are masterly portraits, and, touchingly, the couple are portrayed holding hands for all eternity. On the sides are lengthy inscriptions testifying to their merits and deeds, and

Exterior view of Santa Maria de Vitória, Batalha, begun 1388

Decorative ceiling at Batalha

Tomb of João I and Philippa of Lancaster, Batalha

in pride of place on the head of the tomb is carved the insignia of the Order of the Garter, already the most prestigious order of knighthood in Europe, of which João I was a member. It is also a reminder of the alliance between England and Portugal, the longest on record; the treaty of 1373 has never been abrogated.

Detail of the vaulting in the chapel at Batalha

But the real treasure of Batalha is yet to come. Beyond the east end of the original church lies the pantheon planned by Duarte, a huge octagon with seven octagonal chapels leading off it. These were to have six pentagonal chapels in the spaces between them, an intricate geometric groundwork which echoes the medieval love of patterning as seen in Frederick II's Castel del Monte. The eighth side of the octagon is a massive portal. Not surprisingly, this hugely ambitious project was never completed, and lies open to the sky: it is known as the Capelas Imperfeitas (the unfinished chapels). It represents the last flowering of Gothic, in the extraordinary Mannerist style known as Manoelino after Duarte's son Manoelo I. It has been called a maritime architecture, in which decoration accumulates on the surfaces as weed and barnacles might grow on a ship, encrusting them with a living, writhing overlay. Sacheverell Sitwell, an enthusiast for the Manoelino, compared the doorway into the Capelas to a great Indian gateway to an empty city, such as might be found at Fatehpur Sikri, and calls it 'unparalleled in fantasy'. And as we look at the luxuriant, exuberant decoration, we soon realise that the artist who designed this was not thinking simply in European terms; there are elements of Moorish art and, most strikingly, of Hindu ornament. This is Gothic which transcends the bounds of Europe.

For Portugal had become the most adventurous of the European kingdoms. Prince Henry the Navigator, brother of King Duarte, had laid the foundations for an extraordinary campaign of exploration. The Portuguese caravels which he sent out made their way down the west coast of Africa, slowly mapping out the unknown territory to the south; by Henry's death in 1460 they had reached modern Sierra Leone. Thereafter, the voyages became bolder, culminating in Vasco da Gama's discovery of the sea route to the Indian Ocean in the last decade of the fifteenth century. In 1494, Spain and Portugal agreed to confine their activities to west and east respectively; the immense riches to be made in trade with India, especially in spices, meant that Portugal at first got the best of the bargain, and the wealth from this commerce lies behind the creation of the architectural masterpieces of Manoelo I's reign. The Hindu patterns at Batalha reflect this new-found world and the prosperity that it had brought with it.

To the left of the nave lies the cloister, where more wonders of Manoelino Gothic await us. Medieval cloisters conform to the same four-square arcaded pattern throughout Europe, and any originality lies in the detail rather than the layout. That at Batalha is on the grandest scale; it is not filled with sculptures like twelfth-century cloisters, but

Entrance to the unfinished Octagon Chapel, Batalha

Doorway cloister arch at Batalha, with ornamental tracery

Carved grille, Batalha

instead has tracery of extraordinary complexity, added at the same time as the Capelas Imperfeitas were being built. This tracery has clear echoes of the Moorish buildings of southern Spain; the Alhambra in Granada had been captured by the Spaniards only twenty years earlier. There are two designs, one that seems to entwine briar roses with the 'device' of Manoelo I, the armillary sphere used by the Portuguese navigators, while the other blazons the cross of the Order of Christ entangled in what may be lotus blossoms. The caravels that sought the passage to the east, to the Hindu world where the lotus design reigned supreme, bore on their sails this red cross, which the Order of Christ had inherited from the Knights Templar. These windows, in an architectural style whose roots lie in France three centuries earlier, look back to the early days of the Crusades and forward to the new horizons of art and commerce opened up by the expeditions mounted by the Portuguese kings.

The home of the Order of Christ was not far from Batalha, at Tomar. Here there had been the headquarters of the Knights Templar in Portugal, founded by royal command in 1160. When the Templar Order was destroyed by the king of France and the pope in 1307, in most of Europe their property went either to the Knights Hospitaller or to the state. In Portugal, however, where the Order had helped the kingdom in its lengthy struggle with its Moorish neighbours in the south of Spain, the Order was popular, and much valued by the king, Dinis. Dinis succeeded in arranging for the Portuguese Templars to retain their position, but since the suppression of the Templars was irrevocable, this was achieved by founding a new order, the Order of Christ, which had the same personnel and the same possessions. Prince Henry became administrator of the Order when it was secularised in 1420, and used its resources to launch his expeditions: the red cross of the Order became a naval symbol. With the success of the enterprises in Africa and India, the Order grew

139

The decorative exterior of the Convento de Cristo, Tomar, begun 1160

South window of the Chapter House, Convento de Cristo, Tomar

Reliquary-like interior of the church at the Convento de Cristo, Tomar

Window detail, Convento de Cristo, Tomar

wealthy, and the rebuilding of their headquarters at Tomar reflects both their new-found wealth and their new interests. The entrance is through a highly decorated Gothic doorway, which hints at the wonders to be found further on in its use of unexpected forms, swags and curves which are more rococo than medieval. Inside, we find ourselves halfway down the nave of the church; at the east end is the extraordinary Charola, a twelfth-century Templar oratory, originally the plainest of structures, which has been decorated like some precious image of the Virgin in sumptuous and totally inappropriate clothing. The reworking of this holy of holies in the late Gothic period is overlaid by sixteenth-century paintings and gilding, to make it a strange treasure casket, a giant reliquary perhaps, but with nothing at its centre. The rest of the nave is a stark contrast, simple and spacious; but when we go outside, to the south end, another surprise awaits us. The wall itself is four-square and massive; but on it there grows like seaweed the richest of ornaments and strangest of fantasies. Above, a porthole window takes the place of the

traditional rose window; but it is a porthole surrounded by a sail, furled and brailed by ropes, with a rope around the perimeter which sprouts into luxuriant vegetation. The flanking pillars could be on a Hindu temple: only the gargoyles and the hovering angels and statues of Portuguese kings bring us back to reality. Flowing forms are juxtaposed with surfaces of utter plainness or simple fluting; everywhere there are ropes, fastened to stone eyes and running through stone rings whose carving is sheer bravado. In the centre of the façade is the plainest of diagonal grilles, again surrounded by a jungle of exotic vegetation and exuberant fantasies. Above, the cross of the Order of Christ stands above the royal arms, with armillary spheres to left and right. Below, a mysterious bearded ancient entangled in a rope bears a root on his shoulders. No wonder that one writer declared that this was 'the most stupendous creation of architecture of all times'.

The third of the great abbeys of the Manoeline era is on the edge of Lisbon, between the city and the sea. Belém stands guard at the mouth of the Tagus: it should be a fort, not a monastery, and indeed, just beyond the gates, is the Tower of Belém, which was built at the same time and acted as a lookout for the ships coming into the river. It has the stone

ropes we saw at Tomar; here a rope with great knots in it moors the tower securely round the battlements. Again, Manoelo's armillary sphere and the cross of the Order of Christ are prominent: the courtyard overlooking the river and the battlements blazon the crosses defiantly to all comers. A rhinoceros head on the river façade and dolphins and lions echo the theme of distant voyages. But the tower is too practical a building to indulge in the full panoply of exotic ideas that are found in the cloister at the monastery of Belém a few hundred yards inland.

The abbey at Belém owed its origin to Prince Henry the Navigator, who founded a chapel there which he gave to the Order of Christ. Vasco de Gama prayed there when he set out on his great voyage in 1497, and on his safe return Manoelo I ordered an abbey to be founded there. Portugal's victory over the sea was to be commemorated in the same way as João's victory over the Spanish a century earlier. In the cloister, the lines of Gothic are tempered by the curves of the Renaissance, and the simplicity of the cloister walk becomes a full-blown double arcade, with theatrical corner doorways set at an angle and with a great balcony above. This is architecture as theatre, and the nautical decor might suggest that this was to be the setting for a mock sea-fight in the flooded

cloister. Ropes and anchors abound, forming patterns of extraordinary ingenuity. It stands as a symbol of Portugal at its greatest, the enquiring spirit of exploration and of the Renaissance looking outward to new physical and intellectual worlds. That the flowering of Portugal was brief makes the art of the Manoeline architects all the more poignant: it is a kind of *ne plus ultra*, and Portugal itself went no further: in 1578, King Sebastião, in a romantic attempt to revive the crusading spirit, invaded Morocco and was disastrously defeated. Portugal became part of Spain and declined into a provincial torpor.

View of the Tower of Belém, near Lisbon, built 1515–21

Spectacular cloister decoration, Monastery of the Jeronimos, Belém, built 1502–52

Cloisters of the Monastery of the Jeronimos, Belém

SEVEN WONDERS OF THE RENAISSANCE WORLD

Theodore K. Rabb

BETWEEN the late fourteenth and seventeenth centuries, in the era of the Renaissance, Europeans began to impose a military, intellectual and cultural stamp on the rest of the world. In our own age of globalisation, we tend to emphasise reciprocal influences: the interweaving of the many distinct civilisations and traditions that make up our planet. But during the Renaissance Europe was the main outward-moving force, generating a dynamism that none of its neighbours could match. In this period, therefore, one can argue that it would not be inappropriate to take our seven wonders solely from the West, from those striving cultures that were in the midst of an expansion and encounter that were to transform human history.

By its very nature, a choice limited to just seven creations has to be both idiosyncratic and invidious, and in this case the limits are even more stringent, since non-Western marvels of the period, such as the Taj Mahal, Aztec architecture, Mixtec jewellery and the renovation of the Great Wall of China, are excluded. But even within Europe there is an abundance that is dismissed at one's peril. Michelangelo, for one, seems discriminated against, since he created at least four serious candidates for the list in Rome alone: the luminous paintings that dominate the Sistine Chapel; the architectural harmony of the Piazza del Campidoglio; the soaring dome of St Peter's; and the majesty of the Farnese Palace. His most famous architectural forerunner, Leon Battista Alberti, also deserves consideration for his masterpiece, the classically elegant Malatesta Tempio in Rimini, which still looks pristine. No less gleaming is the magnificently restored Ducal Palace in Urbino, built by Luciano Laurana with a delicate arcaded courtyard that has never been bettered, perched on what is arguably the most spectacular site of any Renaissance palace in Italy.

If one stretches the chronology, one might also include in this category of a single artist's crowning achievement the Scrovegni Chapel in Padua, where Giotto's paintings achieve a sense of perspective and a level of human emotion that transformed European art; or (at the very

Taj Mahal, Agra, built 1632–48 for the fifth Mughal emperor Shah Jahan as a mausoleum for his second wife, Mumtaz

145

beginning of the Renaissance) the glowing Brancacci Chapel, painted by Masaccio in the church of the Carmine in Florence. Both these chapels became shrines, visited and revered by artists for centuries.

Moreover, all of the sites that have been mentioned are not merely splendid monuments, but are generally regarded as essential treasures of Western culture. They would qualify as wonders on any serious list: they offer overwhelming splendour at first sight, followed by a deep contentment that remains in mind and eye as one recalls their qualities. And the same is true if one seeks memories of the Renaissance outside Italy.

The stunning astronomical clock created by Conrad Dasypodius in Strasbourg cathedral, for instance, is a tempting candidate for our list – a combination of aesthetic and mechanical brilliance that embodies the experimental as well as the artistic commitments of the age. A similar case could be made for the Gutenberg Bible, or indeed (to return to Italy) for the entire output of the Aldine Press in Venice during its early pioneering decades. If one cherishes beauty as well as the power to transform the world, there are few artefacts as compelling as the first printed books. But one could say much the same for the oldest surviving cannon and hand-held firearms, and that does cause a problem: multiple small objects simply do not generate the awe that we feel when confronting more massive single constructions.

There are cityscapes that would certainly qualify: the Piazza del Campo in Siena or the Piazza della Signoria in Florence, both graced by distinctive towers; Old City Square in Prague, with its own great clock; the little Tuscan town of Pienza, designed to be the perfect urban space by the humanist scholar and pope Pius II; the Grand' Place in Brussels; or any of a dozen stretches of the Grand Canal in Venice, preferably one that includes the lovely Rialto Bridge. But there is an eclecticism about these ensembles that makes them, though marvellous, somehow less than majestic: the grandeur is assembled by the viewer rather than by the succession of architects who made their individual contributions to the whole.

Individual buildings, too, compete for inclusion. The Mauritshuis in The Hague is a virtual distillation of the Dutch Golden Age, and is one of the most perfect museums in the world. Not far away, the home of Peter Paul Rubens in Antwerp evokes the sumptuous, grandiose and radiant vision of the artist himself – a feeling of being in the presence of genius that one finds, too, in Rembrandt's house in Amsterdam, in Dürer's in Nuremberg and in El Greco's in Toledo. Further north, and very different in feeling, is the Stock Exchange building in Copenhagen, with its fantastic spire of entwined tails, which remains one of the most distinctive sights in Europe. Other splendid candidates might be the monumental castle in Heidelberg, the graceful palace of Chenonceau, or one of the many exquisite country homes that the English and French gentry and nobility built: Montacute, Longleat, Hardwick Hall or Burghley House in England; the Châteaux d'Anet or de Maintenon in France, not to mention the town houses, like the Hôtel Sully in Paris. All, however, seem to carry echoes, either of one another or of analogous buildings not too far away. Their very profusion renders the individual examples – sadly – less than overwhelming.

Thus far we have considered only visible monuments. Which means that one of the productions of the Renaissance that ought to be on a list of the seven wonders of all history is missing: the plays of Shakespeare. And yet, although a case could easily be made that this monument is as remarkable and enduring as any of the physical wonders we will describe, in my view it is crucially different from, say, a work of architecture, because it does not stand on its own. Reading Shakespeare is a life-enhancing experience, but his full glory is achieved only in performance. We see and hear him through intermediaries, and we can never know whether we connect with him or with his interpreters. It is for that reason that I put him to one side, though with enormous reluctance. And the same is true of the masterpieces of Monteverdi, not to mention the invention in Venice of a setting for the new art form he established, the opera house.

To make choices, therefore, is to acknowledge that there are both private inclinations – prejudices, perhaps – and formal, public reasons for the outcome. Above all, for this writer, history is central to the selection: places that stirred the imagination not only at the time but also for generations thereafter, and thus set their stamp on the age, have a high claim. In the end, however, this is a highly personal list of sites that have captured the attention and have kept it ever since. They are the seven places, above all others, that this particular historian wants his readers to see and experience, in wonder, for themselves.

SANTA MARIA DEL FIORE, FLORENCE

By common consensus, the age we call the Renaissance, characterised above all by efforts to bring the achievements of the ancient world back to life, began in Florence. If Venetians, with their senators and their empire stretching across the Mediterranean, liked to think of themselves in political terms as the heirs of Rome, it was the Florentines who first sought to revive, more broadly, the thought, spirit and culture of their distant Roman ancestors. And the path-breaker in the campaign to restore Italy's ancient glories was a fourteenth-century poet, philosopher and diplomat, born in nearby Arezzo, who thought of himself as a son of Florence even though he lived most of his life far from the city: Francesco Petrarca, known in English as Petrarch.

Looking to make a living at the papal court, Petrarch was so dismayed by the corruption and immorality he saw all around him that he determined to find a better guide for the virtuous life. The alternative he found was in antiquity. For him, the only example of upright and public-spirited behaviour worth following came from the great figures of Rome. Writing a pure Latin, not the debased version in use by the 1300s, they had embodied the high purpose and selfless sense of service that he found nowhere in his own age. After reading Livy, for example, Petrarch felt impelled to write to the long-dead historian: 'I wish that I had been born in your age, or you in ours. I should thank you, though, that you have so often caused me to forget present evils and have transported me to happier times.' He therefore urged his contemporaries to imitate the ancients. The more one acted and thought like them, the better one's chance of attaining virtue.

Thanks largely to his friend and avid propagandist Giovanni Boccaccio, Petrarch's message was taken up with enthusiasm by Florence's elite in the years around 1400. Intellectuals who came to be known as humanists sought to write like Cicero and other models of correct Latin; schoolchildren had to learn by heart pages of Horace and Ovid; admirers of Rome foraged for texts, inscriptions and relics that had survived from antiquity; and artists tried to recapture the feel and the forms of ancient painting, sculpture and architecture. The new commitments in the arts were particularly notable, in that they made the turn to the distant past visible, and also created the masterpieces which, to this day, epitomise the age of the Renaissance.

Without this cultural transformation the extraordinary burst of creativity that exploded in Florence in the first half of the fifteenth century

Petrarch (Francesco Petrarca). Portrait from an illuminated letter in *De Remediis Utriusque Fortunae*, fourteenth century

La Divina Commedia illumina Firenze. Fresco by Domenico di Michelino, 1465. In this allegorical fresco, Dante, his book and the layered paradise he imagined bring light to a Florence symbolised by Brunelleschi's dome

would never have happened. But there was also another stimulus, no less essential: the zest for competition. In the early 1400s there were around fifty thousand people living in Florence, crammed into close proximity within their city's walls. Fights and disputes were part of the scenery. In Machiavelli's view, Florentines were free precisely because they argued so much. Among the leading families the constant struggles could have serious consequences, because losers often suffered the most grievous of punishments inflicted on these fiercely devoted citizens: exile. Dante and Machiavelli are merely the most famous of the many who were banished. In the early 1400s even the head of the Medici family had to depart for a few years. To this day, the formidable walls presented to the outside world by the *palazzi* of the Rucellai, the Strozzi and the Medici hint at the families' defensive concerns amidst the perennial quarrels with their rivals.

If competitiveness was rife within Florence, it was even fiercer in relations with neighbours. The leading cities of Italy were almost always at war with one another. Yet the quest for superiority was not confined to the battlefield. Magnificence, beauty and talent were also standards for comparison. A major distinction for the Florentines, for example, was that they could claim Dante and Giotto, who were both revered throughout Italy by 1400, as native sons. They became increasingly jealous of Siena, therefore, as this rival Tuscan city began to build a great cathedral in the thirteenth and early fourteenth centuries. The cathedral was universally admired, even though the Black Death forced abandonment of plans to make it the largest church in the world. The envious citizens of Florence soon determined to do even better.

This was the conjunction of forces that led, slowly but inexorably, to the creation of the first great wonder of the Renaissance world. Seeking to outdo the Sienese, the Florentines had torn down an old church in the centre of town, had cleared the surrounding area and begun building what they promised would be the 'most beautiful temple' in Tuscany. The foundation stone had been laid in 1296, seventy years after the Sienese had started their cathedral, but by the 1360s only the walls and roof of the nave had been completed. At this point construction slowed down, because the plans called for a huge crossing between apse and nave at the eastern end, to be covered by a dome with a diameter of over 140 feet (43 m). This was larger than the two most famous domes that had survived from antiquity, the Pantheon in Rome and Hagia Sophia in Constantinople, and since nobody was certain how to proceed, the enormous gap remained open to the sky above for more than half a century. The rest of Italy, meanwhile, confidently predicted disaster. By the time construction of the dome began in 1420, however, Petrarch's call for the emulation of antiquity had become the Florentines' rallying cry, and the man to turn that vision into stone had been found: Filippo Brunelleschi.

The three founding fathers of the transformations in painting, sculpture and architecture that took off in the first decades of the fifteenth century were Masaccio, Donatello and Brunelleschi. These Florentines all knew one another and had spent time in the fount of inspiration, Rome, even though the city, poor and with a shrinking population, was no longer the cultural force it had once been. Here, however, they had been able to measure and study the relics of antiquity (often arousing the suspicions of the locals) and, on returning to Florence, had startled their contemporaries with their mastery of perspective, emotion and lifelike representations. Their influence was to last for centuries, but even in this august company it was Brunelleschi whose fame eclipsed all others'.

Filippo Brunelleschi was born in 1377, just three years after Petrarch died. By the time construction of his dome began, he was in his early forties and generally regarded as gifted but eccentric. Never married, volatile, short, bald and often dishevelled, he joined a long line of great artists who have given their calling its reputation for the unconventional – even the peculiar – combined with the brilliant. He was clearly exceptional in both senses of the word. Even so admiring a biographer as Giorgio Vasari felt compelled to comment on his physique as well as his talent:

There are some whom Nature has created little of stature, but with a soul of greatness and a heart of such immeasurable daring that if they do not set themselves to difficult and almost impossible things, and do not complete them to the wonder of those who behold, they have no peace in their lives. Thus it was with Filippo di Ser Brunellesco, who was small in stature like Giotto, but great in genius.

Brunelleschi came from a well-to-do family, and was trained as a gold-smith, the elite artistic profession of the time. But he hardly had a straightforward career. He did achieve the rank of master goldsmith at the age of twenty-two, but three years later he left that trade for good. The occasion was one of the competitions by which the Florentines liked to make major artistic decisions. Bronze doors were to be commissioned for the centuries-old Baptistery that stood next to the new cathedral. Brunelleschi's designs were judged equal to those of his fellow goldsmith and sculptor Lorenzo Ghiberti, and it was suggested that they work together. But Brunelleschi, proud and always secretive about his ideas and his working methods, refused to share command of the project, and instead left for Rome.

He remained there, on and off, for over a decade, studying ancient architecture in detail. When he returned to his native city, the enormous cathedral, over a century in the making, was at last nearing completion, with the notable exception of its most problematic feature: the dome that was to cover the opening at the crossing of apse and nave. The space was an octagon, with a diameter of over 140 feet (43 m): wider even than the Pantheon. Even the drum on which the dome was to rest was finished — with 14-foot-thick (4-m) walls to support the millions of pounds of stone and brick that were to come. At its top, the drum was already 170 feet (52 m) above the ground, and now the question had to be faced: how was

The Pantheon, Rome, first built *c.*25 BC. Photograph by George Anderson, *c.*1900. This ancient domed building was both inspiration and object of study for Brunelleschi

one to raise a dome that would more than double that height? For the officials in charge of the works there was only one way to find an answer: a competition for the building of the dome.

What it was to look like had been decided over fifty years before. There were to be two shells: a much thicker, heavier inner dome was to help support the more delicate, but higher-reaching, outer dome. The shape was to be a so-called pointed fifth, which meant that the eight curved sides would rise at a sharper angle, and meet at a higher point, than a hemispherical dome like the Pantheon or Hagia Sophia (or later versions like St Peter's in Rome, St Paul's in London or the Capitol in Washington). The dome would thus tower dramatically over the city, but the practical problems seemed insurmountable. How was one to support it while it was being built? Where were trees large enough to build scaffolding? Equally difficult: how was one to raise gigantic weights (some of the marble and sandstone building blocks weighed several tons) more than 300 feet (90 m) into the air?

To this day, we do not know exactly how Brunelleschi solved all these problems. Some of the answers remain hidden within the massive walls of the dome. But we do know that he caused a sensation when he submitted a proposal that omitted all mention of scaffolding. What ensued, as the works committee grappled with the entries for their competition, was described by Vasari. Since he knew the outcome, he could relish the disbelief that greeted Brunelleschi's plans:

Filippo alone declared that he could make a vaulted roof without much wood, without pillars or supports, and with little expense of arches. It seemed to all who heard him that what he had said was foolish, and they mocked him and laughed at him, saying he was speaking like a madman. Then Filippo, being offended, said, 'Though you laugh at me, you will find out that it can be done in no other manner.' And as he grew warm in explaining his ideas, they doubted him the more, and held him to be a mere chattering fool. And when they had bidden him depart several times and he would not go, he was carried out by force, all supposing him to be mad. And this was how it came about that Filippo used to say afterwards that he dared not at that time pass along any part of the city lest it should be said, 'There goes that madman.'

The derision notwithstanding, the competition was eventually decided in favour of Brunelleschi, and in August 1420 the gigantic effort began. To hedge their bets, the works committee had appointed the runner-up, Ghiberti, as co-supervisor of the project. This time, however, Brunelleschi did not walk off in a huff. Unlike Ghiberti, he was already a widely respected architect, with commissions for a number of buildings under his belt, and he knew he would be able to show up his old rival. The opportunity arose in 1423, when he contracted a diplomatic illness at a crucial moment in the construction: the installation of the first of the four sandstone chains that circled the dome, and countered the sideways thrust of its huge weight. Ghiberti was unable to tell the masons how to proceed, whereupon Brunelleschi arose from his sickbed, triumphantly pointed the way ahead, and thereafter was never seriously challenged as master architect.

It took another thirteen years for the dome to reach its summit. To make the construction possible, Brunelleschi had to come up with a staggering succession of inventions. He devised a hoist of pulleys, gears and screws, driven by oxen, that raised the massive stones hundreds of feet, higher than any such machine had ever attempted before. To make it work, he even had to create a special bolt that enabled the stone to be attached to the hoist. He also had to build a crane that permitted the masons to move the stone sideways, once it reached the right height, and place it precisely where it belonged. For the structure itself, Brunelleschi figured out a herringbone design of bricks which was self-supporting, and thus obviated the need for scaffolding, along with a system of nine retaining bands that circled the dome at regular intervals in order to hold the masonry in place as the walls inclined away from the vertical. He also took into account the fierce wind that swirled around so tall a building, leaving openings to lessen its impact. And he built special platforms that made it easier for the masons to work at great heights; astonishingly, only one worker fell to his death during the construction. As for the design, Brunelleschi was able to taper the width of the two shells that formed the dome so that their weight, and thus the pressure they exerted, diminished as they rose ever higher. The inner shell, which bore most of the weight and created pleasing proportions when viewed from below, tapered from 7 to 5 feet (2 to 1.5 m) in thickness; the outer, which gave the cathedral its height, tapered from just 2 feet to 1 foot (0.6 to 0.3 m).

With Florence at war during much of the construction, and new practical difficulties arising almost every month (whether it be bad weather, mortar that did not set fast enough, or the problem of transporting marble large distances), the enterprise had to endure regular setbacks even as it marched relentlessly forward. The enemies Brunelleschi acquired in this fiercely competitive world even had him briefly imprisoned in 1434 on a trumped-up charge of failing to pay guild dues. But the architect and his workforce persevered, and two years later, in a dazzling ceremony that brought all Florentines together, the pope himself consecrated the completed Santa Maria del Fiore. The dome, soaring over the city, was in place, and the church became the bustling centre of devotion it has remained to this day.

But one job remained. Like the Pantheon, the dome ended in an

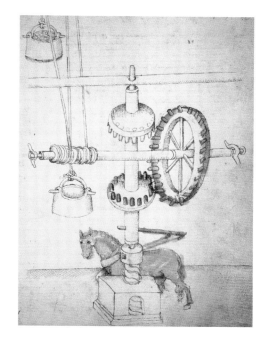

Horse-driven version of Brunelleschi's ox-hoist. Pen-and-ink drawing by Mariano di Jacopo (called Taccola) from his notebooks, 1431–3. A contemporary drawing of one of the machines invented by Brunelleschi for the construction of the dome

Construction of the lantern for the dome of Santa Maria del Fiore, Florence. This contemporary drawing shows the scaffolding Brunelleschi designed

oculus, a circular opening that allowed light to stream down to the church below. Anyone who has visited the Pantheon in a rainstorm knows what that means: a large and messy pool of water on the floor. With Florence's climate, and a high altar under the dome, that was not to be tolerated. The works committee therefore launched another competition, for a lantern at the summit of the dome – an elegant pinnacle that would keep out the elements but still allow light to enter. Once again Brunelleschi had to fight off rival proposals, as he had done repeatedly when designing the dome itself, inventing the construction machines, and making plans for transporting the materials. The committee wanted a model of the lantern and also explanations of how machines (which could no longer be stationed within the busy cathedral) would raise over 1 million tons of stone 300 feet (90 m) to the top of the dome. Once again Brunelleschi won the victory, with a classical octagon of marble arches

154

and Corinthian pilasters, topped by a bronze globe that sat 350 feet (107 m) above the piazza below.

But the architect did not live to see this final feat completed. Soon after the first stone was laid, in 1446, he died, and it was to be another twenty years before the lantern was finished. The final touch, the bronze globe, was to be fashioned by another Renaissance master, Andrea del Verrocchio. By then, Brunelleschi had been buried in the cathedral below – a unique honour, and a testimony to the admiration of his fellow citizens, because the only other tomb in Santa Maria del Fiore is of St Zenobius, bishop of Florence in the fourth century and one of the patron saints of the city.

Despite lightning strikes and earthquakes, this most remarkable of the world's domes continues to loom over its surroundings. One catches sight of it in all corners of the city, and from balconies even 200 yards

Lantern and globe of Santa Maria del Fiore. Lantern by Filippo Brunelleschi, built 1446–66, and copper globe by Andrea del Verrocchio, 1474

155

View of Florence with Santa Maria del Fiore, built 1296–1436. From this angle, the bell tower designed by Giotto looks equally prominent, but in fact it is Brunelleschi's dome that dominates all of Florence

(183 m) away it so fills the horizon that one imagines one has only to lean forward to reach it. Because Florence lies in a valley one can look at it from above, but still it dominates the city near and far. Thus, although he was exiled to the nearby town of San Casciano, Machiavelli could take some comfort in his homesickness because the cathedral was clearly visible some 8 miles (13 km) away. For this author, the building's grandeur took on almost other-worldly beauty when, wandering in the Boboli Gardens across the river during a rain shower, he looked up, and there was a shining rainbow that looked as though it had placed a perfect, natural dome over a perfect, man-made dome. Over five hundred years old, and the symbol of both Florence and the Renaissance, Brunelleschi's engineering and aesthetic triumph continues to evoke wonder from all who see it.

PALAZZO TE, MANTUA

If any building can bring to life Coleridge's idyllic dream-place,

> In Xanadu did Kubla Khan
> A stately pleasure-dome decree,

it is the Palazzo Te in Mantua. This is the ultimate palace of delight, an exuberant setting that offers its guests nothing but relaxation and enjoyment. Here frivolity is made sublime, and the result may well be the most appealing Renaissance structure in all Italy.

Those who flock to Florence, Venice and Rome have rewards aplenty, but the many small cities of the Italian peninsula would, in any other country, be the principal destination for those in search of art, beauty and history. And in this galaxy, which would include at least Bergamo, Bologna, Ferrara, Lucca, Padua, Parma, Pisa, Verona and Vicenza just in the north, none outdoes Mantua for the riches on offer. The Gonzaga family who ruled the city and the surrounding area in the Renaissance were among the most discerning patrons of the age. Indeed, when the line died out in the seventeenth century, and England's King Charles I bought the Gonzaga collection, he transformed London in one stroke into the home for the finest art of the time that it had never been before.

Mantua sits on an easily defensible site, a peninsula surrounded by three lakes formed by the river Mincio. The enormous Gonzaga Palace, begun in the fourteenth century, and dazzlingly decorated by Mantegna, dominates the city. But the palace is not merely a formidable showplace. The suite of rooms, grotto and garden in the palace where Isabella d'Este, wife of the marquis of Mantua, liked to entertain her guests is a small-scale, delicate and numinous space. Here this most discriminating of patronesses – the one person to have been portrayed by both Leonardo and Titian – not only assembled beautiful objects, but also gathered the most innovative poets and musicians of the age. The concerts and conversations that took place under her encouraging eye were renowned, and the setting was without peer. As the inventory of 236 precious items drawn up after her death indicates, the art on display included antiquities and works by Mantegna, Perugino, Michelangelo and Correggio. To this day, Isabella's *studiolo* remains one of the glories of Italy.

Isabella's instinct for art belongs to our story, because she clearly passed it on to her son, Federigo, the ruler who commissioned the Palazzo Te. Te was the name of an island in one of Mantua's lakes (now filled in), which for some time had served both as a stable for the family's

Isabella d'Este, duchess of Mantua. Oil painting by Titian, 1534

stud farm and horses and as a recreation spot in good weather. In 1459, for example, Federigo's great-grandfather had entertained a group of notables on the island by having them watch a leopard run free. But in the 1520s the young prince decided to build a retreat that would be worthy of his ambitions as a patron. To make that possible, he asked his friend (and ambassador to the papacy) Baldassare Castiglione, author of one of the most famous books of the day – *The Courtier*, the treatise that defined manners for gentlemen and ladies for centuries to come – to intercede with Raphael's most distinguished pupil, Giulio Romano, and persuade him to come to Mantua from Rome.

The artist, already widely admired for his architecture as well as his paintings, was described by his friend Giorgio Vasari as being 'of medium stature, rather plump than thin, dark-skinned, a handsome face, black and laughing eyes, most amiable, of courtly manners, a small eater, and elegant in his dress and bearing'. The pope, however, thought of him as part of his own entourage, and it took three years of negotiation before Romano was finally, in 1524, allowed to move north. Soon thereafter took place a scene described by Vasari:

Giulio rode a bow-shot out of the S. Bastiano Gate, where the marquis had a place and stables, called the T, in the middle of a meadow, where he kept his stud. When he arrived there, the marquis said that he wanted, without destroying the old building, to have a place where he could resort for amusement and take refreshment. Giulio, after examining the site, set to work. [He built the structure and also] richly decorated the interior, and this led the marquis to create the present fine palace [which Vasari had visited] from this humble beginning.

It is clear from archaeological investigations that Romano did indeed use the foundations, and possibly part of the walls, of the old stables, but what he fashioned over the next ten years was a building whose proportions, fabric and decoration no longer suggested either utility or practical function.

As one approaches the palace, one's attention is caught by the façade, which manages to be both asymmetrical and harmonious at the same time. Decorated with incisions that suggest huge blocks of stone, some rusticated and some not, and pierced by rectangles, squares and arches that are topped with exaggerated but split keystones (a Romano speciality), the façade warns one of the play with forms and the departure from Renaissance regularity that lie ahead. The façade was the last element that Romano put into place, and it is an apt preparation for what is to come. In particular, the western and northern façades, where the main entrances are located, seem to echo one another but in fact are strikingly

different. On the west, a large, heavy arch, off-centre and level with the ground, marks the entrance; on the north it is a more delicate triple arch, again off-centre, but at the top of a wide flight of steps. There are arched niches on both sides, but set irregularly. And as one nears the entrance on the west side one is surprised yet again, for one looks through to a classical perspective of utter symmetry, with arches and a triangular pediment flanked by simple columns.

Once one has passed beyond the massive stone face that the palace shows to the world, one is likely to be caught unawares yet again. One is now in a courtyard, but the eastern side of this essentially square building is once more different: a gracefully colonnaded loggia, absolutely symmetrical, with a smooth front topped by a large pediment that seems almost the antithesis of the powerful western and northern façades. And wherever one looks there are little oddities that keep one off balance. Contrasting with the ornate pilasters and the smooth pillars of the loggia are rough rustic columns that look unfinished. And everywhere, in different sizes and squeezed into gaps helter-skelter, are carved emblems, or 'devices', all associated (through esoteric references) with the Gonzagas. There is a salamander, a noseband, a glove, musical instruments, a dog, a crucible: a veritable cornucopia of random objects and animals. Then,

Western entrance, Palazzo Te, Mantua, built by Giulio Romano, 1524–35

159

View of the eastern façade and garden of Palazzo Te, Mantua

beyond the building itself lie fish ponds, an inviting garden and a perimeter marked by a free-standing semicircle of arches (an 'exedra') that was probably in Romano's original design but was not completed for over a century. In the open air fountains (now gone) and fish ponds evoked the surrounding lake. This, in other words, was a constantly changing setting, filled with anomalies and unexpected touches, all intended to enhance the pursuit of pleasure that was the main reason for the palace's existence.

But it is in the lavish rooms, as one moves inside, that the main astonishments await. Romano starts one off quite gently in the first suite of rooms on the west. They are named for Ovid's *Metamorphoses*, those stories of transformation and human folly that might almost stand for the concept of the Palazzo Te itself; indeed, one wall is given over to a painting of the palace as it looked in mid-construction/transformation. Each room in this area looks different – panelled ceiling in one, vault in another – but the subject matter of Ovid, landscape and references to the Gonzagas is consistent. The basic intention, moreover, is made clear on the fireplace, dedicated to Federigo, Romano's patron. It shows one of his favourite devices, the salamander, which was famous not only for its changeability, but also for being able to procreate (so the legend had it) without 'going into rut', as one contemporary put it. Above the salamander is inscribed the marquis's motto: *Quod huic deest me torquet* (What this lacks torments me). Federigo's intentions for the place could hardly have been clearer.

The decorations underline the message. There is Venus with a satyr and maenads, Paris as he judges the beauty of the goddesses, Dionysus in

The horse 'Dario'. Fresco by Giulio
Romano in the Hall of the Horses, Palazzo
Te, Mantua

a state of drunkenness, and a set of dancing nymphs and musicians. Love,
wine and music were to be omnipresent. Even the ceiling of the third
room, dedicated to the Sun, is suggestive. Here Apollo takes off into the
sky in his chariot, a brilliant Sun outlining his raised arm as he whips his
horses along. But we see the scene from below, in dizzying foreshorten-
ing, and stare straight up Apollo's flapping robe to his bare anatomy,
more finely shaped but still echoing the rears of the horses that pull his
chariot. Nothing here can avoid the sensual.

A small Loggia of the Muses, covered in learned references and dedicated to another joy, poetry, separates this suite from the first of the
palace's grand chambers, the so-called Hall of the Horses. The animals
stand around the viewer in mute splendour, with paintings behind them.
Cunningly portrayed to fool the eye, they seem almost to step forward
from the walls. They are all Federigo's own horses, a reference both to
the traditional function of the island and to his pride in his stable. Four
of them are even named. This large hall, lit by sizeable windows, was
used for entertainments, and if guests tired of the horses they could
enjoy the *trompe-l'œil* busts and statues, the gods, the landscapes and the
myths (notably the Labours of Hercules) that covered the walls. Pillars,

pilasters and deceptively real stretches of marble and bronze keep every surface sparkling. It is a room in which one cannot imagine conversation ever flagging.

Next door is another large hall, the Chamber of Cupid and Psyche, which is the focal point of the palace. Here the emperor Charles V was entertained at lunch, and here once stood a statue of Venus that, according to the most famous commentator on fleshly pleasures of the Renaissance, Pietro Aretino, was 'so real and alive that it filled with lust the thoughts of anyone who gazed upon it'. The room, though, hardly needs the statue to accomplish this end. The inscription around the walls may state that this is where Federigo came to restore himself in tranquillity after his labours, but the imagery suggests anything but tranquillity. Using the heated love affair between Cupid and Psyche as inspiration, Romano lets the eroticism unfold without restraint. Even the Playboy Mansion might hesitate to show such scenes – in particular, a depiction of Jupiter about to make love to Olympia that leaves nothing to the imagination (and, when I was there a few years ago, proved hugely amusing to a troop of local schoolchildren who, with fingers pointing, must have regarded the Palazzo Te as the best school excursion ever).

Banqueting, bathing, eating, drinking and amorous pastimes surround the viewer. All is given over to the pleasures of the flesh. There may be emotions other than joy that are prompted by love. In one scene an angry Mars is chasing his rival Adonis, in dishabille, while Venus holds him back, but even here Romano has a light touch. He recalls the legend that, as she ran, Venus stepped on a rose thorn, and the drop of her blood turned the original white rose red. To emphasise the reference, Cupid looks down at her foot in amusement. A century after it was painted, Rubens came to visit the Palazzo, and this scene obviously stayed in his mind. When, decades later, he took up the powerful theme of 'The Horrors of War', the composition, with Mars as its central figure, came straight out of Giulio Romano.

That homage apart, it is hard to think of anything but delight in this room. Exotic animals – a giraffe, a camel, an elephant – parade around, and the gods descend to earth to dally with beautiful mortals or other creatures (including a swan and a bull). There are tribulations on the road to love, to be sure. The lovely Psyche, who made Venus jealous, had to pass a series of tests before she could marry Cupid. But the story ended happily, and eventually we see the contented couple on their wedding bed, with their aptly named daughter, Voluptuousness. Even one of the less pleasant figures of myth, the one-eyed giant Polyphemus, who looms up in disorientating fashion, holding a massive club and pan pipe over a disproportionately small fireplace as one enters from the Hall of Horses, is shown smitten by love. Nobody can escape its magic, and its

The words visible in the fresco: ·ET·REIP·FLOR· CAPITANEVS· GENERALIS·

many forms and effects swirl in dizzying array around the room.

The adjoining room, the Room of Winds, calms things down. The gods are still here, but now they are more quietly linked to astrology. Romano employed a whole team of artists skilled in the small-scale to produce elaborate decorations, portraits of emperors, floral patterns, and hunting and fishing scenes, all held together by learned references to the months of the year and the signs of the zodiac. The images are no less exotic than before. Among fishes alone we can spot a whale, a dolphin and a sea monster. But all these fanciful creatures disport themselves under the gentle auspices of the winds of fortune, symbolised by masks on the ceiling which blow forth the destinies of mankind from the stars above.

We now enter the private area of the palace. The emphasis on myth and on decorations of opulent colour continues, though the smaller size of the rooms and paintings lowers the sense of drama. Yet the instinct for caprice and surprise is undiminished. Who would have thought that the room that served as Federigo's bedroom would be adorned by four stucco

The feast of the gods. Fresco in the Chamber of Cupid and Psyche, Palazzo Te, Mantua. This is Romano's homage to the joys of food and wine

163

The fall of the Giants. Fresco in the Room of the Giants, Palazzo Te, Mantua, by Giulio Romano

reliefs of famous rapes? Hardly the impression a welcoming host might wish to convey. But that is exactly what we find in the Room of the Eagles. Although this *camera* may be named after its four standing heraldic figures, derived from the Gonzaga coat of arms, it is the four assaulted ladies – Europa, Proserpina, Amphitrite and Amymone – who give the room its distinct atmosphere.

The private quarters continue in the so-called Apartment of the Secret Garden, an area tucked beyond the fish ponds and surrounding a charming small garden courtyard. This was intended for Federigo's private meditation, and echoed the small suite of rooms and garden that formed his mother's *studiolo*. It has a small loggia, and the entire area is ornately decorated with stucco and painting, though in a lower key than the public rooms we have left. The main themes are the simplicity of agriculture, the deeds of King David and the heroism of ancient warriors, all of which carry references to the interests and ambitions of the Gonzagas. But there is one extraordinary public room to come, and it is a fitting capstone to Romano's complex, overwhelming scheme.

The Room of the Giants was singled out by almost every visitor as the most astounding of the many astonishments they had encountered at the Palazzo Te. What Vasari noticed at once was that it was almost not like a room at all. It was built, he wrote, 'with roughly rounded stones, and almost in a disjointed way, so that it seemed to lean in on one side and to be really falling down'. Moreover, the entire wall and ceiling was seamless, covered in a single shattering painting. The subject is the destruction of the rebellious Giants by Jupiter, a scene of horror that terrifies even the gods and muses who witness it. Vasari captured the effect perfectly:

To make it more frightening and terrible, Giulio had the great giants of strange stature fall to earth, some in front and some behind, some dead, some wounded and some covered by mountains and ruins. No one ever thought to see brushwork more horrible and frightening or more natural than this. Whoever enters the room and sees windows, doors and other such things twisted, as if about to collapse, and the mountains and buildings falling, cannot but fear that everything will crash down upon him, seeing especially that in heaven the gods are rushing here and there in flight. What is marvellous is that the painting has no beginning or end. It is so well joined together that things that are close appear large, and those that are far off are lost in infinity. The room looks like a stretch of countryside with villages.

It took a fellow artist to notice how the impression was achieved. The ordinary visitor, however, has no choice but to rear back under the oppressive power of the massive figures collapsing towards him, hurtling downward in a hail of lightning bolts, smashed columns and enormous boulders. It is an unforgettable experience, unique in its impact amongst the many achievements of Renaissance Europe. In one stroke, Romano has completed the spectrum of pleasures, from bodily delights to the frisson of artificial terror, that is the essence of the Palazzo Te.

VILLA BARBARO, MASER

One can scarcely think of Venice without admitting that the entire city is one of the wonders of the world. Nothing fashioned in antiquity came close to this majestic apparition, built over many centuries by tens of thousands of engineers, workmen, architects and masons to rise from the sea itself. There have been a few who disliked the place. The fastidious English ambassador Dudley Carleton, otherwise known as a fine connoisseur, complained in the seventeenth century that he did not like it because it smelled and he found its inhabitants untrustworthy. Napoleon dismissed it as tyrannical and dangerous, and for a few decades after he brought its independence to an end, it was fashionable to deplore Venice as the home of a repressive government, as a crumbling ruin or as a haven for plots and dark deeds. But these voices have been swamped by a chorus of love, esteem and amazement.

From the late Middle Ages, as the city became a major naval power in the eastern Mediterranean, to the present, it has perhaps inspired more artists, writers and composers than any other single place on earth. Their temperaments may have been as different as those of William Turner and James Whistler, Lord Byron and Mark Twain, Richard Wagner and Peter Tchaikovsky, but all seemed to share the admiration that William Wordsworth felt for 'the eldest child of liberty ... a maiden city, bright and free'. And multitudes of pilgrims, tourists, diplomats and merchants have echoed the delight, making Venice the quintessential playground for travellers from Geoffrey de Villehardouin, chronicler of the Crusades, to Cole Porter, and beyond.

But how can one possibly encompass an entire city as a wonder of the world, especially when its construction extends across more than a single age? The basilica of St Mark's is a medieval marvel, yet the completion of St Mark's Square as we know it had to await the nineteenth century. For the Renaissance there are, of course, splendours aplenty: the series of Carpaccios in the chapel of the Slavic community, glorious Bellini and Titian altarpieces, any number of palaces or churches, the Rialto Bridge, the vistas created by Palladio and Longhena throughout the city. Yet it seems most appropriate to settle on a development quite distinct from what came before or after: an entirely new artistic and architectural invention that was brought to aesthetic perfection in its very first generation, and was conceived by Venetians not in a moment of triumph but as a response to disaster.

Probably the single most devastating trauma the Republic experienced in the millennium or more between its foundation and its destruction in 1797 was the so-called War of the League of Cambrai that started in 1509. For centuries Venice had grown ever more rich and powerful, and in the 1400s that power had begun to spill, not into new strongholds around the Mediterranean, as had traditionally been the case, but into the Italian mainland – the so-called Terrafirma. Here Venice had conquered a substantial territory that extended as far as Bergamo, near Milan, where her symbol, the Lion of St Mark, can be seen to this day. But a land empire brought her new neighbours and new enemies, and in 1509 almost all Europe was united in a league by her most bitter enemy, the pope: the result was catastrophe. Her troops fell back, and within a few months she was driven out of almost all of the Terrafirma.

What happened next was one of the fundamental turning-points of Venetian history. Thanks to its astute and dedicated patricians, the city had the best diplomatic corps in Europe, and by a combination of good luck, clever negotiation and some well-timed military successes, she was able by 1516 to regain just about all the territory she had lost. But the trauma left its scars. Chastened by the defeats, and aware that powerful new rivals – especially Spain, France and Turkey – were eroding the power Venice had long enjoyed at sea, her patricians began to rethink their commitments. It is from the decades after the League of Cambrai that one can date a slow erosion of the devotion to a naval and mercantile career that had marked the Venetian patriciate for centuries, and indeed had prompted Machiavelli to sneer that they were not true gentlemen. Now they turned their attention increasingly from the sea to the land: to the very set of pursuits that were the mark of nobility in Renaissance Europe. Flocking into the Terrafirma, they established country estates that put them into the same category of great landowners as other aristocrats throughout the West, and they thus laid claim to a gentility that Machiavelli had denied. This major shift in their commitments may have been yet another blow to the Venetian economy, but it had momentous consequences in the world of the arts.

For what the Venetians created in the area surrounding their original home, the Veneto, was the model for the country house that was to dominate the European landscape for centuries. There had been grand country residences before. The Medici, in particular, had built splendid villas around Florence, thus emulating the emperors and senators of ancient Rome. But these had been retreats: places to rest, to entertain or to attract artists and intellectuals. What now appeared were genuine homes. They may have been inspired by antique models, but they were functioning centres of large estates. They were neither the fortified strongholds built by medieval nobles nor the luxuries built by the Medici. And the finest representative of this new kind of dwelling – a

Villa Barbaro, Maser, built by Andrea
Palladio, 1560–1

masterpiece of art and architecture that is one of the Renaissance's most
remarkable wonders – was the Villa Barbaro at Maser, some 30 miles
(48 km) north of Venice.

The Villa Barbaro was primarily the work of four men: the two
remarkable patrons who owned the property, the brothers Marcantonio
and Daniele Barbaro, and the renowned architect and painter whom they
commissioned to design and decorate the villa, Andrea Palladio and
Paolo Veronese. The building they put up remains, to this day, a real residence, the heart of a working farm. Indeed, the lowest floor is still mainly
a storage area for agricultural implements. On the main floor, however,
and in the structure and setting as a whole, these four men set a standard
for elegance that has never been surpassed.

The brothers Daniele and Marcantonio Barbaro came from an ancient Venetian family. Their ancestors reputedly arrived in the eighth
or ninth century. Firmly established within the charmed circle of some

168

150 families who made up the city's ruling oligarchy, they had served as leading churchmen, government officials, military commanders and diplomats over the centuries. Their palace on the Grand Canal – a marvellously delicate yet imposing fifteenth-century structure, not far from St Mark's Square, which was to become internationally renowned much later when an American family, the Curtises, bought it, and played host to such luminaries as Robert Browning, Henry James, Claude Monet and John Singer Sargent – reflected their position at the very pinnacle of Venetian society, though they never quite made it to the top. No Barbaro was ever elected doge. Nevertheless, their contribution as public servants and patrons was essential both to the history of the city and now to the shift of interest among its elite to the mainland.

Daniele and Marcantonio exemplified the sophisticated, public-spirited life of a Venetian aristocrat. Both served as diplomats for the Republic. Daniele (born in 1514) led an embassy to England in the 1540s before reluctantly giving up his secular life, at the behest of his government, to take over the strategic ecclesiastical post of patriarch of Aquileia. Two of Marcantonio's sons were to follow him into the position, a dignity that stood at the summit of the Church's hierarchy, but was particularly crucial for Venice because it ensured control of the province north of the city that was an essential buffer against Habsburg power in Austria. Marcantonio (born in 1518) remained in government all his life. A senator, holder of most of the principal offices in the regime, and ambassador to France, the papacy and the Ottoman Turks at crucial diplomatic moments (he was in Constantinople when a Catholic fleet defeated the Turks at Lepanto), he was also entrusted with the reform of the University of Padua.

But these were not public servants alone. Both brothers were deeply learned and highly cultured. Early in his career Daniele oversaw the construction of the Botanical Garden in Padua, to this day one of the glories of the Renaissance. It is circular, in emulation of the globe, and its plants are grown in the quadrant where geographically they are at home: southern flowers in the south, and so on. Goethe considered it one of Italy's marvels. Daniele became one of the leading humanist scholars of his day, the erudite writer and editor of massive tomes on Aristotle's rhetoric and natural science. Even while attending the Church council at Trent, near his patriarchate, he was completing a multi-volume commentary on the works of the ancient architect Vitruvius that was a major influence on Palladio, among others. Meanwhile, Marcantonio tried his hand at history, and also wrote some of the shrewdest and silkiest ambassadorial reports ever put on paper. He was also no mean sculptor. These were statesmen-intellectuals of an order rarely seen in European history. At home in the highest political circles, they were also among the most

Portrait of Daniele Barbaro. Oil painting by Paolo Veronese, *c.*1566

intelligent patrons of their time. Not only did Veronese paint Daniele's portrait, but Titian did so twice, putting him in a league with emperors, popes and kings.

One first sees the villa across a long rectangular lawn, precisely divided by a gravel path that leads to the front door. Symmetry is much in evidence. One scarcely notices the central block where the family lives – a two-storey classical structure, divided into three equal parts by Ionic pilasters – because the façade is dominated by two long arcaded wings stretching out on either side of this block, each with eight arches. The final three arches at the end are topped by identical curved roofs reaching up to classic pediments, and enclosing enormous sundials and hidden dovecotes. These wings serve to store the villa's agricultural artefacts, and it is not until one comes quite close that one realises they are of secondary importance to the seemingly smaller central block. But this rectangular centre of the villa, mainly two storeys high (with bedrooms above, including an austere little room where Daniele stayed while attending the Council of Trent near by), makes the classical origins of the entire structure unmistakable.

The man who designed and built it in the 1550s, Andrea Palladio, was in his mid-forties at the time, a native of a city ruled by Venice, Vicenza. He was known, mainly in that city, for having constructed an arcade and new roof around the city hall, usually known as the Basilica; for a fine two-storey columned *palazzo* that is now the city museum; and for the perfectly square Villa Rotonda, with just four rooms for entertaining guests, almost identical temple-like façades on all four sides, and a small dome at its centre. This last, a place for entertaining that brought antique architecture back to life, may be the most imitated building in all Europe and America. When he started work on the Villa Barbaro, however, Palladio was not yet a household name. His great churches in Venice – San Francesco, San Giorgio and the Redentore – lay well into the future. Yet for the learned Barbaros he was the one architect whose mastery of ancient models (Palladio was later to publish a treatise that updated Vitruvius) made him capable of building a home in their country estate that was worthy of the Romans.

The result is about as pleasing a domestic space as has ever been constructed. As one comes up the stairs to the family's quarters from the ground-floor level one enters a cruciform hallway (an appropriate shape for a patriarch), linked to a further hall. From these halls one can enter the four major rooms of the villa. The impression throughout is of light and of endlessly opening vistas that make the space seem far larger than it is. This is to some extent the result of high ceilings and windows, but is mainly the achievement of the second of the masters who created the villa, Paolo Veronese.

Palladio's work was finished in the late 1550s, and it was probably in 1560 that Veronese began the decoration. Now in his early thirties, Veronese had moved to Venice from his native Verona (close to Vicenza) seven or eight years earlier, and was already establishing his reputation as a particular favourite of the patricians. He excelled in scenes of aristocratic elegance, showing fine figures, wearing splendid clothes and jewels, amidst grandiose architectural settings. His mastery of delicate colour, perspective, and a sensual rendition of people and landscapes made him an ideal choice for the Villa Barbaro.

The two hallways set the tone for the celebration of the countryside, the family and Roman culture that permeates the villa. The ceilings open up to the sky, while all around classical deities are interwoven with members of the Barbaro family and their servants. Throughout, Veronese tries to fool the eye with figures coming out of doorways or peering down from above. Two, in particular, draw immediate attention as we climb from ground level and enter the cruciform hallway.

171

Lute and violin players and girl leaning
through a doorway. Detail of a *trompe-l'œil*
painting in the central cruciform hall,
Villa Barbaro, Maser, by Paolo Veronese.
Both the door on the right and the
little girl coming through it are painted
illusions

In this hall, under pediments that make it seem there are more openings than there really are, Veronese has painted two figures who seem to
lean through doorways as they, too, enter the space. One is a little girl,
probably the daughter of a Barbaro servant, who has charmed visitors
ever since she was painted. The other, a young man, probably a page,
adds to the impression of a bustling hallway with people coming and
going. Elsewhere, alongside the real doors in the hall, are archways and
balustrades, with landscapes beyond, that suggest the room is surrounded
by open-air balconies. On the remaining wall spaces we see musicians
carrying the variety of instruments that doubtless would have entertained the Barbaros and their guests in this area; mock cameos of
classical figures; and other *trompe-l'œil* scenes that suggest, for instance,
that some banners and spears have been propped up in one corner.

A splendid archway leads us from the cruciform hall towards a large
arched window. As we approach, we enter another hallway, the Hall of
Olympus. This time, however, we have a real window, and we can look
out on to a lovely hidden garden with a fountain and statuary. Using the
slight slope on which the villa is set, Palladio has ensured that, although

we had to climb stairs to get to this floor at the front of the villa, we are now at ground level.

We soon realise that the Hall of Olympus is the centrepiece of the entire decoration. The ancient gods after which the hallway is named are of course present in full array. It is easy to spot the seven so-called planetary deities: Mars in armour, Jupiter with his eagle, aged Saturn with his scythe, Mercury with his caduceus, Venus scolding Cupid, and the twins Apollo (the Sun) and Diana (the Moon). Other gods help represent the four seasons (Bacchus, for instance, prepares his grapes in autumn) or the four elements (Neptune for water, Juno for air). To complete the mythic description of the world and of time the decoration includes the twelve signs of the zodiac.

But the figures which make the hall so memorable are not divine at all. Veronese fools us once again with a real-seeming balustrade just below the ceiling, from which Marcantonio's wife, Giustiniana, standing next to her son Alvise and an old servant, looks down at us. Across from her, on another balustrade, stand her two other sons, Francesco reading a book and Almoro playing with a dog. And if we look left and right through the

Giustiniana Barbaro, her son Alvise and a servant behind a balustrade. Detail of the ceiling in the Hall of Olympus, Villa Barbaro, Maser, by Paolo Veronese

173

The exedra-fountain of the nymphaeum in the garden, Villa Barbaro, Maser. Statuary by Marcantonio Barbaro and Alessandro Vittoria, 1560–1

two rooms that lead off the hallway, we again find, in the distance, two figures coming through make-believe doors. One, a huntsman with a large dog, has always been regarded as a self-portrait of Veronese; and the other, a lady with a fan, his wife.

Both the spectacle and the light touches continue throughout the four rooms that adjoin the hallways. There are shimmering landscapes seen through *trompe-l'œil* windows: a ferry crossing a river, sheep grazing in a meadow, classical buildings and even a panorama that includes a tiny version of the Villa Barbaro itself. There are also grand allegories: Abundance, Fortitude and Envy beneath a sky with summer clouds; Faith and Charity under a similar sky; History and Time perched, through a trick of perspective, just below an ornate ceiling with books at their feet. Yet the humour ensures that nobody can get too solemn in this home.

One room is named for the dog who sits quietly at the foot of a wall, waiting for master or mistress. Across from him is a cat, but he takes no notice. Another room, devoted to Bacchus, has a leafy and grape-laden pergola that soars to a blue sky, while grapes flourish on the walls below and Bacchus teaches man the joys of the grape. Here there is another musician, who adds to the celebration of pleasure. But a third room is more ambiguous. It honours love with symbols of fertility and harmony, but a Tribunal of Love, which gives the room its name, seems to offer a sterner lesson. The judges are listening as a bride pleads her case, but Venus herself seems to be hushing the woman so as not to be too forward. One has a hard time imagining Giustiniana Barbaro, herself the daughter of a powerful patrician family, approving such a message. The final room is named for the real lantern, always kept lit, that hangs from the ceiling.

Again we look out at peaceful landscapes, but the theme here is religious: in contrast to the enjoyment of antiquity or the senses we see elsewhere, here it is faith and contemplation that dominate.

Nymph and Giant. Detail of the exedra-fountain of the nymphaeum in the garden, Villa Barbaro, Maser

It is a villa, in other words, that inserts into a country estate a world of gentility and refinement. This is cultivation in both meanings of the word. And the final touch is the peaceful, elegant hidden garden we have glimpsed from the Hall of Olympus. As at the Palazzo Te, the borderline is marked by a kind of exedra, a semicircular wall. This one is graced by sculptures by Marcantonio Barbaro himself and by Alessandro Vittoria, a master of stucco who created elaborate chimney-pieces and cornices within the villa and classical sculptures on the outside. Water is the theme of the garden: behind a placid pool stands its main feature, the exedra in the form of a nymphaeum, a celebration of water nymphs. Within this curved wall, topped by a classical pediment, are four sculptured giants attributed to Marcantonio, and a series of nymphs made by Vittoria. At the centre, an archway that echoes the arches in the villa encloses the spring from which all the water for the villa flows.

The vision is complete: even a placid rural setting echoes with memories of classical antiquity. It is the ultimate country home for the cultured aristocrat. Hundreds of such residences were to be built in the centuries to come, but none has surpassed the wonder of the Villa Barbaro.

175

EL ESCORIAL

It is not often sufficiently appreciated that the dominant power in Europe during much of the Renaissance was Spain. We think of the period's cultural splendours as primarily Italian, forgetting that from the late fifteenth century until the middle of the seventeenth the Spaniards controlled most of Italy. They ruled Sicily and Naples directly; they were the chief outside influence in Rome; they had close financial ties with the Genoese; and everywhere else in the peninsula they were a force to be reckoned with. One of the families that set their stamp on the era, the Borgias, came from Spain, and there were Italians who went in the other direction. Baldassare Castiglione, for example, author of the book that defined tastefulness and proper behaviour for the upper classes for centuries, *The Courtier*, spent the last five years of his life as papal ambassador to Spain.

It is true that the great age of Spanish literature and art came later than the Italian. The century of El Greco, Velázquez, Lope de Vega and Calderón, starting around 1600, arrived nearly two hundred years after Brunelleschi, Donatello and Masaccio began to create their masterpieces, and there were many more Italian than Spanish stars during these centuries. But the Spaniards of the 1600s were still pursuing the artistic ideals drawn from antiquity that had driven their predecessors, and in the sixteenth century the rulers of Spain may well have been the most important single patrons of the artists of Italy. It is no accident that the Prado Museum in Madrid is one of the world's principal repositories of sixteenth-century Italian art.

The two kings of Spain who so determinedly amassed these treasures ruled the country from 1516 to 1598: the Habsburgs Charles I and his son Philip II. Charles, who also reigned in central Europe as Emperor Charles V, spent time in Italy and had a particular fondness for the Venetian painter Titian. The story had it that, just as Alexander the Great had been willing to stoop to retrieve a brush that the painter Apelles had dropped, so too Charles picked up Titian's brush while he was having his portrait painted. But his most elaborate tribute to the aesthetic ideals of his Italian subjects was a palace that he planned for Granada in southern Spain.

Granada had been the capital of the last Muslim kingdom on the peninsula, and it had been captured by Charles's grandparents, Ferdinand and Isabella, in 1492. Its most famous building was the extraordinary Moorish palace known as the Alhambra. Deeply devout, and moved by crusading instincts, Charles resolved to build a palace right next door

that would outshine its Muslim predecessor. Work began in the late 1520s, under the supervision of a Spanish architect, Pedro Machuca, who had been a pupil of Michelangelo and reportedly got the initial design for the palace from Giulio Romano. Though left unfinished when Charles died in 1558, the palace became one of the finest examples of Italian Renaissance architecture ever built. The design is extraordinary: an enormous square, each side of which is nearly 200 feet (61 m) long and over 50 feet (15 m) high, decorated with classical motifs. Fitted within this square is a magnificent circular courtyard, open to the elements, which is surrounded by a colonnade on each of the two storeys of the palace. So large is this space that it used to serve as an arena for bullfights. The building remains a breathtaking example of powerful Renaissance architecture, a dramatic and exuberant challenge by the Christian victors to the delicate beauties of the Moorish Alhambra next door.

Rather than finish this building, Philip sought to do his father one better, with a gigantic monastery-cum-palace that also conveyed the religious message of a crusading faith. That palace, whose formal title is the Monastery of San Lorenzo el Real, is usually referred to as El Escorial, after the tiny hamlet in central Castile where it is located. The

Courtyard of Charles V's palace at Granada, designed by Pedro and Luis Machuca, 1526–50

choices of name and site give one a good sense of the man who brought it into being.

Even more than his father, who lived out his last two years in a remote monastery, Philip II exuded devoutness and conscientiousness. It happened that, after his father's retirement in 1556, he was the official commander of a Spanish army in a war with France, though he was 25 miles (40 km) from the battle when his troops won the decisive victory that led the French to sue for peace. The battle took place on 10 August 1557, the saint's day of St Lawrence, an early Roman martyr who had been born in Spain. When he heard of the victory, later that day, Philip vowed to honour the saint with the finest church in Spain. A year later, his father died, having asked his son to erect a fitting tomb for himself and his wife. The two missions were to be combined in an enterprise that was to consume Philip for most of the rest of his life.

The immediate question was location, and Philip, a stickler for logic and an obsessive bureaucrat, soon had an answer. Spain's capital had never been fixed, and one of the new king's first decisions was to place it permanently as close to the geographic centre of Castile, the country's main province, as possible. He lighted on the small town of Madrid which, despite being hard to reach – nearly 2,000 feet (610 m) high on Castile's central plateau – and also deficient in the resources and history that made a number of other cities, such as Toledo, more likely candidates, had the decisive virtue of centrality. The choice was a token of the meticulousness and the control over the smallest details that was to characterise Philip's rule.

It made sense for the monastery/palace/tomb to be no more than a day's ride from the capital, and the place Philip chose was a flat area next to the village of Escorial (or 'slag-heap', a reminder of the iron mines that had once been worked near by) in the foothills of the Guadarrama mountains about 30 miles (48 km) north of Madrid. The region was abundant in wood and granite, essential for construction, and in early 1562 the work began, with the cornerstone laid the following year. Eventually there were to be over a thousand masons, carpenters and other craftsmen and labourers on the site. Construction took twenty-one years – remarkable speed for so vast a complex of buildings and grounds – but the consecration of the church at its heart did not take place until 1595, just three years before Philip died. That he thought of it as his life's work is therefore not far from the truth.

As befitted the Continent's richest nation, which was importing unprecedented wealth from the mines of its New World empire, the Escorial became the largest and most expensive building in Europe. It is best seen from above, in the surrounding hills, where one can gain a comprehensive view of its beige/grey granite immensity, its towers, belfries

and domes, its dark roofs, and the basilica that looms over it all. The size is not easy to grasp, for the building extends in a rectangle that is nearly 700 feet (213 m) long by 500 feet (152 m) wide. Those are the outside dimensions. Within, there are thirteen outdoor courtyards, including a cloister that is over 150 feet by 150 feet (46 m by 46 m), some 80 miles (129 km) of corridors and hallways, eighty-six staircases, over two thousand windows and 1,200 doors.

One might think that the structure of a building on this scale would be hard to decode. Yet the Escorial follows the fondness for logic of its first master. Its dedicatee, St Lawrence, was reputedly martyred by being roasted on a grill, an attribute that identifies him in his many portraits. 'I'm cooked on one side; turn me over and start eating,' he is supposed to have said. Philip would not have been amused by such irreverence, but he did insist that his monastery/palace be built in the shape of a gigantic gridiron. A look at the ground plan makes this clear. The outside walls form the frame, a rectangle. In the middle, parallel to the longer side, runs a crossing along the length of the building, from which, at right

View of the west façade, El Escorial, built by Juan Bautista de Toledo and Juan de Herrera, 1562–83

179

Bird's-eye view of El Escorial. Oil painting
by an unknown artist, *c.*1600

angles – linking the crossing to the front – extend the four parallel lines
that form the grill. But the design goes one step further. The solid block
of the church runs down the middle of the rectangle from the crossing to
the back of the building, and from this block protrudes a smaller rectangle, containing the royal apartments. This smaller rectangle, anchored
in the church, becomes the handle for the grill. And the theme was followed down to the tiniest detail: restorers recently found a cache of the
trowels the workers used, each one marked with the outline of a grill.

There is a huge plaza in front of the main entrance, and as one
approaches it, one begins to understand how profoundly the building
reflects the values of Renaissance Italy. It was a country that Philip himself had visited; where the first of the Escorial's architects had been
trained; and where the second had spent formative years. That the king
had asked the aged Michelangelo for a design indicates where his tastes
inclined. Moreover, the man he eventually picked, Juan Bautista de
Toledo, was a disciple of the Florentine master and had spent most of his

life in Rome, including a period working on St Peter's itself. Juan Bautista died just four years after the cornerstone was laid, but the architect who took over, Juan de Herrera, was his closest associate and had also benefited from study in Italy. It is that background that is immediately apparent as one looks across the immense front façade of the Escorial.

What strikes one at once is the absolute symmetry, enlivened by the classical central ensemble, which is over seven storeys high, and more than 100 feet (30.5 m) in length. At its peak is a triangular pediment, capping two rows of massive half columns: Doric on the first level, Ionic above, with obelisks topped by globes as decoration. The largest single feature is a statue of St Lawrence, though the façade also displays the arms of Philip II. There can be no doubt where one is standing.

The sense of being overwhelmed is never absent in this building. Its major portion was given over to a monastery, which at one time contained hundreds of monks pursuing their three major commitments: prayer, study and manual labour. It was said that Philip loved to hear

Main entrance to El Escorial, with a statue of St Lawrence over the door their chanting as he passed through the complex, and he had his own private door to the upper choir of the basilica through which he could join them, unobtrusively, during services. Of the devoutness that animated his ambitions there could have been no doubt. Even as he gathered construction materials from his far-flung territories, Philip was seeking sacred relics that could be revered in his church. The quest took his emissaries throughout Europe, from Portugal to Poland, and eventually he amassed over 7,400 relics, including twelve complete bodies of saints, 144 complete skulls and 306 complete arms, all certified as authentic by the pope himself. If the religious character of the Escorial seems less apparent today, as the number of monks has dwindled to less than two dozen, the consequences of their presence are nevertheless still evident.

The Hieronymite order which administered the monastery had been founded in Spain some two centuries earlier, and it had been to one of their houses that Charles I had retired at the end of his life. Inspired by the asceticism and the devotion to contemplation and study that was associated with St Jerome, after whom they were named, the Hieronymites followed the rules of the Augustinians, which emphasised a strict regime of simple food, periodic fasting, hard work and periods of silence. It was amidst these holy men that Philip chose to live, and he gave them ample opportunity to pursue their prayers, studies and labours.

As one passes through the main gate, one enters the largest of the courtyards, the nearly 200-foot-long (61-m) Court of the Kings. It is named after the larger-than-life-size statues that stand over the façade of the basilica at the far end of the court: the six biblical kings who were associated with building the temple in Jerusalem. If the implication was that Philip deserved to be in their company, that merely suggested the extent of his ambitions for the Escorial, and indeed there were contemporaries who saw it as a new Temple of Solomon.

As one enters the huge church, however, one is struck by its simple design and austerity. Most of the walls are bare, as is the interior of the dome. But there are three striking exceptions. The retable behind the altar is an enormous and glittering assemblage of paintings, gilt and semi-precious stones, with fine frescos in the archway above. And on balconies on either side of the nave are two of the most splendid Renaissance sculptural groups in Europe. Commissioned from the Milanese sculptors Leone and Pompeo Leoni, who had portrayed both Charles I and Philip, these groups, again larger than life-size, represent the families of the two kings. Made of bronze and finished in gold, they show, on one side, Charles with his wife, daughter and two sisters; and, on the other, Philip with three of his wives and his son and heir, Don Carlos. All the figures are kneeling in prayer, and the gold in which they are covered shines brilliantly throughout the church.

Statue group of Philip II, his three wives and his son Don Carlos, by Pompeo Leoni, 1570

If one explores further, there are other artistic delights. In one of the chapels is a powerful marble crucifixion by Benvenuto Cellini and, in the high choir on the upper level (where Philip liked to sit), there are 128 beautifully carved wooden choir stalls. The close watch the king kept on every aspect of construction, putting his signature on thousands of plans and invoices, is epitomised by these stalls. He was in Portugal when Herrera designed them, and he insisted that a sample be sent to him for approval before the carpenters could proceed.

Philip probably knew every corner of this vast structure, but as one leaves the church today one cannot see, even over the course of an entire day, more than a few highlights. The most beautiful room, at least to this visitor, is the library, once the centre of the monks' second duty, study, but now a tribute to the elegance that books could inspire during the Renaissance. None of the other examples from the period that have survived – not even Michelangelo's Laurentian library in Florence – is more stunning than this one. It is a 175-foot-long (53-m) gallery, lined with gracefully carved bookshelves and pillars made of different woods, under a barrel-vaulted ceiling frescoed with depictions of the liberal arts. Down the centre are display cases that show medals, coins and other treasures that Philip collected. Not all of the forty thousand books in the library come from the king's own collection, because many were destroyed in a ruinous fire in 1671, but they still evoke his era and also honour his unusual interest in Hebrew and Arabic as well as Christian

183

texts – possibly a reflection of the triple religious heritage of Spain. The room is so magnificent that the setting threatens to become a distraction from serious study.

The library reminds us that, for all his austere demeanour, his piety, his devotion to the minutiae of paperwork, his gravity and the conscientiousness that led Spaniards to nickname him 'El Prudente', Philip was a lover of beauty. Like his father, he had a special fondness for Titian, though in his case it was often for the Venetian's lush nudes and sensuous scenes. A distinguished modern art historian, Erwin Panofsky, jokingly called Philip Europe's chief pornographer. But his collections of the finest work of the leading artists of Spain, Italy and the Netherlands covered the entire spectrum of the subjects of the day, and it is clear that devotional themes outnumbered the depictions of myth, antiquity or allegory. Had his patronage not ranged so widely, neither the Escorial nor the Prado would have been as artistically rich as they are today.

Yet it was not only formal beauty that captured the king's attention. He was known as a young man to have had an eye for the ladies, and the grounds of the Escorial were another arena for his tastes. Today the courtyards are muted, but in Philip's time they were alight with a constantly changing display of colour. He had a passion for flowers, and amongst the many opportunities for manual labour that he offered the monks – working in a mill or cloth-making were among the options – gardening was high on the list. This was an enterprise Philip liked to supervise personally, and he is said to have reprimanded sternly a monk he overheard complaining because a pear tree was not growing well. There were olive groves and vegetable gardens around the complex, but it was the pleasure he took in flowers that one must recall before dismissing Philip (as he often is in the Anglo-Saxon world) as a cold and ruthless monarch, devoid of finer feelings.

He certainly wanted the monastery-palace to pay tribute to his family's glories. A Hall of Battles even longer than the library contains depictions of Spanish victories, including one painting, covering nearly 3,000 square feet (280 m²), which commemorates a 1431 battle. Even here, though, the arched ceiling is covered in decorative motifs that come straight from Renaissance Rome. We are reminded yet again that this is a monument, not merely to a powerful family, but also to an era of artistic achievement.

Still, for many visitors the most distinctive feature of the Escorial is its pantheon of royal tombs. Keeping his promise to his father, Philip built a splendid mausoleum for his parents immediately below the high altar. This was later expanded into a burnished bronze, gold and marble chamber that now houses the tombs of eleven Spanish kings and most of their wives. Near by is another vault for royal children who died before

The library, El Escorial

185

Patio de los Reyes (Pantheon of the Kings), El Escorial

reaching adulthood. For some, this reverence for the dead, and the central place they have been assigned, has seemed to set the tone for the entire building.

Nor is the impression dispelled by Philip's private apartment. The rooms are tiny and decorated with simple elegance. They are the quarters of a disciplined, self-denying man. Two features in particular catch the eye. First is the small desk from which Philip ruled his vast empire. Though now bare, in his day it would have been piled high with the papers and requests for decisions on which he spent most of his working hours. Second is the small bedroom's four-poster bed, from which he could see the high altar and where he was determined to die. Philip's final illness in fact began in early June of 1598 in Madrid, but he insisted on being brought to the Escorial, despite the agony of a journey that lasted seven days instead of the usual one. Here he lingered until 13 September, enduring terrible suffering with a self-control that led an

186

ambassador who visited him to say that Philip died so well, it was as if he had practised it before.

Because of its grey stones, its veneration for the dead and the austerity of its builder, many do think of the Escorial in terms of gloom and fore-boding. It is an impression perhaps best summed up in a letter written by Alexandre Dumas after a visit in 1846:

The day dawned grey . . . and I was glad, for that seemed to me the right light in which to see the Escorial. At a turn of the road, we caught sight of its sepulchral immensity, truly worthy of the man who chose the desert for his capital and a tomb for his palace . . . No one can imagine how austere, how mournful, the Escorial looks . . . No one could call it beautiful. It evokes not admiration, but terror. Have you ever descended a mine and felt that a whole mountain was pressing down on you? That is how one feels on entering the Escorial.

But such views ignore the colours of the library and the works of art; the memory of the flowers that filled the courtyards; and the triumphs of Renaissance architecture one encounters at every turn. Within a few decades, tastes began to change, and Spain's kings spent less and less time in the palace. But its restoration in the twentieth century has demon-strated that, rather than succumbing to Dumas's glum appraisal, we should accept the judgement of Philip's contemporaries, who called El Escorial *la octava maravilla del mundo* – the eighth wonder of the world.

PIAZZA DI SAN PIETRO, ROME

Although emulation of ancient Rome was one of the central aims of the Italian Renaissance, it took a while for that ambition to capture the very city whose past was inspiring its neighbours. Not only Florence but a number of princely courts had taken up the challenge of reviving antiquity long before Rome herself joined the campaign. The reason was simple. For seventy years during the fourteenth century the papacy had left Rome for Avignon, and after its return, in 1377, its power and resources were devastated by a schism that saw two, and for a while three, claimants to the throne of St Peter. Even when that split was settled, in 1417, the papacy could not resume its full powers for over thirty years, because to heal the schism ultimate authority had been given to a general council of the Church. Not until yet another pope had been deposed and it became obvious that conciliar rule caused more problems than it solved, could a pope finally reassert unhampered control both over his flock and over his city. Decades after Brunelleschi, Donatello and Masaccio had visited an impoverished and lacklustre Rome, and long after major new artistic and intellectual initiatives had been launched elsewhere in Italy, Rome was at last ready to play a leading part in the transformation of European culture.

The renewed vigour began in the papacy of Nicholas V (1447–55). In 1449, the last challenge to his authority ended, and from then on the determination to revive the fortunes of Rome gathered momentum. Nicholas himself was a distinguished scholar, a patron of humanist learning and a collector of books, though he is perhaps most famous as the founder of the Vatican Library. But he was also committed to making Rome's physical appearance once again worthy of its status as the centre of western Christendom. He repaired the city's fortifications; he began the restoration of the ancient aqueducts so that Romans again had fresh water that did not come from the muddy Tiber; he started the expansion of his residence in the Vatican; and he also set in motion the demolition of the ancient church that, since the time of the emperor Constantine, had stood on the site of the martyrdom of the first pope, St Peter. To some, this last enterprise bordered on sacrilege, but to Nicholas the ruinous state of the old basilica was an affront to the dignity of Rome, and for the next two centuries his successors on the papal throne pursued, with ever-growing ambition, his dream of magnificence for the entire city and for St Peter's in particular.

Landmark events in the campaign to enlarge and beautify the city can be identified in almost every decade, as each pope sought to set his stamp on his surroundings. The steady improvement of the water supply, as ancient viaducts and pipelines were brought back into operation (following Nicholas V's pioneering refurbishment of the so-called 'Aqua Virgo' that feeds the Trevi Fountain), was one of the signal achievements of these years. That effort not only benefited the health of the citizens but also made possible the spread of the fountains that symbolised Rome's revival. And there were also more visible interventions.

Essential to the transformation of the city was the clearing away of semi-dilapidated areas, the raising of fine new buildings and the improvement of communication. New streets and open areas were laid out in the 1500s – notably Michelangelo's Piazza del Campidoglio and the surrounding buildings on the Capitoline hill; the piazza inside the gate at the northern entrance to Rome, the Piazza del Popolo; and the three streets that fan out from the Piazza, the Via Babuino, the Via del Corso and the Via Ripetta, which form the armature of central Rome to this day. The splendid secular buildings that were commissioned in the sixteenth century ranged from the enormous papal chancellery, the Cancelleria, an exemplar of Renaissance style, to Raphael's modest Villa Madama and Michelangelo's grandiose Farnese Palace. And there were, of course, major new churches, both small (such as Bramante's elegant circular Tempietto on the Janiculum) and large (the restoration of the huge basilica of San Paolo Fuori le Mura).

Not surprisingly, there was a particularly ambitious effort to beautify the Vatican itself. A new chapel, completed by Sixtus IV in the 1480s, and named the Sistine Chapel after him, was built to the exact dimensions of Solomon's Temple and soon housed some of the greatest masterpieces of the age. Under Julius II and Leo X in the early 1500s the finest artists of the day – Raphael and Michelangelo among them – were brought to Rome, and set to work in the Vatican. Julius's favourite architect, Donato Bramante, began in 1504 the construction of a magnificent garden and courtyard, the Cortile del Belvedere, which soon became a unique open-air museum of ancient sculpture. The so-called Apollo Belvedere had been found on one of the pope's properties, and it became the first star attraction, soon to be joined by the Laocoön, unearthed in 1506 and immediately recognised because of a famous description by the Roman author Pliny the Elder. Although the courtyard has now been converted, sadly, into an enormous parking lot, its original purpose deserves to be remembered.

The heart of the beautification campaign, however, remains a triumph to this day: the basilica of St Peter itself. This was to be the largest church in Christendom, and like the new cathedral in Florence, it was to draw on the ideas of a number of architects and was to take some two centuries to

St Peter's Square, Rome, designed by
Gianlorenzo Bernini, 1657–67

complete. Progress was particularly slow during the fifty years or so after
Nicholas V started the demolition of the old basilica and asked the distinguished humanist and architect Leon Battista Alberti to plan the new
building. It was not until the papacy of Julius II that the process began to
accelerate. He completed the demolition of the old St Peter's, put Bramante in charge of the new building, and at last laid the foundation stone
in 1506. But Julius died in 1513, and Bramante the following year. During
the next century and a half, over a dozen architects had charge of the
enterprise at various times. They included some of the most distinguished figures in the history of architecture, notably Michelangelo, who
came to the project at the age of seventy-two and designed the dome
which, however, he did not live to see. Even after the basilica was consecrated in 1626 (exactly 1,300 years after the consecration of Constantine's
St Peter's), there was much work to be done, and from 1629 onwards the
person in charge was the leading sculptor and architect of the day, Gianlorenzo Bernini.

One still feels Bernini's presence throughout central Rome. In the
Villa Borghese Museum we can see his sculptured self-portrait on the
face of a vigorous young David about to kill Goliath. In the city's squares
and streets we can see his fountains, his charming little elephant and
the façades of his buildings. His sculptures grace more than a dozen
churches and palaces. But he was proudest of the work he did for the

Church. The Cornaro Chapel in Santa Maria della Vittoria, built to celebrate a famous Catholic victory over heresy, shows his patrons, the Cornaro family, sitting in theatrical boxes as they gaze on the Ecstasy of St Teresa. For good reason, it is one of the best-loved treasures in Rome. Perhaps most pleasing is his oval-shaped church of Sant'Andrea al Quirinale. His son one day came to pray in this gem, and was surprised to see his father (who was usually his own worst critic) looking happily around. The son asked what he was doing there, and the architect replied: 'I feel a special satisfaction at the bottom of my heart for this one work of architecture, and I often come here as a relief from my duties to console myself with my work.'

Two popes in particular, Urban VIII and Alexander VII, seemed insatiable when it came to Bernini. Later in life, the sculptor is said to have regretted some of the commissions he accepted from them. The story had it that he drew the curtains in his carriage whenever he passed through the Piazza Navona, so that he would not have to look at his elaborate Four Rivers Fountain. It may be that he remembered the cries of a hungry Roman mob, furious that popes were spending money on decorations instead of food: *Pane, non fontane*, they shouted (Bread, not fountains). But his work for the Church was central to his career, and nowhere more so than at St Peter's. In 1629 Urban VIII made him the basilica's chief architect, and it was for Urban that he constructed the

Sunburst at the west end of the nave, and the *baldacchino* over the *Cathedra Petri*, the throne of St Peter, St Peter's basilica, Rome

baldacchino, the tall bronze canopy that marks the grave of St Peter; oversaw the decoration of the four massive piers that support the dome; and made the giant St Longinus that stands below the relic of the Roman centurion whose lance pierced the side of the crucified Jesus.

But there was far more to come from Alexander VII, who more than any other pope put his stamp on the city. One observer noted that before the Sun set on his first day on the papal throne (in 1655) he summoned Bernini. It is certainly true that the pontiff, who came from one of Italy's richest families (the Sienese banking house of Chigi) and was determined to establish himself as the most lavish patron of the age, was the sculptor's greatest fan. In his diary, 40 per cent of his references to the arts concern Bernini – a rate eight times more frequent than the mentions of his next favourite, Pietro da Cortona. He had him build a church (a remarkable small-scale homage to the Pantheon) in his country residence at Ariccia; he brought him into the Vatican to design an immense staircase, the Scala Regia, climaxed by an equestrian statue of Constantine; and in St Peter's he asked him to complete the interior of the western end of the basilica. Here Bernini created the *Cathedra Petri*, the papal throne, which he set against a sunburst in the window that rises over the throne, centred on the dove of the Holy Spirit – a fitting climax to the passage of the devout through the church.

These were all redoubtable achievements. But the best was yet to come: a vast undertaking that remains one of the chief wonders, not only of Rome, but of all Europe. Having decided to raise Christendom's largest church, the papacy now had to place it in an appropriate urban context. The area running from the basilica towards the river Tiber had been the site of a circus in ancient times – a public space that had also been used for the execution of Christians, one of whom had been St Peter. As the plans for the new church developed, the successive popes from Nicholas V onward gave considerable thought to devising a fitting approach from the river to the basilica. One of the problems was a settlement of fairly shabby houses on the river's edge, known as the Borgo, which blocked access to the Tiber and the imposing papal castle on its banks, the Castel Sant'Angelo. Despite various schemes to clear the area, it was to remain built up until Mussolini constructed the rather grim Via della Conciliazione from the side of the castle towards St Peter's in the 1930s.

Even without major demolitions, however, there was a fairly large open space east of the church, as one approached its main entrance, and this was substantially expanded in the 1560s by Pope Paul IV, who created approximately the area that is now occupied by the Piazza di San Pietro. But the question remained: what should one do in this space to make it an appropriate setting for the basilica at its head? A number of plans were suggested over the decades that followed, and Bernini himself worried about the appearance of the façade in his days as principal architect under Urban VIII. To make it more imposing, he designed bell towers for the two ends of the façade, but the project was such a disaster – it caused cracks to appear in the foundations, and in 1646 the part that had been completed was pulled down – that during the rule of Innocent X, between Urban and Alexander, he received no new papal commissions. When Alexander brought him back on the scene in 1656, therefore, the aim was to find a way to make the façade the culmination of the piazza without, however, changing the front of the church itself.

A number of requirements had to be taken into account. Alexander had a fondness for processions, and it was important that there be a special place for the most important of these, on the feast of Corpus Christi each year. There had to be a way for carriages as well as pedestrians to

Aerial view from the Benediction Loggia
of St Peter's basilica to St Peter's Square,
Rome

approach the church. And the architect had to bear in mind that the pope
gave his blessings from two different places to the faithful who gathered
in the piazza below. Depending on the occasion, he might use the so-
called Benediction Loggia above the main entrance to St Peter's, or he
might appear to the crowd from the papal apartments in the Vatican
Palace, which rose over the piazza to the right of the basilica. It had to
seem natural for those who looked towards him to face in either of these
directions. Finally, there were already two objects in the piazza that
Bernini had to incorporate.

The more commanding of the two was a superb pink granite obelisk,
some 80 feet (24 m) high, that had been brought from Egypt by the
emperor Caligula to adorn the circus at this site. Through the centuries
it had stood to the south of the basilica, but in 1586, using 900 workmen,
140 horses and forty-four winches, Sixtus V had it moved to a central
position in the piazza in front of St Peter's. In the succession of popes
since Nicholas V, Sixtus had been the most determined rebuilder and
beautifier of Rome, responsible for shaping the Piazza del Popolo, carving out the Via del Corso (along which horse races took place that made
the Palio in Siena seem like a gentle jaunt), and much else besides.
Columns and obelisks were a particular favourite. He restored the
column of Marcus Aurelius now in the Piazza Colonna, and he raised

Aerial view of St Peter's Square, Rome

obelisks in the Piazza del Popolo and on the Esquiline hill as well as at St Peter's. Bernini's plans now had to take into consideration not only this unmovable monument, but also a large fountain that had been placed near it in the piazza a few years later.

His solution to these many challenges was extraordinary. In just ten years, from 1657 to 1667, he gave the piazza the appearance that has been familiar to millions of pilgrims ever since. The first master stroke was to link the church to the space in front of it. This he did by constructing two 394-foot-long (120-m) covered galleries, which extend from the edges of the façade into the piazza. The gallery on the left as one faces St Peter's has rooms for the guards (and now various tourist shops), and is linked to the church by an archway over one of the main road entrances to the Vatican. The other gallery encloses a magnificent staircase, the Scala Regia, which leads into the papal palace. As we will see, the two galleries not only help enclose the space in front of the basilica, forming a trapezoid that draws one into St Peter's, but also play a crucial role in the design of the entire square.

Colonnades, St Peter's Square, Rome

Sweeping out from the ends of the galleries are two huge semicircular covered colonnades. These are quadruple colonnades, made up of two pairs of columns, one on the outside of the circle, the other on the inside. Each pair is fairly close together, though there is enough room for pedestrians to pass. The pairs, however, are set well apart from one another, because down the middle between them the space had to be wide enough to allow a carriage to go through. The columns themselves, while made of marble and 43 feet (13 m) tall, are remarkably self-effacing, even though there are 284 of them. They are of the simplest classical order – Doric – greyish-white in colour and unadorned, and they are echoed by pilasters which continue the design along the two galleries to the front of St Peter's. Their simplicity and unobtrusiveness, moreover, is reinforced by their openness, which allows people and light to pass through at will.

The power of the colonnades derives, not from their inherent quality, but from their immense size and the shape they carve through the piazza. The two constructions are 1,050 feet (320 m) long, and 787 feet (240 m) across at their widest point. Although Bernini had planned a final colonnade to define the piazza at its eastern end, this was never built, and the result is to reinforce the feeling of openness, especially when tens of thousands fill the square on major occasions. Because of the circular design, which the gap between the two arcs turns into an oval, it becomes entirely natural for those in the piazza to face either the Benediction Loggia on St Peter's or the papal apartments in the Vatican Palace to the right. And they could easily follow the Corpus Christi procession as it made its way around the colonnade.

Saints atop the colonnades, St Peter's Square, Rome

To anchor his design, Bernini made sure that the obelisk would align both with the centre of the basilica's façade and with the mid-point of each colonnade. Then, so as to emphasise the symmetry, he moved the existing fountain to a position halfway between the obelisk and the middle of the northern colonnade, and as balance placed an identical fountain in the same position on the southern side. To ensure that the elegance of the geometry was unmistakable, he set two porphyry discs in the stones of the piazza, between the fountains and the obelisk. From these vantage points, the four columns are perfectly aligned, like spokes on a wheel, and the spectator sees only one row of columns.

The main decoration of the colonnade is at its roof, where a balustrade brings it up to a height of 69 feet (21 m). On top of the balustrade stand a series of 10-foot-tall (3-m) statues, 140 in all. Of these, ninety-six were designed by Bernini himself, and were put in place over the next decade. The remainder were gradually added by others. They represent saints of the Church of the most amazing variety. Here one can find Joseph, husband of Mary; Thomas Aquinas; Ignatius Loyola; Francis of Assisi; and other famous figures like St Benedict and St Catherine alongside figures of arcane obscurity: St Norbert, St Hyacinth, St Techla and so forth. It is the entire panoply of the history of the Church, unfamiliar as well as celebrated, that looks down on the faithful below.

And it is indeed from above that the full significance of Bernini's

St Peter's Square, Rome. Oil painting by an unidentified Italian artist, *c.1665*

achievement is best appreciated. The main purpose of the design is of course to hold the crowds who come to hear the pope. His regular blessing is given *urbi et orbi*, to the city and the world, and at that moment the Church reaches out to people everywhere. This is precisely what Bernini had in mind. He conceived of the linked galleries and colonnades as a gigantic pair of arms that extend from St Peter's in order to encircle humanity. If the obelisk is considered a symbol of man reaching up to God, then the piazza in which it stands is a way of embracing all God's children. The immensity of the ambition is matched by the immensity of the design.

Despite his natural cynicism, the Venetian ambassador, on seeing them for the first time, wrote that 'the colonnades which encircle the Piazza di S. Pietro will be an achievement to recall the greatness of ancient Rome'. That was as high a compliment as he could pay; for us, it is to recognise the piazza as one of the most enduring wonders of the age.

VERSAILLES

Second only to Italy in the development and embrace of the new ideals of the Renaissance was France. Petrarch had begun the campaign to revive the ancient world in the papal enclave of Avignon, today in southern France, and there are some scholars who regard Provence as the ultimate origin, antedating Florence, of the challenge to medieval values. When the French invaded Italy in 1494, the interaction between the two cultures only accelerated – the most famous consequence being the departure of Leonardo da Vinci from his homeland, to spend his last years in France.

Leonardo's patron François I, who became king in 1515, deserves to be seen as the father of the Renaissance in France. Among the literati of the day he was widely admired, an appreciation that won him a mention in Castiglione's handbook of refinement, *The Courtier*, where he is described as the great hope for the intellectual and artistic future of his homeland. Such fame was not inappropriate, because in addition to Leonardo François attracted other Italian notables, such as Benvenuto Cellini, to his court. Equally important, he made it his mission to import the latest Italian ideas. The atmosphere he created was summed up in a poem by Robert Browning, commenting on the unhappy outcome (involving the theft of royal funds) of a visit to the French king by another major artist, Andrea del Sarto. Andrea returned to Italy, and there Browning gave him a telling line: 'How I could paint, were I but back in France.'

François also collected books and manuscripts, and made his country's leading humanist scholar, Guillaume Budé, royal librarian. His other major literary interest was in poetry, which he himself wrote. He must have been delighted that, towards the end of his reign, a group of his subjects, to become known as the Pléiade, were to give new life, in French, to the form for which Petrarch had been celebrated, the sonnet. These poets, especially Pierre Ronsard and Joachim du Bellay, demonstrated that Renaissance ideals had taken root in France.

Yet it was in architecture that François probably did most to transform the taste of his countrymen. His predecessors on the throne had lived in forbidding fortresses, but he now brought an airy light and a sense of style to their residences. He began the renovation of two redoubtable castles on the Loire, at Amboise and Blois, and set new standards of elegance in the nearby Château de Chambord. In Paris, meanwhile, he took on a complete rebuilding of the Louvre. But his principal achievement was the reconstruction, from 1527 onward, of a 350-year-old royal chateau at Fontainebleau, near Paris, into a luxurious palace.

Château de Fontainebleau, begun by
Philibert Delorme and Jean Bullan,
sixteenth century

The building we see today owes a great deal to the further efforts of
François's son Henri II and the king at the end of the century, Henri IV.
But the look of the palace is primarily a reflection of the vision of
François I. His aim was to set a standard for royal architecture, and the
French and Italian masters he relied on lived up to his expectations.
Using classical motifs – the arch, the pediment, the pilaster – and design-
ing harmonious courtyards, embellished with formal gardens and water-
ways, his architects created a palace worthy of a great king.

If the exterior was subdued and restrained, like many an Italian villa,
the interior was sumptuous. Here François and his son employed some
of the leading artists from Italy. In these years, from the 1520s to the 1550s,
the dominant aesthetic was no longer the calm serenity achieved by such
masters as Raphael, but the energetic, sometimes troubling movement
known as Mannerism. It was the Mannerist ideal of beauty (apparent in
religious as well as mythological scenes) that dominated not only the
palace but also much of French art, which soon adopted the so-called
'Fontainebleau style'.

The most renowned example was a gallery that François commissioned, to run from his private apartments to the chapel. This was the
first such gallery in France, inspired by Italian models, but deliberately
on a larger scale than its predecessors: nearly 200 feet (61 m) long and
almost 20 feet (6 m) wide. The splendid inlaid panelled ceiling, the
marble, the fine windows, and especially the elaborate stucco decorations, surrounding paintings full of swirling figures, still astound the
visitor. It was the masterpiece through which François brought the
Renaissance definitively to France, and earned him a decisive influence
on the history of French taste. It also provided an inspiration and set a
standard that only extraordinary ambition (as we shall see) was to exceed.

The tradition that François I set in motion was nowhere more brilliantly represented than at the chateau and gardens that some consider the finest in France: Vaux-le-Vicomte. Built by a royal minister, Nicolas Fouquet, in the 1650s, the residence and its surroundings were the work of the finest artists of the day. The design was by Louis Le Vau, royal architect and already famous for his work at the Louvre and for his buildings on the previously uninhabited Ile St Louis in the heart of Paris. The decorations were by Charles Le Brun, regarded as the most talented disciple of the greatest French painter of the day, Nicolas Poussin, and soon to be named the king's premier painter. And the gardens and waterways, integral to the beauty of the whole, were laid out by Adrien Le Nôtre, son and grandson of head gardeners at the royal park of the Tuileries, a man destined for his profession who was to become a landscape artist without peer in French history. This splendid chateau (a rival even for Fontainebleau) became a centre of French culture, entertaining the playwright Molière, the poet La Fontaine and the sparkling letter-writer Madame de Sévigné, among many others. But its heyday was brief. Accused of corruption, Fouquet was suddenly dismissed by Louis XIV in 1661. Rumour had it that the decision was made when he visited Vaux-le-Vicomte, and felt that his minister was living better than his monarch. There is little basis for the story, but what is unquestioned is that at the

Aerial view of the Château de Vaux-le-Vicomte and gardens, by Nicolas Fouquet, 1650s

201

chateau he encountered a harmony of the arts that he was to draw on and overwhelmingly to outdo when, a few years later, he decided to build himself a new palace.

The origins of Versailles lie in the turbulence of the French political scene in the mid-seventeenth century. All over Europe there was upheaval, as newly powerful central governments (products of the military and bureaucratic developments of the Renaissance) faced resistance and rebellion from subjects trying to hold back their ever-growing demands. There was domestic conflict in Spain and Portugal, in Italy, in Germany, in Scandinavia, in England and also in France. Although the form it took varied widely – from urban revolts in Barcelona or Königsberg to nationwide civil war in England – it engulfed much of the Continent, and was exacerbated by a devastating international struggle, the Thirty Years War. The war may have come to an end in 1648, with the Peace of Westphalia, but the troubles within particular countries festered on, in some cases until the 1660s.

In France the upheaval began in the very year of Westphalia. Louis XIV was a child of nine at the time, and his mother and her minister, Cardinal Mazarin, had run the government since his father's death five years earlier. In May 1648 the members of the principal court in Paris, the Parlement, denounced a new tax that Mazarin, facing increasing financial difficulties, was trying to impose. When Mazarin had their leaders arrested in August, the city erupted into revolt. The narrow streets of Paris were ideal cauldrons of resistance, and its citizens had resorted for centuries to barricades that prevented troops from pursuing them. The barriers went up again in the summer of 1648; the threats to the court intensified; and in October, soon after his tenth birthday, Louis and the royal family had to flee the city. It was a memory that stayed with the king. Although he was soon able to return to the Louvre, he never trusted Paris again. As soon as he took full charge of his government, after the death of Mazarin in 1661, he resolved to move himself and his court to a safer home.

But where? One answer might have been Fontainebleau; in fact, however, Louis was much more attached to a small hunting lodge that his father had built on an estate owned by a leading aristocrat near the village of Versailles, some 12 miles (20 km) from Paris. Louis XIII had built the original lodge in 1623: a small building of five rooms that ran north–south. It was less than 20 feet (6 m) wide and slightly over 70 feet (21 m) long, with the beginnings of wings at right angles at either end. In the words of one observer, it was a 'miserable' place, unworthy of a king.

Over the next seventeen years it became somewhat more grand (though hardly grandiose) as it tripled in size, with the two wings extended to form almost a square, though the fourth side was left open.

By then, too, Louis had bought the entire 500 acres (203 ha) of the estate; he had built a terraced walled garden in front of the house; and he had cut alleys through the surrounding wood towards a circular plot about 900 yards (823 m) west of the lodge where he built a small pond. What is remarkable is that, although both house and gardens were to be expanded beyond recognition by his son, the original lodge still forms the set of buildings at the centre as one approaches the palace today, and the elaborate park to the rear takes its starting point from the landscaping put in place by 1640.

Twenty-one years later, after Mazarin died, Louis XIV began the transformation of this modest structure into a palace fit for Europe's most powerful monarch, ruler of its richest and most populous kingdom. His first task was to redo the interior of the lodge to create properly lavish living quarters for himself and his immediate family. He divided the second storey between himself and his wife, and the location of the king's apartment in the northern half, with the queen next door to the south,

Bird's-eye view of the palace and gardens, Versailles, before Louis XIV's expansion of the palace. Detail of an oil painting by Pierre Patel, 1668

Entrance to the Palace of Versailles

was never to change. At this point, too, Le Nôtre was brought in to lay down flower beds and start expanding the gardens. Construction also began on the stables and kitchen buildings that have flanked the forecourt ever since. Eventually the stables were to have space for thousands of horses, perhaps as many as twelve thousand. And the wide forecourt, narrowing towards Louis XIII's three-sided lodge, focused the attention of all who approached the palace on the central importance of the original building and the royal apartments it contained.

Over the next fifty years, Louis XIV transformed this relatively small structure into the largest palace in Europe. France had replaced Spain as the Continent's dominant power, and in his quest for ever-greater glory he was determined that his residence should outshine not just the Escorial but every princely and royal home that had come before. By the time he made it the official seat of the monarchy, in 1682, his goal had been accomplished. The most extravagant feature, the Hall of Mirrors, was not finished for another two years, and the elegant chapel, at the edge of the royal apartments, was not consecrated until 1710, just five years before Louis died. But it was the whirlwind of activity during the first two decades of expansion – overseen by the trio from Vaux-le-Vicomte: Le Vau, Le Brun and Le Nôtre – that gave the palace and grounds the basic look they retain to this day.

The immediate response of a visitor is to marvel at the enormity of the enterprise. Had some thirty thousand workmen not been employed in the construction, one cannot imagine the palace being completed as quickly as it was. Its western façade alone, overlooking the gardens, is

204

well over 600 yards (549 m) long, and a 25-mile-long (40-km) wall was required to encircle the gardens. Big enough to house approximately five thousand people, with another fifteen thousand who came in each day, it was the most concentrated hive of human activity in the world.

Astonishingly, though, the second response is to recognise the human scale of this gigantic enterprise. Except for its size, there is nothing obviously assertive about the appearance of the palace. The exterior is quite modestly decorated and, apart from the chapel, the building remains at a comfortable height of three storeys. The balustrade at the roof line is crowned by evenly spaced statues and urns, but these are relatively self-effacing and do not tower over the viewer. The classical façade, moreover, though immensely long, has a uniformity that makes it easily absorbed. On the lowest floor are some two hundred arched windows at regular intervals; above them, behind a low balustrade, are larger rectangular windows, with arched windows above; and on the much smaller top floor the windows are square. To make the huge length comprehensible, encompassing as it does two vast wings that stretch out from the central

View of the western façade of the Palace of Versailles

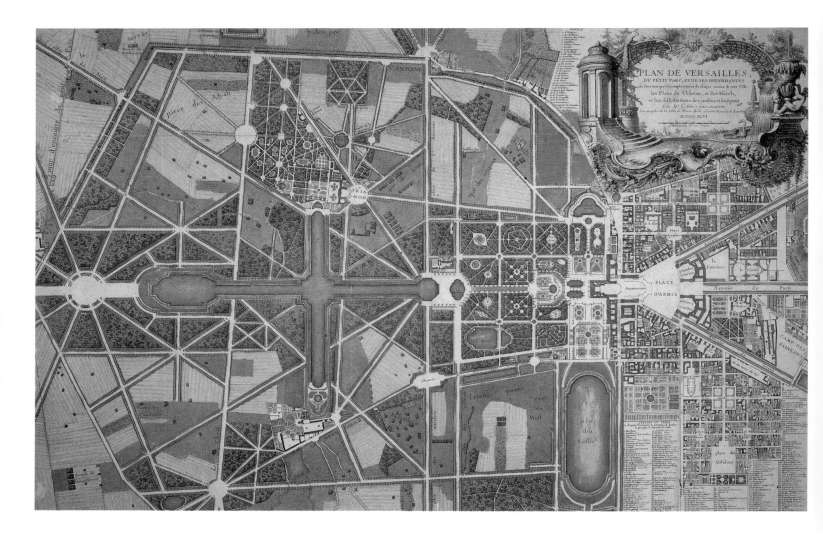

Plan of the gardens at Versailles. Engraving by the abbé of Lagrive, 1746

section (essentially Louis XIII's original building), the façade is divided symmetrically by slightly protruding two-storey-high porticoes. These are marked on the second storey by groups of paired columns, topped by statuary. The interruptions, built of the same beige stone as the entire building, divide the expanse into readily graspable units, and modify the impression of almost endless length.

Seen as a whole, the architectural motifs represent a climax of the Renaissance classical spirit. Palladio and Michelangelo would have recognised all the elements of the palace's façade (one is sometimes tempted to see it as a gigantic extension of Michelangelo buildings in Rome). But its size was beyond anything they could have imagined.

In the gardens, too, there is a restraint that tempers the vastness of the conception. This is Le Nôtre's masterpiece, and its symmetries, endlessly varied features and vistas have never been equalled. The large open area in front of the western façade, marked by flower beds, pools and fountains, is certainly grand. And the panorama to the west, along the axis first laid out by Louis XIII, but then hugely expanded by Le Nôtre with a nearly mile-long (1.6-km) canal that took thirteen years to

complete, is also spectacular. Perhaps most stunning is the nearly oval pool on the site of the circular plot and pond towards which Louis XIII had built alleys through the woods. From the edge of this pool emerges the gilded figure of Apollo, in a chariot drawn by four horses, riding eastward towards the palace and the beginning of his daily transport of the Sun across the sky. There is no question that these are dazzling sights. Yet the sense one has, at the end of a stroll through the park, is of successive small pleasures rather than repeated awesome spectacles.

Thus the lovely summer palace that Louis built as a retreat at the edge of the park, near the village of Trianon, is a charming smaller version of Versailles. Its single storey includes the same tall arched windows as the second storey of the main palace, and it has the same balustrade at the roof line. To add colour, the windows are divided by pink marble pilasters; these, together with pink marble Ionic columns in a walkway between the two wings of the building, reinforce the sense of classical simplicity even amidst the splendour. With woods covering much of the palace's grounds, and decorative statues, peaceful waterways and

Apollo's chariot, Versailles

207

South façade of the Petit Trianon,
Versailles, built 1763–8

refreshing fountains throughout, the gardens encourage quiet satisfaction rather than jaw-dropping amazement. So proud was the king of the pleasures the park offered that he himself wrote its first guidebook, *The Manner in Which the Gardens of Versailles Are to Be Shown.*

If the emphasis on graceful detail moderates the grandeur of the exterior, there is no such restraint within the palace. Here the sumptuousness, the trumpeting of French power and wealth, is inescapable. The marbles and fine stones, the grand staircases, the majestic hallways, galleries, rooms and salons, and the glittering paintings and decorations leave no doubt that the intention is to overwhelm. Le Vau died in 1670, when the building was still in its early stages, but his successor, Jules Hardouin-Mansart, remained true to his spirit. It was Mansart who built the Trianon, and it was he who created the palace's most astounding space, behind the royal apartments and overlooking the park: the Hall of Mirrors. This 250-foot-long (76-m) gallery, which seems to be a combination of gold and glass, has seventeen arched windows facing the view, and behind them seventeen matching arched mirrors that reflect their light onto enormous chandeliers and gilded decorations. Above is a vaulted

208

ceiling on which Le Brun painted extravagant celebrations of the king's triumphs, such as *France's Supremacy Recognised by Spain*. There had been famous princely galleries before, notably a splendid hall of mirrors in the Gonzaga Palace in Mantua, but none of them even approached the scale Mansart here achieved.

The other rooms the royal family used may have been smaller, but they were no less flamboyant. They have been much altered since Louis's reign, but the opulence persists. Today's Apollo Room, for instance, was where Louis granted his official audiences as sovereign. In his day it was a throne room, with the throne itself, of carved silver, standing nearly 9 feet (3 m) high and adorned in winter with velvet and in summer with

The Hall of Mirrors, Palace of Versailles, built *c.*1678

brocade, all embroidered with gold and silver to match the decorations of the room. Above, in the centre of the ornate ceiling, is a painting of Apollo, again in his chariot hauling the Sun. As the Sun King, Louis had himself surrounded by reminders of his symbol, and one wonders if anyone has ever been able to count the number of gilded sunbursts that decorate palace and grounds. Given that image, however, it was entirely appropriate for Louis to demand that gold be the dominant colour in the royal rooms. Gracious in their proportions, embellished with crystal, marble, rich fabrics and fine ceilings, they have dazzled their visitors ever since.

Although life at Versailles was punctuated by elaborate ceremonies, firework displays, theatrical and musical performance, and superb banquets, one must not think of it as a seat of luxury alone. Gondolas from Venice might ply the canal, but among them would have been the prince of Condé, a cousin of the king who had revolted against him during the Fronde but ended his days rowing ladies on the waterways. For Versailles was also a way for Louis to keep an eye on his nobles. A thousand of them lived in the palace at any one time, but there was a large turnover every few weeks, and most had to live in appallingly cramped and often stifling conditions in the small rooms that made up the palace's third floor. In summer the heat could be unbearable, and in winter the water in the glasses at the banquets sometimes froze. For many residents, a visit was hardly a time for glamorous living. In addition, large sections of the palace were given over to bureaucratic offices. Versailles was the seat of government as well as the home of the monarch, and Louis wanted his officials at hand as he pursued his duties amidst his pleasures.

Little of this other side of the palace is apparent to the visitor today. The stiff, regulated behaviour required of all who came is forgotten. The many discomforts have been swept away. The division that the move to Versailles created between the king and his people, between the formalities of the court and the energies of Paris (symbolised by the march of Parisian women to Versailles in 1789) has been superseded by revolution and political change. But the sheer ambition of the place, and the genius of those who built and decorated it, has survived the alterations and deteriorations it has suffered over the centuries. The wonder it arouses is palpable still.

Chapel Royal dedicated to St Louis, Versailles, designed by Robert de Cotte, completed 1710

GREENWICH

The Renaissance came late to England, and it is apt that our last example of a wonder from the years 1400 to 1700 should be English. Not until the years around 1500 did it become apparent that the new ideas coming from Italy might migrate this far to the north. Soon thereafter, however, it became clear that humanist learning had found a significant outpost across the English Channel.

The first stirrings were noticeable in the world of scholarship. On three occasions between 1499 and 1509, the most famous humanist of the day, Erasmus, visited London. There he formed an abiding friendship with Thomas More, a future Lord Chancellor and also, in *Utopia* (1516), the author of a classic of Renaissance thought. In 1509 a friend of both men, John Colet, founded St Paul's school, which was to be a bastion of the new learning. And there was growing direct contact with Italy, notably through the historian Polydore Vergil, a papal envoy who arrived in 1501 and was to write a highly influential history of England. Polydore had been secretary to the duke of Urbino, whose court had been graced by some of the most glittering figures of Italian art and letters, and the interchange he represented gradually transformed the culture of his adopted land.

By the time of the reign of Elizabeth I in the second half of the sixteenth century, the English were beginning to make a major contribution to Renaissance culture. Unlike their neighbours, however, they were making their mark primarily through their literary achievements. The poet Sir Philip Sidney was known through much of Europe, and indeed had his portrait painted by Veronese. His contemporary Edmund Spenser bore comparison with Italian masters like Ariosto and Tasso. And the playwrights who were being performed in London's lively theatres were without peer. No other European country could boast a succession of masters of the stage to compare with Marlowe, Jonson and, above all, Shakespeare.

In the arts, however, it was a different story. The dominant painter of the reigns of Henry VIII and his son Edward VI was a German, Hans Holbein. Under Elizabeth the main focus was on the delicate but hardly revolutionary art of the miniature. But during her reign some imposing country houses were beginning to appear, freed (by gunpowder's effects) from the traditional need to build a defensible castle. Among these fine aristocratic mansions, one can single out Robert Smythson's two masterpieces at Longleat and Hardwick Hall, and such other achievements as Montacute and Burghley House. But these houses were not shaped by the classicising impulse that had transformed architecture in Renaissance Italy – notably in the work of Brunelleschi, Alberti, Palladio and Michelangelo – or elsewhere in southern Europe, as at the Escorial. They did draw on Renaissance elements, but there was much else involved, including reflections of the Gothic, and the results were certainly not intended to recall the style or the decorative features of antiquity.

That was to change in the early years of the seventeenth century, when Continental developments captured English architecture, largely as a result of the influence of one man, Inigo Jones. He was born in London in 1573 to a Welsh cloth-worker, but his first thirty years remain fairly obscure. We do know that he spent time in Italy, which he visited again in 1613; that he seems to have been for a while in Venice, where he must have become fully acquainted with the work of Palladio; and that eventually he was invited by Christian IV of Denmark, an avid patron of the arts, to his kingdom. Here Jones would have seen one of the first major Renaissance buildings in northern Europe, just a few miles up the Øresund from Copenhagen: Kronborg Castle, set spectacularly on a hill overlooking the sea. Its proximity to a small town gave it the name for English speakers that was to make it world-famous: Elsinore Castle. For Jones, however, it served as an introduction to the adaptation of Renaissance styles to northern climes.

After returning to England he found employment at the royal court, where the queen since 1603, Anne of Denmark, was the sister of Christian IV. At first Jones was employed designing scenery for theatrical performances – he is said to have been the inventor of the movable stage set – but eventually he was able to pursue his *métier* as an architect. Many of his elegant and deceptively simple buildings survive, including two in London: the Banqueting House that was part of Whitehall Palace and the church of St Paul in Covent Garden. He was also active outside London, and it was he who designed the first of the buildings that was to transform the riverside a few miles from the capital down the Thames at Greenwich.

For centuries this site, sloping gently up to a prominent hill south of the Thames, on a long U-bend of the river, had been a favourite recreation area. The Romans had been here, and in the Middle Ages there was laid out a park of nearly 200 acres (81 ha) that forms the basic topography to this day. At the river's edge was a fortified palace that was a favourite of Henry VII and Henry VIII as a place for hunting and tilting. Here both Queen Mary I and Queen Elizabeth I were born, and it continued to be used in early Stuart times. But it was becoming increasingly dilapidated, and in 1662, after the Civil War, it was demolished. Long before, however, Anne of Denmark had decided she would like a place of her own near by, and she commissioned Jones to build what was to become the Queen's

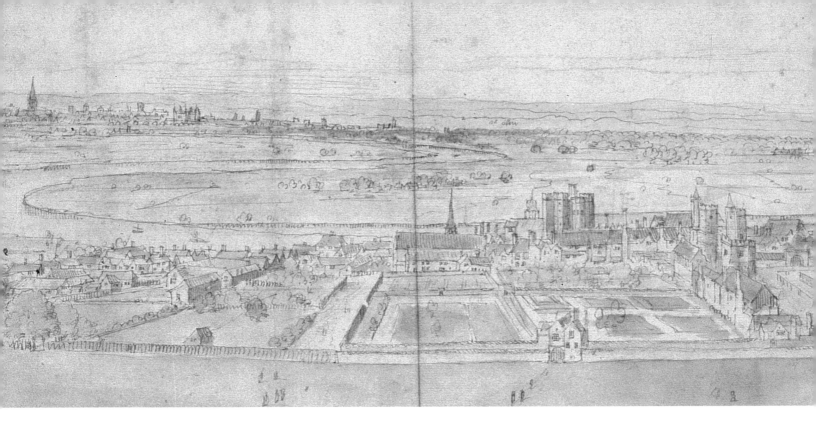

Greenwich Palace and London from Greenwich Hill. Detail from 'The Panorama of London'. Ink-and-watercolour drawing by Anthonis van den Wyngaerde, c.1544. This panorama from the summit of Greenwich Park in the 1540s shows the towers of the old Greenwich Palace and the surrounding village on the bank of the Thames. The figures in the park indicate the scale of this vast bird's-eye view. In the distance on the left is the city of London, with the Tower just visible at its eastern edge. The view, probably as much imagined as observed, is from the approximate position of the Royal Observatory today

House, though it was unfinished when she died in 1619 and its first occupant was to be her daughter-in-law, Queen Henrietta Maria.

The house has been enlarged and reworked since Jones finished working on it in 1638, but the façades are much as he left them, and one can still appreciate the graceful building he created. For those who had seen an Italian villa, it must have been a revelation to see one on English soil. Growing numbers of England's social elite were coming to recognise that a journey through the Continent – the beginnings of the Grand Tour – would be the capstone on their education. Many were heading for Italy, and the first travel guides aimed at this market, with tips about major artistic monuments, were being published. Particularly important in this process of familiarisation was England's ambassador to Venice, Sir Henry Wotton, an ardent advocate of the new Italian aesthetic and the author of a summary in English of the writings of a revered source for Renaissance architects, the Roman theorist Vitruvius. Wotton may well have introduced Jones to the work of Palladio, and he certainly fostered an appreciation of the new style among his countrymen.

The Queen's House is full of echoes, not only of Palladio but also of Medicean villas and Vignola's recently completed Palazzo Farnese at Caprarola. It has the first open, colonnaded loggia in England, Italianate marble floors with geometric patterns, a balustrade around the roof, a shell-shaped circular staircase and a myriad other touches that brought the Renaissance to life in stone. A little over 100 feet square (30.5 m square), with two high storeys and symmetrical classical façades, broken only by an imposing double set of steps that curve up to the front

214

entrance, this light and harmonious house has always seemed the epitome of grace.

Henrietta Maria hoped that the interior would complement the distinction of the building. To adorn its two-storey great hall she brought to England the well-known Italian painter Orazio Gentileschi and his daughter Artemisia. There were also plans to install a Tintoretto and to commission from Jacob Jordaens (the prime pupil of Rubens, who had painted the ceiling of Jones's Banqueting House) a series of pictures on the theme of Cupid and Psyche. Less graphic than Giulio Romano's depiction of the story in the Palazzo Te in Mantua, these paintings symbolising the power of love would have established the Queen's House as a major monument of art as well as architecture. Sadly, however, civil war intervened. The plans had to be shelved, and although the house has remained, through ups and downs, a pioneering embodiment of the Renaissance, it is the overall design, rather than the contents, that have set it apart as one of England's most remarkable buildings.

The second new structure to be constructed in the park at Greenwich was Flamsteed House. Crowning the hill that overlooks the river, this was to be the main building of the newly founded Royal Observatory. At this point architecture intersected with the movement that transformed Europe in the seventeenth century, and, by undermining the superiority of the ancient world, was to bring the Renaissance to an end: the Scientific Revolution.

The structure that stood on the top of the hill until the 1660s was a tower and lodge built by Humphrey Duke of Gloucester in the fifteenth

Queen's House, Greenwich, designed by Inigo Jones, 1616–38

Tulip staircase, Queen's House, Greenwich, designed by Inigo Jones

century. Since the building was crenellated, its official name, Duke Humphrey's Tower, was often shortened to Greenwich Castle, and its hill is known as Castle Hill to this day. It was badly damaged during the Civil War, and pulled down, together with Greenwich Palace, in the 1660s. This was the very decade of the founding of England's premier scientific organisation, the Royal Society, whose aims and interests were now to intersect with Greenwich.

A major concern of the Royal Society was astronomy, a subject that had been transformed during the 120 years since Copernicus had made it the focus of ever more revolutionary study. One of the society's members, Isaac Newton, was to bring these developments to a climax with the publication of his *Principia* in 1687, but it is important to realise that a major stimulus to his work was the fact that he was surrounded by fellow investigators, sometimes rivals, who were also intensely interested in the workings of the heavens. Among his colleagues in the Royal Society, for example, Christopher Wren was Savilian Professor of Astronomy at

Oxford, and both Robert Hooke and Edmond Halley were to make distinguished contributions to the field.

A central aim of the Royal Society was to produce useful knowledge, and one of the practical problems on which it focused (natural in a maritime nation) was a means of calculating longitude. This remained unsolved for another century, until the clockmaker John Harrison, addressing the need to compare shipboard time with time at a fixed point on land, produced a chronometer that remained accurate even at sea. In the interim, however, a number of other approaches were tried, and a favourite in the Royal Society in the 1670s was associated with the astronomer John Flamsteed, who believed accurate calculations of the movements of the Moon against the stars could lead to a solution. To make those observations Flamsteed was appointed England's first Astronomer Royal in March 1675. The hill at Greenwich, high above London's smoky air, seemed an ideal place to build him an observatory, and it was Wren who suggested they use the site of Duke Humphrey's Tower. Assigned to design the new building, he saved money by using the tower's foundations (to Flamsteed's dismay, because the walls were not aligned with the meridian), and by July 1676 the Astronomer Royal had moved into his new quarters.

The building, named for Flamsteed, is not an especially distinguished piece of architecture, despite its provenance. It is almost square, just under 40 feet (12 m) on each side, with twin towers at the end of the front façade. The upper of the two storeys has a grand octagonal room, with large windows, through which observations were to be made, but in fact Flamsteed tended to use a courtyard behind the building. Fifteen years after he moved in, he added small buildings with walls properly aligned to the meridian and continued his work, but most of his observations (which included a first sighting of what was to become known as the

Duke Humphrey's Tower. Detail from 'A View of Greenwich'. Etching by Wenceslaus Hollar, 1637

Flamsteed House, Greenwich Park.
Aquatint by Thomas Hosmer Shepherd,
1824

planet Uranus) were published only after his death in 1719.

The Flamsteed Building today sits alongside a modern observatory, and is famous primarily because it marks zero degrees longitude and is the reference point for Greenwich Mean Time. But its contribution to the vista from the river is nevertheless vital. In aesthetic terms it provides a pinnacle for the hill; far more resonant, however, is the unique historical presence it brings to the site. As a symbol of the intellectual revolution that transformed Europe and then the rest of the world, it is without parallel.

But the most commanding building at Greenwich was yet to come. It was clear that Charles II, who had given the Royal Society its charter and Flamsteed his position and his home, had high hopes for an area which once had held a royal palace. Having spent the era of the Civil War in exile in France, he was particularly drawn to French gardens, and in 1662 he asked Le Nôtre, already famous for his work in the Tuileries and Vaux-le-Vicomte, and soon to be the landscaper of Versailles, to suggest new designs for Greenwich Park. Only a small part of Le Nôtre's plans were put into effect, because they were linked to dreams of a new palace that Charles never had the money to build. Instead, it was his niece, on the throne from 1689 as Mary II (jointly with her husband William III), who set in motion the project that gave Greenwich its full majesty.

The story begins, ironically, with two of the worst tragedies to befall England in the seventeenth century: the Civil War and the Fire of London. The first prompted calls for the government to aid the growing numbers of ageing soldiers, often in poor health, who had no means of supporting themselves. The latter made the architectural reputation of Christopher Wren. Wren had been a childhood friend of Charles II in the 1630s, and when the king returned to the throne in 1660 he encouraged his former playmate, known primarily for his scientific work as a professor of astronomy, to follow up the interest in architecture he had expressed after reading the ancient Roman theorist Vitruvius. Wren's promising potential was evident from two commissions that came his way in 1663 and 1664: a chapel for a Cambridge University college, commissioned by his uncle, and a theatre commissioned by the chancellor of Oxford University. He visited both Rome and Paris to hone his skills, but the decisive moment for his career came when much of London burned to the ground in 1666. Within three weeks Wren had drawn up a plan to rebuild the city, and while no master plan was adopted – though he did supervise the rebuilding of fifty-one of London's churches – he was clearly coming to be recognised as England's premier architect.

In the 1670s, in addition to the Royal Observatory and a multitude of other projects, Wren began the largest of his London churches, St Paul's Cathedral. Long before it was finished, however, Charles in 1681 had given him a new task on an even bigger scale: the design of a hospital for old soldiers, to be established in Chelsea. Completed in 1692, this was Wren's most extensive undertaking to date: a harmonious set of three quadrangles, with rooms and services to accommodate nearly five hundred men. But it proved to be just a foretaste of the single largest undertaking of his career, which was to bring him back to the Greenwich he had already adorned with the Flamsteed Building.

The original idea for a hospital to serve sailors, the equivalent of Chelsea for soldiers, came from Charles's brother, King James II. But it was James's daughter Mary who in 1691 took up the idea. Terrible casualties in a naval battle the following year gave urgency (and initial funding) to the project, and in 1694 the queen granted the land for a building 'for the relief and support of Seamen ... who by reason of age, wounds or other disabilities shall be incapable of further service'. Mary died later that year, but her husband, William III, determined to realise her wishes.

When the old palace at the river's edge had been demolished in the 1660s, Charles had begun a new one, but the building that had been started, named after him, had remained unfinished when money ran out in 1672. Wren's first contact with the naval hospital project was a visit to this building in 1693 to see what could be done with it, and eventually he was to incorporate it into his overall design. More problematic was the vista down to the river from the Queen's House that had been opened by the demolition of the old palace. Even though the unblocked space

Royal Naval Hospital, Greenwich. Note the central opening, which allows the Queen's House an uninterrupted view, and also creates a harmonious ensemble when seen from the river

bisected the site of the hospital, Mary insisted on keeping her view. Various attempts were made to evade this provision, which prevented construction of a single building, united around a grand centre (Wren even drew up such a plan, with a large dome as its focus). Mary's sister, Queen Anne, even proposed doing away with the restriction. But in the end it was never overturned, and one could argue that the effect was to stimulate Wren (as the problems of the Piazza di San Pietro had stimulated Bernini) to produce one of his most inspired creations.

It was to take 140 years to complete the Royal Hospital (which thirty years later ceased its existence as a hospital and became the Royal Naval College). Some of England's most distinguished architects, including Nicholas Hawksmoor and John Vanbrugh, were involved in its construction over the years, but the overall design is unquestionably Wren's. A wooden model, built in 1699 and still on display in Greenwich, shows essentially the buildings and façades that we see to this day. The absorption of Renaissance aesthetics and the use of design features from the ancient world served far more grandiose ambitions in the 1690s than they had in the days of Inigo Jones sixty years earlier, but the power of the classical ideal had not diminished. The unlikelihood that the three diverse initiatives at Greenwich – Queen's House, Observatory and Hos-

pital – could form a coherent whole makes Jones's and Wren's buildings the most astonishing architectural ensemble in England.

Greenwich Hospital from the north bank of the Thames. Oil painting by Antonio Canaletto, *c*.1752

The Royal Hospital consists of four buildings, centred on the open vista towards the Queen's House. Looking from the river, the dominant feature is a pair of identical domes over classical porticoes (each looking like miniature versions of St Paul's Cathedral) which frame the Queen's House. The four buildings are all rectangular. At the front, on the river, is the completed King Charles building on the right, and its near-mirror image, the Queen Anne building, on the left. Including slightly extended wings, they cover approximately 175 by 300 feet (53 by 91 m), and are mostly three storeys tall. Behind them stand the King William and Queen Mary buildings, about 210 by 320 feet (64 by 98 m), with identical colonnades, extending towards one another, that add 20 feet (6 m) to their width. The effect from the river is of a single pair of buildings, stepped so as to become narrower at the rear, with the colonnades and domes commanding the central open space that leads to the Queen's House.

Built in white stone, with dark roofs and domes, and decorated with symmetrical classical motifs – pilasters, pediments, Doric and Corinthian columns, balustrades – this enormous set of buildings strikes the observer (as does the view of St Peter's in Rome) as a triumphant

Interior of the Painted Hall, Greenwich, with decoration by Sir James Thornhill

reinvention and expansion of the architecture of antiquity. There are some splendid spaces within, notably the Chapel and the great Painted Hall, but, like the Chelsea Hospital, this was a structure intended for practical use, not display. That the impact is nevertheless so overwhelming, and that the sight from the river of the Hospital and Queen's House, and then the park rising up to the Observatory, is so deeply satisfying, is a tribute to the special qualities of English architecture. Even after many visits, this dramatic ensemble continues to amaze. The values of the Renaissance may have been fading by the 1690s, but they still had the power to produce one final wonder.

SEVEN WONDERS
OF THE
MODERN WORLD

Jonathan Glancey

M<small>Y CHOICE</small> of wonders shifts from the earthiest to the most ethereal. In fact, it includes the Earth itself, or at least an image of it, and a sub-particle of a sub-atomic particle that is not just invisible, to date, even to the most powerful microscope, but may yet prove to be no more than hypothetical.

In between, I have added something very special of ourselves, the DNA double-molecule, which connects all of us back to the very first human beings (or Adam and Eve if you like to give them names); a machine that acts and seems as if it is alive; one of the most dramatic and memorable of all industrial-era structures; an unforgettable architectural skyline; and a twentieth-century mechanical sky goddess that once talked with a voice loud enough to drown out that of Vulcan, or even Jove himself.

I hope this makes some sense. 'The Modern World' could be interpreted more spaciously than I have chosen to do it, but it struck me, when I was making my choice, that our notion of what constitutes a wonder has changed radically in the last two hundred years, and the perspective this offered on more traditional wonders of the world particularly appealed to me. My era may not be very long in historical terms, but it is, to say the very least, packed with incident and invention. It covers the wonders of the Industrial Revolution and those of the heroic Machine Age. It threads its way through the devastation of world wars, leading us to the age of the atomic bomb and those of computers, space travel and global electronic communications. My wonders have to work hard for their living, each attempting to catch something special of the spirit of its own times, while standing up to be counted among the long-recognised wonders of the ancient world, those of medieval Europe with its breathtaking cathedrals, and the beauties of the Renaissance.

All my wonders have been nurtured in the West, for which I offer no apology, except to say that most of them have been created by people from different parts of the world who have either transferred their talents from one country to another, as with the architects who shaped the

New York skyline, for example, or else joined together in various forms of international collaboration, as with the engineers who guided Concorde into the supersonic mesosphere, and the physicists who are currently conducting wondrous research beneath the Franco-Swiss border at CERN.

The Industrial Revolution was, of course, a Western phenomenon, born in England, a country often held up as one of the most conservative in the Western world. Nothing could have been further from the truth. The level of invention, skill and daring on the part of both engineers and those who commissioned them in nineteenth-century Britain was as high as the topmost girders of the Forth Bridge. This very daring, skill and imagination was either exported, or emerged more or less independently, all across the West, and then, through trade and empire, to many other parts of the globe.

Throughout the industrial era and into the age of the atom, the world served as one big and infinitely exploitable resource for humankind to plunder and to experiment with. Although there had been warnings by profound Victorian critics such as John Ruskin (1819–1900), a concern for the harm 'progress' was doing to the Earth itself was slow in coming. Much as poets, painters and theologians, among others, might rail against it, progress was just too exciting. I think of Concorde, the supersonic airliner, as one of the last unalloyed messengers of the nineteenth-century notion of progress at almost any cost. Significantly, it was brought down to Earth for the last time at the beginning of the twenty-first century, when concerns for the ecology of our planet, even if wilfully spurned or deliberately misunderstood, had finally reached most ears. That concern emerged, with a clear and powerful voice, when humans first saw Earth itself from deep space. What had for so many decades been treated in cavalier fashion, often supported by religious dogma, as a source of coal, iron ore, animal fats and oil, was a beautiful living entity in need of truly loving care.

To understand our world better, scientists began to peer ever deeper into its nature and structure. In doing so, they have learned much about us – living, breathing creatures made of the very substance of the Earth and stars that we have so carelessly exploited in the name of progress and 'man-made wonders'. And so I have chosen the model of DNA made by Crick and Watson in 1953, which tells us about our own physical and genetic make-up, along with the experiments into particle acceleration at CERN, which may yet tell us where the components of DNA come from. These microscopic parts are, of course, the building blocks not just of very tiny structures like DNA, but also of the Empire State Building and the New York skyline.

Though it may be considered odd for someone who writes much

about architecture, I have not included individual buildings among my wonders, because to my mind there have been none in the past 250 years, no matter how brilliant, that can better the drama, the craftsmanship and the dreams represented by the ancient ziggurats, stepped or spiral, the Gothic cathedrals or the Renaissance domes. In any case, many of the most inspiring buildings shaped since the Industrial Revolution have been aided by the skill of, all too often, shadowy engineers, or else are engineering structures pure and simple. That said, there are buildings, very much the work of architects, that I would call wonders if my list could go beyond seven. Le Corbusier's pilgrimage chapel at Ronchamp only just dropped from the bottom of my list.

As for 'Big Boy', one of the greatest of all steam railway locomotives, how could I ignore it? It has to stand in, on these pages, for the steam railway locomotive as a whole. Not only did the steam engine power the early modern world, but the steam railway locomotive was one of the most thrilling of all machines yet invented. It is the one that appears not just to live and breathe, but to express emotions. I have never collected the numbers of railway engines, but I can drive a steam locomotive, and continue to find them a wonder to watch in the few corners of the world in which they still perform their sulphurous ministry.

All my wonders, I hope, have the power to stir both the heart and the intellect. Most are the product of men, but, in terms of buildings and machinery, this was simply the case until very recently. A visit to CERN today will demonstrate how far women have come in this world of wonders in the past fifty years. One of the reasons this has been so (aside from any other) is the contraceptive pill, a small wonder in itself that has enabled women to control, more or less, their own fertility. A birth-control pill might not look quite as impressive as a 'Big Boy' or the Chrysler Building, yet it has done a great deal indeed to change the face of the workings of the modern world, and even the results of its relentless researches.

Each of my wonders, whether noisy in the case of Concorde and 'Big Boy', gigantic like the New York skyline and the Forth Railway Bridge, infinitesimally small in the examples of DNA and the theoretical sub-particles of protons, and jewel-like in the image of the Earth, is something special for us to enjoy, remember and nurture before they, or we, cease to be.

EARTH FROM SPACE

Lunar Module Pilot Harrison Schmitt, photographed during extravehicular activity of NASA's final lunar landing, Apollo 17 mission, 13 December 1972

There are something like 250 billion galaxies in the known universe, as far as this can ever be knowable, and possibly very many more. One of these galaxies, the Milky Way, is our very own. Measuring some 90,000 light years across, it is, technically speaking, a flat four-arm logarithmic spiral, with a bulge in the middle. Halfway out on one of those four arms is what we call the Sun, one of the four hundred billion or so stars in the galaxy. And whirling around that familiar yellow star is the planet we call Earth. The world. Our home.

Not even the most informed scientist really knows how many stars or galaxies there are in the universe, nor whether the universe is infinite, or doughnut-shaped, or sitting in a bell-jar in God's library, or even in the palm of His hand. From the Earth, on a clear night and with a good eye, some 2,500 stars are visible in the heavens from any one point. It is possible that one in ten of these, and of all the other billions of stars in the Milky Way, is orbited by planets. So in our own galaxy alone there might be as many as forty billion planetary systems. To date we know of about a hundred. The hundredth, by the way, is a Jupiter-sized planet discovered in 2002, circling the star known only as HD2039. You may, of course, know of more by now.

And yet, for all this ineffable vastness and baffling uncertainty of numbers, there is one planet we can be sure of. Of course, it might be nothing more than a dream in our collective imagination, or in the infinite mind of its creator, yet the Earth seems real enough to the six billion humans and trillions of other creatures, great and small, who swim, crawl, pounce, slither and otherwise leap and bound through its seas, soil and skies.

It was not, though, until December 1968 that the very first photographs of our planet were taken by humans. These were the astronauts of Apollo 8, one of the NASA missions which led up to the first Moon landing by Apollo 11 in July 1969. It was as the Gemini capsule came out from behind the Moon for its fourth pass that the crew witnessed an event never seen before. Earthrise.

Glancing out of the window, astronaut William Anders saw a blue and white orb and realised it was the Earth. He took the first photograph in black and white, and then, later, the more famous colour image, framed in the lens of his hand-held Hasselblad Lunar 70-mm camera and now captioned for posterity, 'Earth Rising from the Moon'.

On 7 December 1972, perhaps the most famous picture yet of the Earth was taken, from Apollo 17 on its way to the Moon. It shows the planet glistening, a supremely alluring blue and white sphere in the infinite inky

blackness of deep space. We can clearly see the outlines of East Africa, the Middle East and, emerging from seas of white cloud, Antarctica. In the following years, this image was reproduced in what appeared to be as many posters as there were stars in the Milky Way. It was an image of astonishing and numinous beauty, and it helped to change the way many humans (though far from all) saw their planet, and, more importantly, felt for it.

This exquisite orb, so wonderfully alive, is where we live. Seen from space, it appears whole and beautiful. Who could ever guess that down below was a world long divided into squabbling states and bickering religions, beset by savage wars and fouled by pollution created by its own inhabitants? From the perspective of deep space, it must have seemed

Earthrise, photographed by the Apollo 8 mission crew, December 1968

227

absurd that any human would ever want to harm this, their own home, yet even the astronauts who brought us this epoch-changing vision knew perfectly well that humans are capable of savage and wilful destruction of their own species, their own kith and kin; of the wildlife they share the planet with yet are so unkind or oblivious to; of whole natural environments; entire cities, even (in certain unthinkable circumstances) the planet itself. Boom! Nuclear war would see to that, if industrial pollution or global warming failed to do the job first.

Unsurprisingly, the Apolline view of this glorious planet had an immense effect on the souls and psyche of contemporary astronauts. 'The Earth reminded us of a Christmas tree ornament hanging in the blackness of space,' recalled James Irwin, the Apollo 15 astronaut, who walked on the Moon in July 1971:

As we got farther and farther away it diminished in size. Finally it shrank to the size of a marble, the most beautiful marble you can imagine. That beautiful, warm, living object looked so fragile, so delicate, that if you touched it with a finger it would crumble and fall apart. Seeing this has to change a man, has to make a man appreciate the creation of God and the love of God.

While on the Moon, at the end of the first day's exploration of the lunar highlands, Irwin said he was reminded of 'my favourite Biblical passage from Psalms'. Speaking by radio to Mission Control in Houston, he quoted the passage, 'I'll look into the hills from whence cometh my help.' Irwin resigned from the Astronaut Corps the following year and became the founding president of the High Flight Foundation, an interdenominational evangelical organisation based in Colorado Springs. He preached around the United States, and looked for the remains of Noah's Ark on two missions to Mount Ararat.

Other astronauts were moved to believe that a world divided by politics made no sense whatsoever. 'For those who have seen the Earth from space,' wrote Donald Williams, 'and for the hundreds and perhaps thousands more who will, the experience most certainly changes your perspective. The things that we share in our world are far more valuable than those which divide us.' Williams knew about the destruction such division can cause. He had flown no fewer than 330 missions from the decks of the USS *Enterprise* in the Vietnam War. His medals include the Vietnamese Gallantry Cross (with gold star), the Vietnamese Service Medal (with four stars) and the Distinguished Flying Cross. He became a NASA astronaut and Space Shuttle commander.

Sigmund Jahn, the first German astronaut, flying to join Salyut 6 aboard the Soviet rocket Soyuz 33 in 1978, said: 'Before I flew I was already aware of how small and vulnerable our planet is; but only when I saw it

Earth photographed by Apollo 17 mission crew, 7 December 1972 from space, in all its ineffable beauty and fragility, did I realise that humankind's most urgent task is to cherish and preserve it for generations.' Ecology was on the agenda, and more so than ever before.

For Shuttle pilot Charles Walker, it was the stuff of some unwritten symphony, the music of the spheres:

My first view, a panorama of brilliant deep blue ocean, shot with shades of green and gray and white, was of atolls and clouds. Close to the window I could see that this Pacific scene in motion was rimmed by the great curved limb of the Earth. It had a thin halo of blue held close, and beyond, black space. I held my breath, but something was missing. I felt strangely unfulfilled. Here was a tremendous visual spectacle, but viewed in silence. There was no grand musical accompaniment; no triumphant, inspired sonata or symphony. Each one of us must write the music of this sphere for ourselves.

'A Chinese tale', said Taylor Wang, a Chinese-American Shuttle crew member, 'tells of some men sent to harm a young girl who, upon seeing her beauty, become her protectors rather than her violators. That's how I felt seeing the Earth for the first time. I could not help but love and cherish her.'

'The Earth was small, light blue, and so touchingly alone . . . our home that must be defended like a holy relic.' This was the view of Aleksei Leonov, the Soviet cosmonaut, and, in March 1965, the first man to walk in space during the Voskod 2 mission.

A holy relic, a beautiful young girl, an unwritten symphony, an ineffable beauty, the most beautiful marble you can imagine, and, above all, home.

'Suddenly, from behind the rim of the Moon,' wrote Edgar Mitchell, 'in long, slow-motion moments of immense majesty, there emerges a sparkling blue and white jewel, a light, delicate sky-blue sphere laced with slowly swirling veils of white, rising gradually like a small pearl in a thick sea of black mystery. It takes more than a moment to fully realise this is Earth . . . home.' Mitchell, a former US Navy pilot and member of the Apollo 14 crew, was the sixth man to walk on the Moon, in February 1971. He went on to found the Institute of Noetic Sciences in 1973, the aim of which was to conduct and sponsor research into areas that mainstream science ignores, including psychic events. As well as writing academic journals, Mitchell has written two books, *Psychic Exploration* and *The Way of the Explorer*. He is '90 per cent sure that many of the thousands of unidentified flying objects, or UFOs, recorded since the 1940s, belong to visitors from other planets,' and that UFOs have been the 'subject of disinformation in order to deflect attention and to create confusion so the truth doesn't come out'. And for Mitchell, as for so many of the other

astronauts and cosmonauts who have seen the Earth from space, 'My view of our planet was a glimpse of divinity.'

This takes us back to the Apollo 8 mission from which the first photographs of Mitchell's 'glimpse of divinity' were taken. Apollo 8 entered lunar orbit on 24 December 1968. It was the night before Christmas. That evening, as they rounded the Moon for the ninth time, the astronauts, Commander Frank Borman, Command Module Pilot Jim Lovell and Lunar Module Pilot William Anders, made a live television broadcast, in

Mitchell's 'glimpse of divinity': view of Earth photographed by the Apollo 8 mission, 24 December 1968 which they showed pictures of the Earth and Moon. Lovell said, 'The vast loneliness is awe-inspiring and it makes you realise just what you have back there on Earth.' Borman described space as 'a vast, lonely, forbidding type of existence or expanse of nothing'. And then the crew took turns to read from Genesis.

[William Anders:] In the beginning God created the heaven and the earth. And the earth was without form, and void; and darkness was upon the face of the deep. And the Spirit of God moved upon the face of the waters. And God said, Let there be light: and there was light. And God saw the light, that it was good: and God divided the light from the darkness.

[Jim Lovell:] And God called the light Day, and the darkness he called Night. And the evening and the morning were the first day. And God said, Let there be a firmament in the midst of the waters, and let it divide the waters from the waters. And God made the firmament, and divided the waters which were under the firmament from the waters which were above the firmament: and it was so. And God called the firmament Heaven. And the evening and the morning were the second day.

[Frank Borman:] And God said, Let the waters under the heavens be gathered together unto one place, and let the dry land appear: and it was so. And God called the dry land Earth; and the gathering together of the waters called he Seas: and God saw that it was good . . . and from the crew of Apollo 8, we close with, good night, good luck, a Merry Christmas, and God bless all of you, all you on the good Earth.

The mission was the most widely covered by the media since the first American orbital flight in 1962 by John Glenn in Mercury 6. The BBC's coverage alone was broadcast in fifty-four countries in fifteen different languages. It is possible that a quarter of the people alive at the time saw the Christmas Eve transmission. When, on a world tour soon after returning to Earth, Borman met Pope Paul VI, the pontiff told the astronaut, 'I have spent my entire life trying to say to the world what you did on Christmas Eve.'

Not everyone was happy with the reading of Genesis, no matter how beautiful the majestic prose of the King James Bible. The militant atheist Madalyn Murray O'Hair was so outraged that she brought a lawsuit against NASA over the reading. She wanted the courts to ban US astronauts from public prayer in space. The case was rejected, yet it made NASA publicly uneasy about issues of religion ever afterwards. Buzz Aldrin, the Apollo 11 astronaut and second man on the Moon after Neil Armstrong, decided it best not to mention the fact that he took Holy Communion on the surface of the Moon after landing. O'Hair and others had missed the point. The crew of Apollo 8 were so moved by what they witnessed that they wanted to express the view from their cramped cockpit in terms that were both poetic and numinous. They wanted to celebrate the sheer beauty of creation. And chapter 1 of the Book of Genesis does exactly that, whether you take its message literally or not at all.

Whether or not there had been a message from God, or the gods, at the time, many people of whatever creed, or no creed, thought that there had. Apollo 8's mission had been at the end of 1968, a year that had witnessed upheaval around the world. Soviet tanks had rolled, unwelcome, into Prague. Martin Luther King Jr and Robert F. Kennedy had been assassinated. The Vietnam War had escalated with the Tet Offensive. University campuses across the United States had witnessed rioting. The events of May in Paris had brought France close to revolution. Troops had opened fire on students in Mexico City, killing hundreds. Apollo 8 brought home the message that there was only one Earth, a beautiful planet, so different from anything else to be seen in what appeared to be the barren reaches of space. It belonged to us. It needed our tender loving care.

The environmental movement was galvanised into fresh thinking and action. The famous image of the Earth sailing through the sea of space taken by the crew of Apollo 17 four years later helped even more. Here was the perfect image for book covers and posters encouraging ecological awareness. Significantly, the economist E. M. 'Fritz' Schumacher published his hugely influential polemic *Small Is Beautiful* the following year.

Photographs of the Earth had been taken from space before, but from 1968 human eyes and human hands worked the cameras that framed these potent images. The Apollo 17 image is a wonder of the modern world, a picture that made the Earth itself a wonder. We knew that all along, but now we could see it with fresh eyes. None of us, ever again, had any excuse to treat the planet badly. Or to squabble over religions and politics. Or to fight wars. But of course we did.

THE FORTH RAILWAY BRIDGE

The Forth Bridge rose in the shadow of Britain's greatest civil engineering failure. The collapse of the earlier Tay Bridge had made not just tragic history, but terrible poetry.

> Beautiful Railway Bridge of the Silv'ry Tay!
> Alas! I am very sorry to say
> That ninety lives have been taken away
> On the last Sabbath day of 1879,
> Which will be remember'd for a very long time.

This, of course, was the immortal Bard of Dundee, William Topaz McGonagall (1825–1902), recording the event for posterity. The 2-mile (3-km) bridge carrying the North British Railway across the Firth of Tay had opened, to imperial acclaim, on 31 May 1878. The queen empress rode across by train. Thomas Bouch (1822–80), the bridge's Cumbrian-born engineer, and inventor of the roll-on, roll-off ferry, was knighted. At the zenith of his career, he began work on his next project, an even more ambitious railway bridge across the Firth of Forth.

Then, on 28 December 1879, the evening Dundee mail train steamed north from Edinburgh Waverly, behind North British locomotive No. 224 – a two-cylinder 4-4-0 designed by Thomas Wheatley eight years earlier. According to McGonagall:

> When the train left Edinburgh
> The passengers' hearts were light and felt no sorrow,
> But Boreas blew a terrific gale,
> Which made their hearts for to quail,
> And many of the passengers with fear did say –
> 'I hope God will send us safe across the Bridge of Tay.'

He didn't. At 7.15 p.m., as the six-coach train was negotiating the bridge, a force 10–11 gale blew it and Bouch's masterpiece into the cold and stormy waters below. Sir Thomas's son-in-law was among the seventy-five officially recorded dead. Karl Marx, so Dundee legend tells, had very nearly been a passenger on the fateful train, too, but his journey north had, for some reason, been delayed. Only forty-six bodies were ever recovered. So, too, four years later, was the locomotive, which was dubbed 'The Diver', and ran without further incident until withdrawn from service in 1919.

Bouch's reputation, unlike Wheatley's or The Diver's, was destroyed along with the Tay Bridge. So, too, were his ambitions and designs for the

Rescuers search for survivors following the Tay Bridge disaster on 28 December 1879, as shown in the *Illustrated London News*, 10 January 1880

Forth Bridge. A public inquiry set up after the disaster revealed that the railway company had sacrificed safety and durability in favour of stringent cost-cutting. Sloppy working practices, such as poor smelting and the reuse of girders dropped into the sea during construction, were factors in the bridge's collapse. Bouch took much of the blame. He retired during the inquiry and died, a broken man, before its findings were published in 1880.

Photographs of Bouch's Tay Bridge show a structure describing an elegant arc across the Firth, as if drawn with a single stroke of the engineer's pen. It does look a bit flimsy. But this is hindsight speaking. No one knew at the time that the bridge, and Bouch with it, was probably doomed from the start. Inspecting engineers quickly determined that the cylindrical cast-iron columns supporting the thirteen longest spans of the bridge, each 245 feet (75 m) high, were of particularly poor quality. Nor had Bouch made allowance for wind loads, although, to be fair, such calculations were not recognised by engineers until after the Tay Bridge disaster.

After the inquiry, the Board of Trade, with designs for the planned Forth Bridge on the same railway line in mind, imposed a specification of 56 lb (25 kg) force per square foot (0.1 m²), sufficient, it was presumed, to keep the new bridge safe and sound even in the strongest gales. The foundations of the Forth Bridge had already been laid, but now Bouch's design

235

was abandoned and the project was handed over to engineers Sir Benjamin Baker (1840–1907) and Sir John Fowler (1817–98), and contractor Sir William Arrol (1839–1913), who had also been put in charge of building the replacement Tay Bridge. This still stands today, handsomely restored, with the stubs of Bouch's McGonagall fodder still visible alongside.

The choice of engineers proved to be one of genius. Together, Baker and Fowler gave shape to one of the wonders of the modern world, a bridge that more than a century on still has the power to take the breath away. Here was proof, if proof were needed, that Victorian engineers, rather than the architects of their day, were the true heirs to those who built the Egyptian pyramids, the Roman aqueducts and medieval Gothic cathedrals. The bridge can be seen from central Edinburgh, itself one of the finest creations of British architects and urban planners. And yet, for all the lure of Edinburgh's fine and sturdy Georgian architecture, the Forth Bridge draws the visitor as surely as sirens did ancient mariners.

Although it is a joy to cross by train today, there are car parks on either side of the bridge for the many sightseers who come this way just to sit and look at the wondrous bridge and to map its many moods as the weather changes with wind and tide. Morning sea mists can hide the entire structure. By night, it is floodlit. There have been many superb bridges built since, yet few have caught the imagination quite like the Forth Railway Bridge. Perhaps, in responding to the Tay Bridge disaster, Baker and Fowler were determined to create a structure that would withstand the test of time. Its beauty, though a product of strict engineering logic and mathematics, cannot be described as accidental. Working at the height of the British empire, the design team must surely have wanted to create a marvel for the world to gawp at and admire. They did.

Benjamin Baker is generally considered to be the driving genius behind the design. Born near Bath, he trained in a South Wales ironworks before joining Sir John Fowler in London. He took part in the construction of the Metropolitan Railway, London, the world's first underground railway. He designed the cylindrical vessel in which Cleopatra's Needle, now standing on the Thames Embankment, London, was shipped from Egypt to England in 1877–8. By this time he was known as an authority on bridge construction. The design of the Forth Bridge beckoned. It would crown his reputation. Later, he was consulting engineer on the original Aswan Dam, and was in Egypt for its opening in 1902. He played a considerable role in the development of the cast-iron construction of London's deep-level Tube lines. He was, quite simply, one of the great civil engineers of his or any other day, and the Forth Bridge was his unquestioned masterpiece.

Located 9 miles (14.5 km) west of Edinburgh, the new bridge was designed to replace the existing Granton to Burntisland ferry, and to

carry two North British tracks 1.5 miles (2.4 km) across the Firth of Forth between South and North Queensbury, at a height of 158 feet (48 m) above the high tide. Baker and Fowler's solution was to lay the lines across a steel track bed supported by three Herculean cantilever towers, each 340 feet (104 m) high and 1,710 feet (521 m) long.

Work began in 1883. Over the following seven years, construction of the bridge consumed some 51,000 tons of steel, 640,000 cubic feet (18,123 m³) of granite, 6.5 million rivets and fifty-seven lives. During operations, rescue boats were stationed under each cantilever, saving at least eight lives. A total of five thousand men had been involved in its construction. The final cost, all told, was £3.2 million. The new Palace of Westminster, by Barry and Pugin and completed in 1860, had cost £2.17 million. The Forth Bridge was, one might say, the greatest and possibly the costliest of all structures built in Victorian Britain or, indeed, across the empire.

To span the Forth with assurance, Baker adopted the balanced cantilever principle. This meant that the bridge was built as three separate double cantilevers. When each had been constructed, they were linked together by 350-foot-long (107-m) girder spans joined to the main structure of the bridge by huge pins, the size of a fully grown man. The whole bridge is balanced by 1,000-ton counterweights on the outside of the outer cantilever structures. This concept is readily understood from

The Forth Bridge, during its construction in 1887

Baker's famous, and thankfully well-photographed, 'human cantilever' model, in which his assistant Kaichi Watanabe, a Japanese engineer studying in Britain, represented the 'live load' or central weight on the bridge. One look at this famous photograph of 1887 and the structural logic of the bridge becomes clear.

The use of a cantilever in bridge design was not a new idea. In fact it has roots in ancient Chinese and Japanese bridge construction. The first modern steel cantilever bridge had been erected to designs by Heinrich Gerber at Hassfurt over the river Main in Germany. The principles he adapted were those published by John Fowler in the late 1840s. What was different in Scotland was the sheer scale of the undertaking. Much of the work on the bridge was without precedent, including calculations for incidence of erection stresses, provisions made for reducing future maintenance costs, calculations for wind pressures and the effect of temperature stresses on the structure. The bridge was designed to withstand wind forces 5.5 times greater than those that toppled the Tay Bridge.

Finally the prince of Wales drove the last gold-plated, and suitably inscribed, rivet home at the opening ceremony on 4 March 1890. The bridge had, in fact, been convincingly tested on 21 January 1890 when two 1,000-foot-long (305-m) test trains, each comprising a locomotive and fifty wagons, and weighing 900 tons, rolled onto the bridge side by side from the south entrance. The bridge passed the test with flying colours. It was also, for the record, the biggest man-made construction of its time and the largest civil-engineering structure of the nineteenth century. It boasted the largest span of any bridge. There was enough material here to keep contemporary newspaper reporters very busy indeed.

Not that everyone was impressed. William Morris (1834–96), the Arts and Crafts designer and socialist critic, described the bridge as 'the

View through the Forth Bridge, 1903

supremest specimen of all ugliness'. But then he would. Morris, although much younger than Fowler and just six years older than Baker, belonged to a generation of artists and writers for whom the mechanical strivings of the nineteenth century were sooty anathema. Morris, along with the hugely influential critic John Ruskin (1819–1900), hated railways. The prologue to Morris's *The Earthly Paradise* (1865) imagines the counties through which the river Thames flows free of the evils of the railway:

> Forget six counties overhung with smoke,
> Forget the snorting steam and piston stroke,
> Forget the spreading of the hideous town;
> Think rather of the pack-horse on the down,
> And dream of London, small, and white, and clean,
> The clear Thames bordered by its gardens green . . .

Yet the steam railway was to become one of the best-loved sights and sounds in Britain. Morris's eyes, like those of so many aesthetes and intellectuals of his generation, were blinkered. If they could see beauty in the structural drama of a Gothic cathedral, then why not in the heroic design of the Forth Bridge? 'A bridge', says Santiago Calatrava, a Spanish

239

The Forth Bridge illuminated in red light for Comic Relief, 2001

architect who is also one of the most artistic of today's civil engineers, 'adds energy to the landscape.' Which, aside from any other virtues it possessed or expressed, is exactly what a medieval cathedral did.

Was it the scale of the Forth Bridge that angered the likes of Morris? Yes. Baker and Fowler needed to make a statement with the presence of their steel bridge. It needed to look strong to break the ill spell of the Tay Bridge and to assure passengers that rail travel across the stormy firths of east-coast Scotland was safe. The Forth Road Bridge, spanning the Firth alongside the railway bridge since 1964, shows how much slimmer and lighter bridges were to become in the twentieth century. Dramatic improvements in materials, and the analytical methods used in their design and construction, meant that massive structures were no longer necessary. Engineers, from Abraham Darby and John Wilkinson with

240

their pioneering cast-iron bridge of 1779 at Coalbrookdale, Shropshire, through Thomas Telford and his Menai Suspension Bridge of 1820, to Gustave Eiffel and Eugène Freyssinet in France and Robert Maillart in Switzerland, worked tirelessly to shape and refine bridges of great economy of means and fine lines. The Humber Bridge (1981), Lincolnshire, by Freeman Fox and Partners, has a suspended central span of 4,624 feet (1,409 m). This has a knife-edge profile to make it as aerodynamic as possible. In this way, the bridge is easily able to withstand the kind of battering by the wind that brought down Bouch's Tay Bridge on the last sabbath day of 1879.

Even so, for all its massiveness the Forth Bridge shares the heroic quality of the original Seven Wonders of the World, and has a majesty very much its own. Will it endure like the Roman Pont du Gard at

Nîmes? It has remained in regular use since completion, carrying the main east-coast line north over to Fife and onwards to Dundee and Aberdeen. Today, stresses placed on the steel bridge are much less than they used to be in the days of steam, when the 'hammer-blow' from pistons acting on wheels gave even the toughest bridges and best-laid track a hard time. In fact, the bridge, for all its grandeur, often seems underused, although between 180 and two hundred trains cross it each day. But at least this means that its life should be a very long one yet, despite its shocking neglect during the early days of the dismal and churlish privatisation of Britain's main-line railways in the 1990s.

In 1996, at the request of the Health & Safety executive, Railtrack, since replaced by Network Rail, began a structural and maintenance assessment of the bridge. The result was a £40 million refurbishment programme begun two years later. This comprised steelwork repairs, surface coating, access improvements and an upgrade of the floodlighting. The contractor undertaking this work gave up the ghost in 2002 due to financial problems, and in the same year Balfour Beatty Civil Engineering won a seven-year £10 million per annum maintenance contract. A materials analysis of the bridge at the time found the Victorian steelwork in good shape, with little variation in quality over the vast length, height and breadth of the structure.

The steelwork has now been blast-cleaned down to bare metal and recoated with a zinc-based primer to prevent corrosion, a glass-flake-epoxy intermediate coat and a polyurethane-gloss top coat in traditional 'Forth Bridge Red'. This system, which the contractors say has been tried and tested in an 'offshore environment', is designed to give a twenty-year life, meaning the bridge may yet be free of its legendary team of painters, doomed, like latter-day Sisyphuses, to repaint the structure ceaselessly and for ever.

Now back to McGonagall and the doomed Tay Bridge:

> Oh! ill-fated Bridge of the Silv'ry Tay,
> I must now conclude my lay
> By telling the world fearlessly without the least dismay,
> That your central girders would not have given way,
> At least many sensible men do say,
> Had they been supported on each side with buttresses,
> At least many sensible men confesses,
> For the stronger we our houses do build,
> The less chance we have of being killed.

Baker and Fowler chose cantilevers instead, making the Forth Bridge one of the great wonders of the modern world.

THE NEW YORK SKYLINE

While researching a radio programme for the BBC in New York, I was introduced to the oral archives of the Ellis Island Immigration Museum. Ellis Island, a ferry ride from Battery Park, was where some twelve million immigrants to the United States were processed between 1892 and 1954, in the long, lantern-lit shadow of the Statue of Liberty. The plaque on the French-made statue still boldly proclaims:

> Give me your tired, your poor,
> Your huddled masses yearning to breathe free,
> The wretched refuse of your teeming shore.
> Send these, the homeless, tempest-tossed to me.
> I lift my lamp beside the golden door.

As for Ellis Island, this golden door has been a fascinating public

The Statue of Liberty with the World Trade Center and Lower Manhattan skyline, New York City. Photograph by Burt Glinn, 1986

museum since 1990, thriving in the even longer shadow of the New York skyline that, between 1892 and 1954, became one of the wonders of the modern world. I listened to the voices of long-dead immigrants recording their first impressions of New York, which for them, of course, was the United States, even though New York is completely unlike anywhere else in America, or for that matter anywhere else in the world.

In particular, I remember the lilting voice of an animated Irishman describing his first view of the city. It was 1913. Someone had shouted in time-honoured fashion, 'Land ahoy!', and what our man saw first as he rushed, aged eighteen, to the deckside was not the Statue of Liberty and her lamp of freedom, but the top and then the Gothic shaft of the Woolworth Building.

Of course it was what he saw first. Newly completed, the Woolworth Building was a staggering 792 feet (241 m) tall, far higher than the spires of the most ambitious Gothic cathedrals back in old Europe. In fact, it was the tallest building in the world, and had cost its client, Franklin Winfield Woolworth (1852–1919), founder of the famous 5-and-10-cent store, $13.5 million from his own unfathomable pocket. Designed by the architect Cass Gilbert, the Woolworth Building, with its gargoyles, turrets and pinnacles, was instantly dubbed the 'Cathedral of Commerce'. It was as much a symbol of New York as the Statue of Liberty, promising to that young Irish immigrant not just freedom, but the chance to think big. This was truly a land of opportunity, and a city where people walked very tall indeed.

After the completion of the Woolworth Building, New York entrepreneurs vied with one another to see who could build the biggest, tallest and best building not just in the city, but in the world. This race had been almost inevitable since 1854, when Elisha Graves Otis (1811–61) first demonstrated his safety lift, or elevator, to a huge, and hugely impressed, public. There had been elevators before Otis's. The invention this Vermont farmer's son patented was the elevator brake. The idea was simple, but no one had thought of it before. If the rope raising or lowering Otis's elevator broke, a tough, steel wagon spring would mesh with a ratchet running the height of the lift shaft; the spring would catch and hold the elevator. In 1854, Otis demonstrated his invention at the Crystal Palace Exposition, New York. With a large crowd watching, Otis ascended above it in an elevator climbing an open-sided shaft. Halfway up, he had the cable cut through with an axe. The crowd gasped; the elevator held fast. The modern lift had been born, and with it the Woolworth Building and the New York skyline.

Almost. For building so high into the sky there was one other necessary ingredient – steel. The very next year, the English inventor and engineer Henry Bessemer (1813–98) developed a process to mass-produce

Cass Gilbert's Woolworth Building

steel from iron. Steel, an immensely strong and stable material, was now available at a reasonable cost to the construction industry, and it was taken up with gusto in Chicago and New York. Although Chicago developed the first tall steel-framed buildings, it was New York that added the vital element of brio or panache to shape a skyline that made the Atlantic city utterly unlike any other.

There were other reasons for the rise and rise of New York, aside from the patents and inventions of Elisha Otis and Henry Bessemer. First there was pride, and competition among dynamic entrepreneurs. Then there was the nature of Manhattan Island itself. It was long, thin and made of granite, and building on it was never easy. And as the island filled up with its famous grid of streets and avenues, so it made sense to build ever higher. Having dug foundations into the all but unyielding rock, it made sense to use building sites efficiently, and the best way to do this, with more than a little help from Otis and Bessemer, was to reach for the sky.

As the towers rose, so the planning authorities began to worry about the nature of these new buildings. They might be exciting, but they blotted light out from the streets they rose from and those they overshadowed. The results were city-planning laws insisting that the new skyscrapers stepped back as they climbed. This 'zoning' shaped a whole generation of skyscrapers that narrowed as they ascended, and, in the case of the very tallest, were topped by the very slenderest of spires. By stepping up in the way ordered by local planning laws, these ultra-modern buildings harkened back to the very first tall buildings of all, the ziggurats, or stepped pyramids, of Mesopotamia, which rose synonymously with the world's first cities and thus civilisation itself. They also recalled the towers and spires of medieval cathedrals, to the extent that it was quite natural for Cass Gilbert to clad the steel-framed Woolworth Building in a limestone Gothic dress.

Yet by the time Walter P. Chrysler, a Michigan mechanic turned motor industry mogul, commissioned the Chrysler Building some fifteen years later, Gothic had given way to art deco. This was the whimsical if elegant style of decoration first shown to the public on a grand scale at the Paris Exhibition of 1925. Clearly Chrysler and his architect, William Van Allen, were enchanted by the style. They incorporated it in bold American ways throughout the sensational 1,048-foot-high (319-m) skyscraper. Chrysler was also determined not just to scrape the sky, but to pierce it. In the spirit that shaped the New York skyline, his was to be the tallest building in the world. Van Allen, however, would ensure that, despite its essentially simple brick-over-steel construction, it was also one of the most elegant.

Chrysler's former business partner, and now rival, H. Craig Severance, was busy at the time building the Bank of Manhattan Tower. This was to

The Chrysler Building, photographed by Fairchild Aerial Surveys Inc., 1931

Gargoyle, the Chrysler Building

be 927 feet (283 m) high, compared with Chrysler's original 925 feet (282 m). In secret, Van Allen devised a sun-motif stainless steel spire for his building that was only revealed at the very last moment. Hidden at the top of the building, the seven-storey spire was raised in just ninety minutes, making Chrysler's the tallest building in the world. With its seventy-seven floors, thirty-two elevators, restaurant, stores, beauty parlour and barber's shop, it was described as a city of its own.

Within just a few months of its opening it had been trumped – by the taller and vastly bigger Empire State Building. This art deco behemoth, clad in limestone, 102 storeys tall and climbing to 1,250 feet (381 m), was simply staggering. An entirely speculative venture, it was designed by the newly formed firm of Shreve Lamb and Harmon, who never did anything so remotely impressive again, despite working on a large number of Manhattan towers.

The Empire State Building reached so high into the Manhattan sky that its top floors were originally meant to serve as an airship terminal, especially for the ocean-liner-long Zeppelins sailing in airwaves high above the Atlantic from Germany. This was a thrilling idea, although best suited to the pages of a brand-new generation of science-fiction comics. In practice, the enormous uplifts of air generated by the building would have made it impossible for Zeppelins to dock or berth safely. Instead, the building won immortal worldwide publicity in 1933 when it played a starring role in the film *King Kong*. It certainly needed publicity. For all its sensational qualities, the Empire State Building opened in the very depths of the Great Depression following the Wall Street Crash of 1929. It was hard to let, and became known as the Empty State Building. It was only after the US entry into the Second World War that its floors filled with government bureaus, sending its seventy-three elevators whizzing up and down at stomach-churning speed.

King Kong atop the Empire State Building. Still from *King Kong*, 1933

And it was a Second World War bomber that nearly proved the tower's nemesis. Just days before the Japanese surrender, a twin-engined USAF B-25 crashed, in fog, into the seventy-ninth and eightieth floors of the skyscraper. These were the offices of the Catholic Welfare Council. Fourteen people died. The great building was dented, but stood firm. Clearly, though, skyscrapers were vulnerable. Had they reached their upper limit? Many commentators during the years of depression in the 1930s believed that they had. The visiting Swiss-French architect Le Corbusier offered a very different view, however. Like so many European architects arriving in New York for the first time, the Manhattan skyline took his breath away. Asked by the *Herald Tribune* what he thought of the city's by now world-famous skyscrapers, Le Corbusier replied to the effect that they were far too small. In fact, Le Corbusier was clearly puzzled by what he saw. The buildings were impressive, but somehow oppressive, too. In one of the lectures he gave at the Museum of Modern

Art during his 1935 trip, he said: 'The skyscrapers of New York are romantic, a gesture of pride, and that has importance of course. But the street has been killed and the city made into a madhouse.' This, from an architect whose dream had been to tear down much of the centre of Paris and rebuild it with tower blocks.

The streets were not killed by the tall buildings. In fact, Manhattan has remained one of the world's great walking cities, and life at the foot of the towers is remarkably animated. The skyscrapers Le Corbusier witnessed did make the city look like some sort of man-made mountain range, and they did shape streets that resembled canyons, deep in shadow at certain times of the day. Yet they were also spectacular, heroic and symbolic of a New York that refused to sleep and was determined to be the world's most successful city – financially, at least.

The skyscraper, and the streetscape it served, was far from dead in the aftermath of the Second World War. Refugees from Nazi Germany brought new ideas about city architecture with their luggage. On Park Avenue, between 1954 and 1958, Ludwig Mies van der Rohe, the great German architect, and third and last director of the Bauhaus, shaped the Seagram Building. This was not the tallest building in New York and far from being the biggest, yet it was an epiphany of Park Avenue cool, a building as elegantly and as powerfully dry as the martinis Mies drank at lunchtime, and as immaculate as his bespoke suits. Standing in its own custom-designed plaza, the Seagram Building was the model for thousands of lesser straight-up-and-down office towers built not just in New York but across the world in the 1960s. Urbane and sophisticated in the hands of a master like Mies, the Seagram Building was not a design to copy on the cheap. But copied it was, and from then on, New York appeared to lose its way with skyscrapers. No more stepped towers, spires and spirited decorative detail – just straight lines; offices that looked like filing cabinets and would be known, quite justifiably, as 'rent slabs'.

Then, in spring 1973, the twin towers of the World Trade Center were declared open. New York had done it again. Designed by the Japanese American architect Minoru Yamasaki, the towers were 110 storeys or approximately 1,368 feet (417 m) high. Designed as hollow steel boxes, they were immensely light structures, their floors supported by birdcage-like steel frames each comprising 240 columns and so framing extremely narrow windows. Here was a new building technology that, perhaps deliberately, perhaps by default, gave the towers a Gothic look. The New York skyscraper had come back to roost alongside the Woolworth Building.

The scale of the towers was mind-boggling. Together they housed fifty thousand office workers. Unmissable, though never pretty, they were

Soaring upwards, the twin towers of the World Trade Center

250

described at the time as the boxes that the Chrysler and Empire State Buildings came out of, while at the press conference held at the opening of the World Trade Center, Yamasaki told a reporter who had asked him why not design just the one tower with 220 floors, that he did not want 'to lose the human scale'.

The towers had their moments. They acted like a vast anchor on the New York skyline, appearing to pin the city to its granite base. From the Windows of the World Restaurant, located at the top of one of the towers, the view looking up towards central Manhattan was utterly thrilling. Small wonder that the terrorists who smashed two jet airliners into them on 11 September 2001 saw themselves as men with a mission to destroy two provocative symbols of US power.

They had missed the point. New York is not the United States. Its skyline represents a city of immigrants of all creeds, colours and ambitions. It measures the heights of financial success in its loftiest skyscrapers, while embracing, in between them, the humblest, in streets lined with a hugger-muddle of single-storey developments. It is a skyline rising from the nominally rational grid of an essentially romantic city that has always ridden high on its own myth. It is a skyline that promises the world. No matter how ragged it is in parts, it remains awe-inspiring even after many visits. You really would have to be dull of soul not to allow the Manhattan skyline into your mind and eyes as you ride a yellow cab from JFK to the city centre. And if you could sit on the terrace of the restaurant at the far side of Brooklyn Bridge at sunset and witness the lights of the city going on, up all the façades of the skyscrapers, and not be moved, then you would be a very cold fish indeed.

The debate over the skyline continues with the unholy row over the future of the World Trade Center. A needle-like Freedom Tower, patriotically 1,776 feet (541 m) high, originally designed by Daniel Libeskind and later by David Childs of Skidmore Owings and Merrill, continues to raise a titanic question mark over New York. Yet it may be that many of the parties involved are being far too self-conscious and questioning. Outsiders might tell New Yorkers to go, gung-ho, for the biggest and the best, just as Frank Woolworth did when he had Cass Gilbert design his 'Cathedral of Commerce' the best part of a century ago.

THE UNION PACIFIC 'BIG BOY' 4-8-8-4 FREIGHT LOCOMOTIVE

It was someone in the Schenectady erecting shop who chalked the legend 'Big Boy' across the frames of the biggest locomotive ALCO had ever been asked to build. ALCO was the American Locomotive Company, Schenectady the upstate New York town where steam trains had first run to nearby Albany in 1831. Over the ensuing 110 years, railroads had spread their steel web the length and breadth of the United States. The most extensive of all was the Union Pacific (UP). By the outbreak of the

The 'Big Boy' freight locomotive UP 4019 crossing Devil's Gate, Weber Canyon, Utah, September 1942

253

The early days of freight: UP 81 at Columbus, Ohio, early 1870s

Second World War, the UP ran trains west of the Mississippi and out in a great fork as far as Seattle and Los Angeles.

In shifting prodigious quantities of freight from west to east and east to west, Union Pacific trains had no alternative but to climb some of the steepest hills between the Rockies and the Appalachians. The most notorious sections of its tracks were between Ogden, Utah and Cheyenne, Wyoming. Running east from Ogden (elevation 4,355 feet/1,327 m), trains were faced a with a 62-mile (100-km) climb to a summit at 6,799 feet (2,072 m). Heading west from Cheyenne (elevation 6,060 feet/1,847 m), they faced a 30-mile (48-km) climb to the top of Sherman Hill (8,013 feet/ 2,442 m). This would have been tough going for a lightweight streamlined express in the years immediately before the Second World War, but for the massive freight trains needed to fuel the United States' war effort, these climbs demanded a Herculean effort on the part of UP locomotives. Now, imagine these great mountainous plains in the white depths of winter: the challenge they posed to railroad engineers was formidable.

This was where, late in the day, the US steam locomotive came to the rescue, making one last supreme effort before the oil-and-diesel lobby forced it into retirement. 'Big Boy' would be a veritable wonder – not the

254

biggest, nor the heaviest, nor even the most powerful of steam locomotives, but in terms of speed, usable power, availability and flexibility, the mightiest of all. The much-needed Hercules of the US railroads, it would push the development of the conventional steam locomotive, effectively devised by George and Robert Stephenson with *Rocket* in 1830, to its upper, outer and logical limits.

Throughout the 1920s and 1930s, the Union Pacific had specified ever bigger locomotives to deal with the Wahsatch and Sherman Hill climbs. Its three-cylinder 4-12-2 class, built between 1926 and 1930, was a good slogger but not particularly fast, and it was unable to cope single-handedly with future wartime loads. The UP's Challenger class 4-6-6-4 of 1936–44, was a maid of all work, able to run smoothly at up to 70 mph (113 kph) and to manage extremely heavy freight trains; yet even these giant machines had to be assisted by a second locomotive over the Utah and Wyoming peaks.

The UP wanted freight trains of at least 3,600 tons, pulled by a single locomotive and crew, over the grades that challenged their Challengers. This made economic sense, especially in wartime when manpower was inevitably going to be in short supply. This was why, in just three very intense months in 1940, the UP vice-president in charge of research, Otto Jabelmann, and his team in Cheyenne, drew up the specification and design for the 4000 class, the one and only 4-8-8-4 type ever built. Jabelmann's brief was to shape an articulated locomotive that could haul 3,600-ton freight trains (something like 110 fully laden British railway carriages) unassisted round the steep bends and up the Utah and Wyoming hills. To ensure a rapid turnaround of locomotives, freight cars and crews, the giant new locomotives would need to run fast, day in, day out. Jabelmann designed the 4000 class so that it would race safely at 80 mph (129 kph), although, except in test conditions, it never needed to run nearly so fast.

In 'Big Boy' – and this was the key to its success – the UP team designed not some muscle-bound monster, but a remarkably lithe machine, rather like a 16-stone (102-kg) marathon runner, or a heavyweight boxer capable of dancing round the ring for an entire match. Twenty-five were built, in two batches (in 1941 and 1944), at a cost of $256,000 each. They were undoubtedly BIG. They were absolutely the largest and weightiest machine the UP could run without entirely rebuilding its trackbed. As this was never going to happen, 'Big Boy' became the ultimate in UP steam power, and because of the precise and uniform nature of the duties it was called on to perform, twenty-four hours a day, it has more than a fair claim to be judged the greatest steam locomotive of them all.

To put the scale of 'Big Boy' into perspective, consider the comparative dimensions of the largest, latest and most powerful British freight

'Big Boy' UP 4019 in Weber Canyon, Utah,
20 October 1942

steam locomotive, the 9F 2-10-0 – designed under the direction of Robert
Riddles for the nationalised British Railways, and built between 1954
and 1960. Without its tender, a 'Big Boy' weighed 345 tons (and with it,
535 tons); a tenderless 9F tipped the scales at 86 tons. 'Big Boy' could
exert a theoretical tractive force of 135,375 lb (61,405 kg) compared to the
9F's 39,670 lb (17,994 kg). This is the brute effort that gets a train away
from rest. In practice, 'Big Boy' could generate a sustained output at the
drawbar – that is the power the locomotive has to pull its train after
subtracting the power it needs to move itself – of 6,290 dbhp at a steady
35 mph (56 kph). A 9F was known, for a burst of a few minutes, to produce
a maximum of 2,800 ihp, a rate measured in the cylinders and so including the power needed to work the locomotive as well as its train. At 132
feet 9.25 inches (40.5 m) long, 'Big Boy' was twice the length of its distant
British cousin.

Now, grasp a few more statistics before steaming out into the wilds
of wartime Utah and Wyoming. Inside 'Big Boy's' vast boiler, pressed to

256

300 lb/square inch (136 kg/6.5 cm²) (high for a locomotive), there were over 1 mile (1.6 km) of tubes and flues to heat. The firebox measured 150 square feet (14 m²). If you had been able to take the intense heat (2,500 °F/ 1,371 °C), you could have held a party inside. This enormous grate swallowed low-grade Wyoming coal, mined near the UP tracks, shovelled automatically from 'Big Boy's' fourteen-wheeled tender by a steam-powered Archimedes screw.

In full cry (and you can hear this in contemporary recordings), 'Big Boy' sounded like a fast-moving thunderstorm or a continuous broadside from a battleship as, with exhaust roaring from its triple blastpipe and chimney, it took 4,200-ton loads (well above its design specification) east and west over the hills that were its stamping ground and its one and only true test. Built for this single purpose, the 4000 class did exactly what it was meant to do, smoothly, reliably and well until the summer of 1959, when diesel traction finally took over the locomotives' regular duties. No individual diesel locomotive could match 'Big Boy's' power output, especially at speed, but several easy-to-service diesels could be coupled together in series and manned by a single crew: these would rival and, eventually, outperform 'Big Boy', a Goliath to their several Davids. A number of 'Big Boys' were kept steaming until 1962, by which time each of the original batch had run more than one million trouble-free miles (1,609,340 km), and US railroads were effectively 99 per cent steam-free. Eight out of the twenty-five were spared the scrapyard, although, to date, none has been returned to steam.

'Big Boy' was clearly an impressive machine. But a wonder of the modern world? I include it because, aside from the fact that to see one in action must have been a spine-tingling experience, 'Big Boy' carries the weight of the history of all conventional reciprocating steam railway locomotives on its broad steel shoulders. It was the steam locomotive itself that was a wonder, and 'Big Boy' was simply the most thrilling of them all. Yes, there were steam locomotives that ran far faster, in England (the streamlined LNER 4-6-2 'Mallard' may have reached 126 mph (203 kph) in July 1938), in Germany, and possibly in the United States.

There were more powerful locomotives in absolute terms, although in practice there was not really very much in it. The sixty-strong Allegheny H-8 class 2-6-6-6s of the Chesapeake and Ohio Railroad, built between 1941 and 1948, and put to work on 10,000-ton coal trains (the equivalent of about three hundred laden British passenger carriages) along the 80-mile (129-km) route up and over the Allegheny mountain passes between Hinton, West Virginia and Clifton Forge, Virginia, generated very nearly 8,000 dbhp: this was, at 40 mph (64 kph), a steam record, as much as five contemporary diesel locomotives combined. On a rolling test-bed at Altoona, Pennsylvania, a Pennsylvania Railroad Q-2 4-4-6-4 produced

The 'Mallard' London & North Eastern
Railway locomotive no. 4468 (built
in 1938 and reaching speeds of 126 mph
(203 kph)) pulling 'The Scarborough Flyer'
on its anniversary run to Scarborough
via the Harrogate–Leeds–York loop,
26 April 1987

7,987 ihp at 56 mph (90 kph). And yet, with diesels on the way, these ambitious freight locomotives were withdrawn from service in 1949, after just seven years. As for the Alleghenies, they were only ever asked to slog along at a steady 15 mph (24 kph) with their stupendous loads; they were almost never asked to tuck up their full metal skirts, and run.

In terms of thermal efficiency, the 'Big Boy' was not up to the standards of the very latest US steam locomotives, such as Paul F. Kiefer's 'Niagara' S1-b class 4-8-4 express passenger locomotives for the New York Central. Built to run from Albany, where electric-hauled trains from New York's Grand Central Station gave way to steam for the all but level 900-mile (1,448-km) run to Chicago, 'Niagaras' were very nearly as economical as the diesels growling at their steel heels. 'Niagaras' could pull 1,000-ton express trains (about thirty British carriages) at very high average speeds on runs with numerous stops. Near-silent in normal operation, and riding as smoothly as the passenger cars behind them, they rasped along at the line limit of 85 mph (137 kph), clocked up to 28,000 miles (45,062 km) a month, developed a steady 5,070 dbhp at 62.5 mph (100.6 kph), and were much loved by crews, maintenance staff and many passengers.

Even a 'Niagara', however, had to bow to the extraordinary efficiency of the locomotives designed, or rebuilt, for the SNCF, the French state railways, by André Chapelon. Chapelon's 242A1 three-cylinder compound 4-8-4 of 1946 weighed a total of 225 tons. An NYC 'Niagara' weighed 397 tons. The French locomotive was a revelation. It could produce 5,500 ihp and was easy on both coal and water. Restricted to running at the SNCF national maximum of 75 mph (121 kph), although it could run very much faster, it was still able to average speeds of just below this figure over pretty much any distance because of its ability to accelerate very rapidly indeed from a standing start. It could spin 700-ton trains over the 160 miles (258 km) from Paris to Lille in 140 minutes without exceeding 75 mph (121 kph). It simply went uphill as fast as it came down, just like an electric locomotive. Chapelon's mercurial 4-8-4 could outperform the latest electrics, and as a result it was nothing but an embarrassment to SNCF officials, who had embarked on a policy of electrification at all costs.

This was just the beginning. Chapelon had already planned a family of super-efficient standard steam locomotives for the SNCF. They included 125 mph (201 kph) passenger locomotives and a 6,000 ihp, 75 mph (121 kph) 2-10-4 freight locomotive, the frames of which were laid down before SNCF management cancelled the entire programme. The 242A1, meanwhile, led a rather tame life running expresses with almost absurd ease across Brittany. It was discreetly withdrawn in 1960, and scrapped.

By this time, 'Big Boy' was reaching the end of the iron road. Generally maintained in tip-top condition, these ruggedly handsome jet-black and graphite-grey locomotives had earned their keep many times over by the time their fires were dropped for the last time. They were much loved as well as highly regarded machines, a symbol of US can-do spirit during the 1940s, and muscular peace-making during the consumer boom that followed the Second World War. A 'Big Boy' had featured on the cover of *Time* magazine during the war, while, as they came up for retirement, the UP made a fine film about them. Called *Last of the Giants* (1958), this was a well-paced black-and-white documentary that captures beautifully the spirit of those mechanical wonders – a class of charismatic locomotives you feel they were not keen to lose.

A part of the wonder of the conventional steam locomotive is that it lasted for such a long time and was so effective. This was down to simple economics rather than affection. For a limited capital outlay, railways the world over were able to build or buy locomotives that offered speed, power and durability at the price no diesel could rival. Steam's luck finally ran out for several clear-cut reasons. Diesels were easier to service. On the whole they had better acceleration from standstill. They needed fewer crews. They could start at the turn of a key. They were

The wheels of the 'Big Boy'

versatile. No line manager would put a 'Big Boy' at the head of a lightly loaded passenger train. 'Big Boy's' job was singular and clear, to move mountains of freight over mountains. And while it did its job well, it was hungry for fuel. Its large tender could carry 28 tons of coal and 24,000 gallons (109,106 l) of water, yet, riding at full blast with a full load over the Wahsatch or Sherman hills, it would have to be refuelled after just 55 miles (89 km). Diesels could run all day on a tankful of oil. And, perhaps more than any other argument in its favour, the diesel appeared (however superficially) to be clean and modern. The diesel lobby, aligned with the oil industry, had considerable political clout. No matter how powerful, reliable, fleet of foot and admired, 'Big Boy' was never going to hold back the diesel for long.

In China, the world's last regular mainline steam locomotives are coming to the ends of their working lives. Significantly, perhaps, these are the Q J, or 'Forward', 2-10-2s modelled on an earlier Soviet Russian design that was, in turn, based on US practice. Despite many experiments over the decades to alter, or even revolutionise, the basic architecture of the classic Stephensonian locomotive, the last, and many of the best, steam locomotives remain true to character. Late-flowering steam engineers, notably the Argentinian visionary Livio Dante Porta (1922–2003), continued the attempt to increase the thermal efficiency and steaming of locomotives, but although they achieved great successes they were working against the grain. Even so, Porta's disciples, including the English engineer David Wardale, currently working on the design of a 124-mph (200-kph) steam locomotive for fast, main-line tourist trains, and Roger Waller in Switzerland, who has built some remarkably efficient mountain locomotives for the Brienz Rothorn Bahn, Zermatt, continue the campaign into the twenty-first century.

The language of the steam locomotive, meanwhile, remains an understandable joy to two centuries of railwaymen and enthusiasts: a compulsive vocabulary of pulsating exhausts, singing injectors, an insistence of pistons, the chatter and ring of connecting rods, the urgent hiss of safety valves, the hum of blower valves, a backbeat of air-brake pumps and the banshee wail or mournful chime of whistles. 'Big Boy' spoke this language with a big, spirited confidence. It was a great wonder of the industrial age.

THE DNA SPIRAL

In the Science Museum in South Kensington, there is a glass box shrouding a particularly delightful piece of early 1950s sculpture. As a child I would stare quizzically at this playful sight, a glorious double helix constructed from metal plates and rods arranged around a laboratory retort stand. I was told that it was important in the development not just of science, but of me. It took many years before I was able to grasp the fact that this captivating model represented one of the basic building blocks of life.

This was Crick and Watson's famous model, made in 1953, of DNA, or deoxyribonucleic acid, which contains the genetic instructions specifying the biological development of all cellular forms of life, and hands on genetic traits from generation to generation. I am much of what my father was and my grandfather before him, and of what my mother was and my grandmother before her, and so on back to Adam and Eve, or the first human beings, because of DNA. Its double-helix structure is made of countless codes or instructions that have determined not only the colour of my eyes and hair but also, to a certain extent, my health. I may have free will, and yet who I am and how I am have partly been decided for me. In this lies something of the conundrum certain religions pose when they claim that a person's life is predetermined even though that person is able to choose between good and evil.

So here it is, the 'molecule of heredity' – for more than a century one of the holy grails of science, finally successfully described and modelled by Crick and Watson, who are twinned in perpetuity like a firm of Dickensian solicitors or a pair of Victorian gravediggers. Certainly their research was forensic, and they dug hard and at great speed late into the night.

DNA, by the way, is not a single molecule; it is a chemically linked chain of 'nucleotides' composed of pairs of molecules twisting around one another, rather like the branches of a vine, to form a double helix. Nor does DNA come in just the one shape; the DNA helix can assume one of three slightly different geometries. The chain of helixes is, chemically speaking, a polymer made of a sugar, a phosphate and four kinds of 'nucleobases'. These bases provide the genetic code: just as a four-letter alphabet might spell out words, the sequence of the four kinds of bases along the length of the DNA molecule spells out the information stored in genes. Each human cell contains billions of base pairs lined up along nearly 6 feet (1.8 m) of DNA, all packed into a nucleus only one-twentieth the width of a human hair. Whatever its composition and exact

Reconstruction of the double-helix DNA molecular model discovered by Francis Crick and James Dewey Watson, 1953

geometry, DNA is a wonder; but the real wonder, for the world at large, was the discovery of its structure in a Cambridge laboratory in 1953 by two young academic research scientists.

Today, DNA is an acronym familiar to anyone who watches, listens to or reads news. The DNA profiling of suspected criminals, one of the most familiar offshoots of Crick and Watson's discovery, was developed in 1984 by the English geneticist Alec Jeffreys, and first used in the Enderby murder cases in Leicestershire. There are few educated people now who do not know that DNA located in blood, semen or hair at the scene of a crime can identify rapists and murderers. They may throw away and burn their clothes, wipe their fingerprints from knife handles and door locks, but not one of them can ever hide or disown their DNA.

Crick and Watson may not, as a result, be popular in criminal circles, but they have been the saviours of those found guilty for crimes they never committed and later proved innocent through DNA testing. More-over, Watson's own 1968 account of the discovery, *The Double Helix*, was hugely popular with the public at large, selling millions and translated into more than fifteen languages.

Scientists are also still exploring the use of DNA as a building material for making tiny devices and powerful computers that might serve us usefully, if controversially, in the future. In 1994, Leonard Adleman, of the University of Southern California, made headlines when he discovered a way of using tools from molecular biology, in particular DNA, for a new form of what might be called 'bio-computing'. A new generation of computers is emerging that will be as much biological as electronic and mechanical. At their ineffable hearts are the tight double-helix spirals of DNA, our link with our first ancestors and so beyond, into the very heart of creation.

The discovery of DNA was almost, if not quite, one of those 'Eureka!' moments, though neither James Dewey Watson (b. 1928) nor Francis Harry Compton Crick (1916–2004) were lying in hipbaths waiting for inspiration to strike on 21 February 1953 when they arrived at their epoch-making conclusions. The astonishing answer to the questions they had been raising and asking for the past eighteen months together in Cambridge University's Cavendish Laboratory, was in fact announced over Sunday lunch at The Eagle, a handsome Georgian pub in Benet Street, a week later. 'We have found the secret of life,' said Crick.

'When we saw the answer we had to pinch ourselves,' Watson told the BBC years later. 'Could it really be this pretty? We realised it probably was true because it was so pretty.' The model in the Science Museum is very pretty indeed. It has something of the look of the ancient Sumerian headdresses found in the royal tombs of Ur, or of the mobile sculptures of Alexander Calder, an artist whose work was fashionable and influential at the time of Crick and Watson's discovery of 'the secret of life'.

DNA itself was not unknown in the early 1950s. During the Second World War, researchers in the United States had demonstrated that the mysterious substance carrying genes from generation to generation was, in fact, DNA. But what did it look like, and how did it work? They even knew what DNA was made of, but had no clear idea of how the various elements in the DNA recipe combined to work as the genetic code.

Research into what would later be known as DNA had begun much earlier with the researches of the Swiss biologist Friedrich Miescher who, working with discarded surgical bandages, and later with the cells of salmon sperm, first isolated nucleic acids in 1868. From these very important early experiments into the nature of nucleic acids, and a wealth of other corroborating evidence, it was clear by the 1940s that DNA was the carrier of genetic information in all living cells.

Enter, in 1951, the researchers Crick and Watson – the first an English physicist, the second an American geneticist. It was a strange meeting. Crick, at thirty-five, still had no doctorate, while Watson, twelve years the Englishman's junior, had graduated from the University of Chicago at nineteen and gained his doctorate at the tender age of twenty-two. He came to Cambridge University, where the two met, the following year. From their first meeting, they lunched together nearly every day, and their colleagues quickly found them a room to share where they could talk away like birds – a booming one in the case of the loud and ebullient Crick – without disturbing anyone else. Both shared the ability to wander and even leap across boundaries and disciplines, to think very freely indeed.

'It was intellectual love at first sight,' says Victor McElheny, author of *Watson and DNA: Making a Scientific Revolution*. Not only did their interests coincide, Crick wrote later, but they shared 'a certain youthful arrogance, a ruthlessness, and an impatience with sloppy thinking'. Crick and Watson twisted around one another, platonically and intellectually, like the DNA double-helix spiral they were soon to uncover.

Francis Crick was born in Weston Favell, Northamptonshire, where his father and uncle ran the family's boot and shoe factory. Brought up a Congregationalist, he chose science over God at the precocious age of twelve, and was to remain a lifelong atheist. He later predicted that once the detailed workings of the brain were eventually revealed, traditional Western culture, with its foundation formed from erroneous Christian concepts about the nature of man and the world, would no longer be tenable; traditional concepts of the soul would be replaced by a new understanding of the physical basis of the mind.

He studied physics at University College London, obtaining a B.Sc. in 1937. During the Second World War he worked on the design of magnetic

Rosalind Franklin, whose X-ray 'Photo 51' of the double-helix cystals, *below*, led directly to Watson and Crick's discovery of DNA

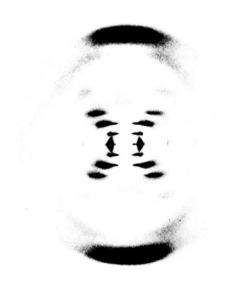

and acoustic mines. He began studying biology in 1947, swapping what he described as the 'elegance and deep simplicity' of physics for the 'elaborate chemical mechanisms that natural selection had evolved over billions of years'. He described this transition as 'almost as if one had to be born again'.

Crick was interested in two fundamental unsolved problems of biology – first, how molecules make the transition from the non-living to the living, and second, how the brain makes mind. Talkative, brash and immodest (he was said to have been an LSD user), he was clearly a challenging intellectual sparring partner and obviously an ideal one for James Dewey Watson.

Watson, born in Chicago, had been keen on birds for as long as he could remember, and became something of an expert ornithologist. At the age of twelve he starred on *Quiz Kids*, a popular radio show that challenged precocious youngsters to answer difficult questions. He enrolled at the University of Chicago aged fifteen. After reading Erwin Schrödinger's book *What Is Life?* in 1946, he changed his direction from ornithology to genetics. He graduated with a B.Sc. in zoology, aged nineteen, in 1947. Like Watson, he was, and remains, a devout atheist. A strong proponent of genetically modified crops, an offshoot of research into DNA, he has also said, repeatedly, that 'if the gene [for homosexuality] were discovered and a woman decided not to give birth to a child that may have a tendency to become homosexual, she should be able to abort the foetus'. Like Crick, his aim has never been to please, but to think – even if this means expressing thoughts that others might find offensive.

'Neither of us had a big ego,' Watson has, however, insisted. 'We just wanted to get the answer. Francis was brains ... I was the emotion.' At a conference in Naples before leaving continental Europe for Cambridge, Watson had seen a ghostly image of a DNA molecule produced by X-ray crystallography, a speciality of Crick's. DNA, he had heard, might be the stuff genes are made of. 'A potential key to the secret of life was impossible to push out of my mind,' he wrote later. 'It was certainly better to imagine myself becoming famous than maturing into a stifled academic who had never risked a thought.'

Meanwhile, as the talents of Crick and Watson bonded, a team of scientists at King's College London had for several years been performing experiments using the relatively new technique of X-ray crystallography Crick had witnessed in Naples. One of them, Rosalind Franklin (1920–58), had taken a now famous image of the X-ray diffraction pattern from crystalline DNA. It was Franklin's jealous older colleague, Maurice Wilkins (1916–2004), who let the ambitious young Watson, already fascinated by what he had seen in Naples, take a surreptitious look at Wilkins's hard-won image on a trip to London from Cambridge. Franklin

Francis Crick and James Dewey Watson constructing their DNA model, 1953

was, in fact, very close to discovering the structure of DNA herself, but Wilkins ensured that she was effectively isolated. Working in a largely male field, in an age when women were not even allowed in the pipe-smoke-filled faculty coffee room, she had no one to bond with, no supportive critic whose knowledge matched the gaps in hers.

Working as a close-knit team, Watson and Crick had already worked out what the X-ray photo of DNA should look like if their model was correct. So when Watson saw Franklin's image, he knew that he and Crick were on to a winner. Late in 1951, building on the X-ray diffraction results of Wilkins, Gosling and Franklin, he and Crick began work on their own model, even though they were not officially working on the subject.

In February 1953 Watson fitted the final pieces of the model into place, with cardboard replicas standing in for the vital bases of adenine, thymine, guanine and cytosine that serve as the vital rungs on the twisting ladder of the DNA spiral, and on 25 April the pair published their famous paper in *Nature*, having tossed a coin to decide whose name should go first. In it they revealed the double helix to the world and hinted at the fact that, because DNA has two strands, it should be able to create identical copies of itself. This was proved in 1958.

At the time, Watson said that Franklin would probably have got to the structure herself later in 1953 if he and Crick had not got there so quickly. Watson, Crick and Wilkins were to share a Nobel Prize for their work in 1962. Franklin herself had died of ovarian cancer, aged thirty-seven, in

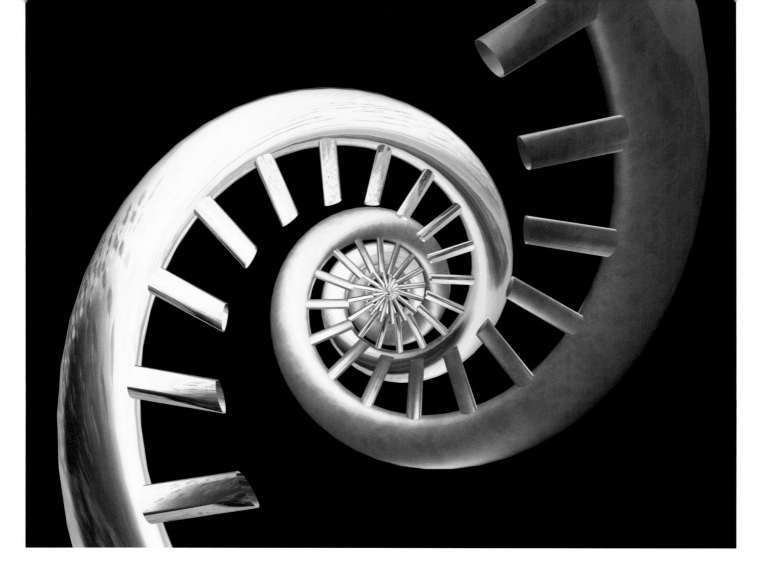

Computer-generated image of a golden DNA double helix unwinding. End-on view

'Dolly', the world's first cloned sheep, goes on display at the Royal Museum, Edinburgh, 9 April 2003

1958, unaware of the full impact of her image and Crick and Watson's now famous model.

From then on, the scientific spin-offs from this key discovery were as daunting as they were widespread. Between 1961 and 1965 the genetic code was cracked. In 1972 the first successful DNA cloning experiments were carried out in California. Five years later, the first human gene was

cloned. In 1982, genetically engineered insulin was approved for use in diabetics in Great Britain and the USA. And still to come were genetically modified crops, Dolly the Sheep and, very probably, the real life Frankenstein-style creations of the future, alongside nano-technology and a new generation of biochemical computers.

An image of a human hand with a strand of DNA. In DNA fingerprinting, a person is identified by the analysis of their own DNA, which carries a genetic code unique to that individual

And yet one of the most wonderful things about DNA is that you do not need to be a top-ranking scientist – neither Crick nor Watson, Franklin nor Wilkins – to create it for yourself in your own kitchen. This is all you need: a ripe kiwi fruit, table salt, non-concentrated washing-up liquid, a knife, a chopping board, measuring scales, a measuring jug, teaspoon and bowl, a saucepan of hot water, a large saucepanful of ice, a coffee filter and funnel, a tall thin glass and some fuse wire. With some patience and jiggling about, you will soon enough to be able to spoon out spirals of DNA from the resulting biochemical goo. There is something truly wonderful in being able to create, as it were, the building blocks of life, by yourself and in your own home. It took, however, leaps of the imagination, daring, cockiness and the quick and resourceful use of another's research to refine that resulting goo, or chemical soup, into the model of the double-helix DNA spiral still proudly on show in the Science Museum, South Kensington.

CONCORDE

Within a biblical lifespan, the Wright Brothers' 12-hp 'Flyer', the first powered aircraft to achieve flight – all 120 feet (37 m) of it – had evolved into a spacecraft capable of taking humans to another planet. This was the evolution of human flight in one logical direction, which reached its breathtaking climax in June 1969 when Neil Armstrong and Buzz Aldrin stepped out of *Eagle* and walked on the Moon. But there was another. On 9 February of that same year, Jack Waddell, senior Boeing test pilot, took off from Paine Field, Everett, Washington state, in a brand-new aircraft that was to revolutionise passenger flight. His mount was the Boeing 747, the 400-plus-seater, twin-deck airliner with a range of 5,500 miles (8,850 km).

Almost from the beginning, powered aircraft flew in two directions. The first headed into the realm of magic, dreams and poetry, of heroism: Blériot, Alcock and Brown, 'Biggles', Lindbergh, Amelia Earhart, Marina Raskova, Saint-Exupéry, 'Chuck' Yeager, Yuri Gagarin, John Glenn . . . the right stuff. They would lead us ever faster, higher, further above troposphere, stratosphere, mesosphere, thermosphere, onwards and upwards above the Earth's gravitational pull into star-spangled space. It was the stuff of nineteen-year-old pilot officer John Gillespie Magee Jr's lyrical poem 'High Flight' (1941):

> I've chased the shouting wind along, and flung
> My eager craft through footless halls of air.
> Up, up the long, delirious, burning blue
> I've topped the windswept heights with easy grace
> Where never lark, or even eagle flew –
> And, while with silent, lifting mind I've trod
> The high untrespassed sanctity of space,
> Put out my hand and touched the face of God.

This young American pilot met his maker in a Royal Canadian Air Force Spitfire in 1941. His was the stuff too, at least in part, of Yeats's ice-cold 'An Irish Airman Foresees His Death' (1922), written in memory of Major Gregory, who flew for the sake of flying against Germans he did not hate for the British he did not love:

> Nor law, nor duty bade me fight,
> Nor public men, nor cheering crowds,
> A lonely impulse of delight
> Drove to this tumult in the clouds . . .

This first direction was a thing of terrible beauty, ineffable sorcery, chariots of fire: an invitation on uncertain wings into the realm of eternal and unforgiving sky gods.

The second direction, the stuff of our everyday lives, was decidedly more prosaic, though no less intriguing. It also produced my sixth wonder. It started, perhaps, in 1935 with the Douglas DC3, the first recognisably modern and comfortable airliner, but came of age in 1958 when the sleek Boeing 707 airliner began to cross the Atlantic with regular ease. From then on, although no European would have known or admitted it at the time, Boeing was making the going: 'If it ain't a Boeing, I ain't going.' Boeing was making flying sewing-machine smooth, ticking away hours spent cruising the world's airwaves with the sure action of a Swiss-made quartz watch.

It was to become the stuff, not of epic poetry, but of a new form of curt blank verse, an international interrogative spoken not by thundering sky gods and jutting-jawed heroes, but, alas, by patronising sky nannies: 'Any wine at all with the meal, sir/madam?' 'Red or white?' 'Chicken or fish?' 'Can you put your seat in the upright position for me, sir/madam?'

And if not these obligatory lines, then the smooth assurances of captains and first officers reciting professional pilot mantras concerning outside air temperatures, height above sea level, and polite commands to fasten safety belts the moment the Boeing, or Airbus, encounters a mild turbulence that threatens to upset the food and coffee festering in the seat next to one's own. This is the world of the passenger aircraft, ever quieter, bigger and easier on fuel, never quite seen, but only glimpsed from those giant out-of-town shopping malls that double up as airports; vast machines attached to umbilical cords through which passengers shuffle in various states of nonchalance, boredom, irritation and fear; aircraft that fly with window blinds drawn firmly down in daylight so that the face of God is blotted out by those of soupy Hollywood actors on blurry video screens. In less than sixty-six years, the invention of the aircraft has taken us on one flight path to the Moon, and on another to planet 'Red or white?'. Poetry on the port wing, doggerel to starboard.

The point of the commercial airliner was to get more and more people from A to B, and eventually from A to Z, ever more cheaply. In such a world, that mechanical sky goddess, Concorde, for all its thundering magnificence, its technical mastery, was always going to be a supersonic sideshow. A century on from the Wright brothers, flight is regarded for the most part as a chore to be endured, a fug of fetid, low-pressure air, crippling seats, medical phobias, permanently engaged lavatories, backrests thrust into your face, stupefying airline magazines, food one would never dream of eating on terra firma, decor adapted as if from a high-street branch of a building society; these, and the occasional

Landing of the Bell-X1 Supersonic Test Plane, 14 October 1947

hard-won view of gloriously mutating skies, of cumulus clouds passing like fantastic white galleons, of cirrostratus whipping overhead like unbottled genies, of frost sparkling in infinite patterns on tiny aircraft windows, of boats bobbing on green seas far below, of another aircraft darting like some sudden arrow above your own: each a glimpse and gone for ever. For a few moments, it is just possible to capture the dream of aviators who took their improbable machines alone across violent seas and eventually up and through the sound barrier ('Chuck Yeager' in the Bell-X1 in 1947) towards the arc where atmosphere becomes outer space and conventional aircraft will, like Icarus, fall to earth.

Concorde was the Icarus of the aviation world. A wonder of the heavens as well as the world, it was the most thrilling of all passenger aircraft.

There were always those who had it in for this supersonic dart. Thunderously noisy, gas-guzzling and first-class exclusive, Concorde was deemed an anachronism by those who believed civil flight should go the way of chicken or fish rather than 'the high untrespassed sanctity of space'. Here was an aircraft flying, in every way, too close to the Sun.

Concorde finally fell to earth, its wings burned, on 25 May 2000, when an Air France machine, F-BTSC, crashed soon after take-off in Paris due to a catastrophic engine failure after a tyre burst. All 109 passengers and crew, and four people on the ground, were killed. The fourteen-strong Concorde fleet, flown by Air France and British Airways since 1976, was effectively grounded for good after this one fatal accident. The aviation expert Elmar Giemulla told Germany's *Bild am Sonntag* newspaper that the aircraft were 'flying time bombs', and that no civilised country should use planes more than twenty-five years old. The last scheduled Concorde flight took off from JFK Airport, New York, bound for London Heathrow, on 24 October 2003. The *Guardian* newspaper carried the story on its front page. I wrote it: 'The sky seems a little lower this morning; a

Soaring like a bird, Concorde takes its last flight, 24 October 2003

cathedral without a spire, a mountain without wolves. Yesterday Concorde, the Anglo-French sky goddess, drooped her nose for the last time in commercial flight, coming in to land among commonplace Boeings and Airbuses at Heathrow Airport.'

And then she turned and pirouetted slowly into her hangar to meet and greet the massed ranks of waiting TV cameras, as a hundred celebrities, captains of industry, competition winners, newspaper editors and at least one ballerina and a fashion model emerged from her nipped and tucked fuselage.

Down we came along the Thames over central London to join up with two other Concordes and to be welcomed by a crowd that was impossible to see through the aircraft's tiny windows. Down came a dream that – as the pilot Captain Mike Bannister was keen to remind us – could fly faster than a bullet, faster than the Earth rotated. A time machine of sorts that could transport those who could afford a ticket from London to New York and arrive at least an hour before they took off.

Concorde was always a star. Born into the glare of flashbulbs and global publicity, she was worshipped by the many who could never have afforded to drink champagne and dine on caviar in her pencil-thin cabin as she boomed across the Atlantic twice as high as jumbos and at twice the speed of sound.

The skies will seem quieter today, too. Concorde could always be heard before she was seen. That trademark thunderous rumble, as if the clouds were being pushed apart by some titan, caused heads to crane from city streets as she took off or came in to land. Generations of the environmentally conscious thought of her as an evil, smoke-belching dragon, a gas-guzzling curse, pandering only to the swinish rich.

Concorde has always been a singular aircraft. 'Look, there's Concorde,' people have said, pointing to the sky ever since she first took to the air in 1969, as if there has only ever been just the one of these dart-like planes. The future we dreamed of in the late 1960s has dissipated somewhere between meso-, strato- and thermospheres. Air travel is rarely glamorous a century on from the Wright brothers.

Captain Bannister, a Concorde veteran of twenty-seven years' standing, spoke of the aircraft's sporty acceleration as if he was letting out the clutch of a 1920s Blower Bentley or 1950s D-type Jag. Concorde, he told passengers, was one of the three great loves of his life, the others, perhaps thankfully, being his wife and daughter. This might be hard for those unmoved by machines to understand, but Concorde is, as pilots testify, one of the world's greatest flying machines – at once a work of art, icon, national emblem and a passenger plane that flies with *Top Gun* verve. But when was champagne ever served in a Mirage, Lightning or Tornado?

Captain Bannister spoke like an RAF or BOAC pilot of yore; his

Touching down at Exeter, 2000. The vortex created by Concorde's smoking tyres is awe-inspiring, but by 2000 cracks had been found in its great structure and the future of the aircraft was under threat

speech pattern and choice of words were those of the age in which Concorde was nurtured. Spitfires had gone out of service with the RAF in the Far East just two years before the supersonic programme that launched Concorde took flight. Her flight deck was adorned with pre-digital analogue dials. Like a Lancaster, she had a flight engineer to monitor her Rolls Royce Olympus engines; even the name of these conjures visions of heavenly realms.

An impulse of delight drove Concorde into the sky as much as any commercial consideration. Old Europe had something over both the superpowers of the 1960s and 1970s. The Soviet Union's Tu-144 Concorde lookalike came to a disastrous end, while Boeing's rival was never built. Boeing knew that the future lay elsewhere, in the 747 jumbo jet that made its maiden flight a month before Concorde did.

From the beginning, Concorde had been a quixotic episode in the history of flight. The international engineering team explored the very frontiers of technical knowledge developing a passenger aircraft that would boldly go where no passenger aircraft had gone before. That

Streamlined service: an air steward serves drinks on Concorde's New York route, September 2000

development occupied more than a decade of research and nearly five thousand hours of test flying.

The demands on the engineers were as weighty as Concorde had to be light. Many compromises were made in the design of the aircraft, yet the result was a beautifully sleek machine that looked wonderful, whether stork-like on the ground or dart-like in the 'delirious, burning blue'. The wing was a thing of wonder in its own right. Stunningly beautiful, apparently simple and all of a piece, close up it proved to be a thoroughly complex aerodynamic form with a precisely calculated degree of camber and taper across the wing structure itself and a combination of droop and twist along the leading edge. Camber, taper, droop and twist all made their contribution to Concorde's excellent characteristics at low speed without prejudicing its supersonic, fighter-like performance.

Featherweight yet immensely strong materials, such as titanium, were incorporated into the structure of an aircraft that would stretch at supersonic speeds, so great was the temperature of its skin (302 °F/150 °C), even though the air temperature around it could be many degrees below zero. The aircraft also had to fly subsonic in temperatures down to −49 °F (−45 °C).

Unlike an up-intercept-and-down jet fighter, Concorde was designed

276

to cruise at Mach 2, or 1,350 mph (2,173 kph), for more than two hours at a time. The engine chosen was the 593-series development of the Rolls Royce Olympus first designed for the RAF subsonic delta-winged Vulcan nuclear bomber and first flown in service in 1956 – a case of swords into ploughshares, if such an agricultural metaphor could ever be applied to such a heavenly machine.

Concorde 001 was rolled out from its hangar at Toulouse on 11 December 1967. Until then the project had been called Concord, but as the British minister of technology Anthony Wedgwood-Benn explained to the 1,100 guests that day, the aircraft would now be known as Concorde, the 'e' standing for 'excellence, England, Europe and entente'. She made her maiden flight on 2 March 1969 with chief test pilot André Turcat at the controls, went supersonic that October and reached Mach 2 in November 1970. More than five years later, British Airways began flying a regular Concorde service from London to Bahrain and Air France from Paris to Rio via Dakar. After many months of discussion over noise levels, both airlines were finally able to fly their Concordes in and out of New York from November 1977.

The maiden flight in England of Concorde 002, at Fairford, 10 April 1969

277

For the next two decades, Concorde was beloved of the rich, famous and otherwise spoilt. Environmentalists railed against the aircraft even though there were only ever fourteen Concordes in service. Originally airlines as diverse as Qantas, Lufthansa and Iran Air had all ordered the supersonic airliner, but one by one they fell by the wayside, leaving the Anglo-French aircraft in the sole hands of the British and the French.

Commercially, Concorde was a doomed wonder from the start. Remember the Concorde-like Pan American spaceliner in Stanley Kubrick's *2001: A Space Odyssey*? Slyly, Kubrick showed us how the sorcery of space flight might quickly become as boring and as routine as commuting to the office, even though the machinery itself would be soaring into infinite space. The interior of Kubrick's Pan American space Concorde was satirically bland. A VIP scientist passenger sucked at glum food served by dolly-bird space-stewardesses. The pretentiously uniformed captain and first officer had nothing to do but smile toothpaste smiles and monitor computer displays while the machine flew itself.

Outside, though, the spaceliner was shown to be pirouetting through a majestic backdrop of stars, Moon and rotating space-station accompanied by Strauss's weightless *Blue Danube Waltz*. The beauty, poetry and wizardry of flight, of air and space travel, Kubrick implied, would be ever further removed as humans learned to live passive, strapped-in, 'red or white' lives. Concorde was never going to break the barrier of routine and banality, but it was an outburst of romance in an industry bent on commercial efficiency, and as such one of the great wonders of our age.

THE CERN PARTICLE ACCELERATOR

What is matter made of? What is the fundamental building block of the universe? If you happen to be a bird or a fish, a cat or a dog, such questions are unlikely to bother you. Life exists for its own sake; it is its own meaning, and ideally, though set about with dangers, its own pleasure and joy. Humans, though, are questioning creatures. We want to know what this universe is made of as well as why it exists, when it was created and how big it is. We want to know whether it is a sentient organism, the product of some divine being, a colossal figment of our own imagination, a mirror of some parallel universe, or a kind of quintessence of stardust, ultimately unknowable even as we hold it in the palm of our hands and blow it away whether in the form of grains of sand, dog hairs, dandelion seeds or sneezing powder.

CERN, the European Centre for Nuclear Research, exists to answer questions along these lines. Largely hidden underground, it straddles the Swiss-French border near Geneva. It is the world's largest particle-physics research centre, employing some three thousand scientists,

An aerial view of the CERN laboratory complex, near Geneva. The circle shows the underground path of the LEP (Large Electron–Positron Collider). The smaller inner circle denotes the tunnel of CERN's existing proton–antiproton collider. CERN's main laboratory, Site Meyrin, is immediately to the south-west of this circle

Particle accelerator inside the Compact Muon Solenoid (CMS) Assembly Rooms, CERN laboratory

technicians and other full-time staff, and host during any year to some 6,500 particle physicists from eighty or so countries. It has often been described as the United Nations of the scientific world. There is nowhere else like it – at least, not in our world.

Its most famous machines, truly giant contraptions, are the accelerator rings running around a circle with a circumference of 17 miles (27 km), 328 feet (100 m) below fields of mulching cows and prosperous vineyards. These extraordinary tools make CERN one of the wonders of the modern world. Its job is to help researchers raise questions about the origins of matter and the universe and to try to find answers by accelerating particles of matter to phenomenal speed, then smashing them together in the hope of finding matter at the heart of matter, and ultimately matter so small that those peering at them will be somehow staring into the essence of the universe, the face of God.

'The most interesting problem about the cosmos, about the universe', says Álvaro de Rújula, a theoretical physicist (which is not to say he does not exist) from Spain who works at CERN, 'is . . . what is there in those pieces of universe where there is nothing?' Masaki Hori, a Japanese research physicist, says, 'My current interest is . . . to understand how these small particles fit into the real world . . . We're made of particles, but it's not certain how these small particles come to be us.'

There are as many questions as answers at CERN. Its range is truly infinite. At its core, though, is the big question relevant to every last dark corner of its immense research programmes: what are the most fundamental building blocks of all matter, the pieces of matter that make up everything from flowers to people to galaxies, and which cannot be broken down into anything smaller?

It was not so long ago that scientists thought the most fundamental building block of matter was a particle called the atom. For some while we have known that the atom is made of many smaller pieces. Every atom contains a central core called the nucleus, made of protons and neutrons.

The nucleus is surrounded by mostly empty space, except for very tiny particles called electrons that orbit the nucleus. Each atom is like a tiny model of a solar system. And just as there are, as yet, unknowable numbers of solar systems out there beyond us in deep space, so each of us is made up of many millions of these tiny solar systems. As such, we are essentially a part of the great spinning structure of nature's million-fuelled bonfire, the star-lit universe. We are, truly, stardust – at once carbon or immortal diamond, as well as the spaces between the nucleus and the electrons orbiting an atom and the elusive particles that bind these together.

Recently, scientists have discovered that protons and neutrons are made of smaller particles known as quarks. Today, physicists do not know for certain if there is anything smaller than quarks and electrons, but there might be. And what, in any case, are quarks and electrons made of? 'Nothing', as King Lear reminds us, 'comes of nothing.' We must speak again of what exists beyond a visible, or apparent, nothing.

How can such sub-particles be found? One way, so CERN scientists believe, is to recreate the conditions that existed less than a billionth of a second after the Big Bang occurred.

Scientists believe that when this cataclysmic event took place, whether by the hand of some almighty god or by chance, the ambient temperature was about 1,859 °F (1,015 °C). At that temperature materials and matter that seem so familiar to us behave very differently. Iron, for example, which seems a solid enough material, and a metal able to conduct electricity and to create a magnetic field, becomes a free-floating gas. By accelerating matter – that is, particles, and in particular protons – to great speeds, and thus to Big Bang temperatures, CERN scientists hope to detect, as the accelerated matter cools down again, something about the forces behind the creation of elementary particles. This force is known at CERN as the Higgs Particle, or Field of Particles. Nominally, this fills the universe uniformly and interacts with all other particles giving them mass. So out of nothing comes something after all. That iron bar. A cow. A park bench. A vineyard. Geneva. A CERN physicist. You and me.

CERN explains the Higgs Field this way:

The Higgs Field clustering effect

Imagine you're at a Hollywood party. The crowd is rather thick, and evenly distributed around the room, chatting. When the big star arrives, the people nearest the door gather around her. As she moves through the party, she attracts the people closest to her, and those she moves away from return to their other conversations. By gathering a fawning cluster of people around her, she's gained momentum, an indication of mass. She's harder to slow down than she would be without the crowd. Once she's stopped, it's harder to get her going again.

This clustering effect is the Higgs mechanism, postulated by British physicist Peter Higgs in the 1960s. The theory hypothesises that a sort of lattice, referred to as the Higgs Field, fills the universe. This is something like an electromagnetic field, in that it affects the particles that move through it, but it is

282

also related to the physics of solid materials. Scientists know that when an electron passes through a positively charged crystal lattice of atoms, i.e. a solid, the electron's mass can increase as much as forty times. The same might be true in the Higgs Field: a particle moving through it creates a little bit of distortion, like the crowd around the star at the party, and that lends mass to the particle.

The original version of this metaphor concerned a prime minister entering a room full of party workers, yet was otherwise identical. It was given voice by Professor David Miller in response to a challenge by the then British Minister of Science, William Waldegrave, in 1993. Given that British taxpayers were putting a lot of money into CERN without understanding what it was, what it did and why we needed it, Waldegrave challenged the physicists to come up with an easy answer to the question, what is the Higgs Particle?

Miller's was a good attempt at an answer for something hypothetical that may or may not exist in some form or other, or even no form at all. Sometimes referred to as the 'holy grail of particle physics', or the 'God particle', the Higgs is a hypothetical particle, which if it does exists has, so far, evaded detection. Its discovery, should it exist, would make the scientists who found it wonders of the universe.

Work on the particle accelerator that would prove the case, or not, began at CERN in the mid-1980s with the construction of the Large Electron Positron Collider (LEP). It resided inside the 17-mile (27-km) underground tunnel which crosses the Swiss-French border with happy impunity. LEP ran from 1989 until 2000 conducting a number of experiments. From 1995 its energy was cranked up to maximum level to search for the Higgs Particle, and anything else for that, or any other, matter. But protons were always going to require more energy to accelerate than the LEP could provide. Though you would not notice if one or the other were placed in the palm of your hand, electrons and positrons, the primary subject of LEP experiments, are much lighter than protons. So in 1994 CERN began work on the Large Hadron Collider (LHC), to replace LEP.

Meanwhile, in the USA, American physicists, determined not to let the Europeans find the Higgs Particle unchallenged, were drawing up their own plans. The USA had a large particle-accelerator centre constructed at Fermilab near Chicago. To search for the Higgs, however, they too would need a higher-energy machine that they had at first. In 1983 the US Department of Energy recommended the construction of a high-energy proton collider. Naturally, it was bigger and, it was hoped, better than anything conceived of or planned in old Europe. The proposed Superconducting Super Collider (SSC), with a circumference of 54 miles (87 km), would in fact have been the biggest machine ever built.

Engineers align elements of the Omni Purpose Apparatus for LEP (OPAL) detector at the CERN laboratory, one of four giant particle detectors at the LEP. It collides electrons and positrons accelerated to an energy of 50 GeV via a circular tunnel 330 feet (100 m) underground and 17 miles (27 km) in circumference. OPAL's apparatus fits together like the layers of an onion around a central point where the particles collide. The photograph shows OPAL's cylindrical central detector, at centre, behind the Hulftegger crane, and its two 'caps', far left and right (the latter partly obscured by the scaffolding), which fit onto either end of the central section

If the Higgs existed in the expected 'mass range' of scientific observation, such a machine might have been expected to find it easily enough. And if the SSC sounded too good to be true, it was. Construction started in Ellis County, Texas, at around the same time as CERN's LEP. After several years of ever-rising costs, from $6 billion to $10 billion, President Clinton cancelled the project in 1993.

Back at CERN, during the final few months of LEP's operation, scientists believed they had evidence of the Higgs Particle. Sadly, this was not the case. The media was predictably tough and cynical, many journalists and mountebank commentators calling CERN a waste of time, energy and money. The CERN physicists, however, have remained optimistic, and their researches have already led to fascinating, useful and world-changing discoveries. Several CERN researchers, including the English scientist Tim Berners-Lee, inventor of the World Wide Web, and Georges Charpak, inventor of the multi-wire proportional chamber (a breakthrough in the technique for exploring the innermost parts of matter), are Nobel Prize winners. They are all excited about work in progress on CERN's LHC, a particle accelerator which will probe deeper into matter than ever before.

Due to switch on in 2007, LHC is designed to collide beams of protons at an energy of 14 TeV. Beams of lead nuclei will be also accelerated, smashing together with a collision energy of 1,150 TeV. A TeV is a unit of energy used in particle physics: 1 TeV is roughly equivalent to the energy of motion of a flying mosquito. What makes the LHC so exciting and so extreme for CERN physicists is the fact that it will squeeze energy into a space about a million million times smaller than a mosquito. Metaphorically, this would be like God squeezing the universe into His, Her or Its clenched palm. It is a terrifying and remarkable thought. And what on earth or, more appropriately, what in the universe will come of it? The Higgs Field, if it is revealed, will only last for a small fraction of a second – and then decay into other particles. So in order to tell whether the Higgs has actually appeared in the collision, researchers will look for evidence of what it would have decayed into so soon after the proton smash. And even if it does exist, does it really matter? Is all this effort to build a gigantic particle accelerator simply there to excite the curiosity of physicists?

The answer is yes and no. Getting physicists excited leads ultimately to inventions, whether we see these as useful or not, or whether the challenge is in terms of good and evil, as with the splitting of the atom which, while threatening to blow us all away, may yet have maintained an uneasy peace among warring humans since the bombing of Hiroshima and Nagasaki in 1945. The discovery of mysterious X-rays, cathode rays, alpha and beta rays, among others, has, however, not only helped our very incomplete understanding of the universe, but offered us along the way such seemingly commonplace devices as television, transistors, medical imaging devices and computers. CERN's up-and-coming LHC will break matter down as humans have never been able to do before, and who knows what good might come of this process.

The machinery itself required to break matter down, and down again, is certainly impressive in scale, although it has few moving parts for visitors to gawp at. Its marathon pipes, in which particles will run ever faster laps of the great 17-mile (27-km) CERN circuit, as they are accelerated to way beyond giddying speeds, gleam into the darkness of the concrete-lined tunnel that curves forever away from sight deep below the Franco-Swiss landscape. The paths of racing protons will be kept in check by batteries of superconducting magnets, the surfaces of which will be kept to a temperature of 1.9 Kelvin (or something like 500 °F/300 °C below normal room temperature), by being soaked in liquid helium. At such way-below-Arctic temperatures they will work with astonishing effectiveness. When the protons, accelerated in tubes in two directions, meet one another in a head-on crash, they will burst into millions of fragments. And, if they look quickly enough, CERN's physicists might just be able to detect something new, the elusive ghost perhaps of the matter at the heart of matter, the universal glue.

Perhaps, then, it is surprising to find CERN so discreet. Yes, it has an interesting website, and yes, it encourages visitors through its doors to see for themselves what progress is being made in the search for the basic building blocks of our universe. And yet there are no grand building blocks in architectural terms to celebrate the special nature of CERN. It can seem rather strange, and rather special too, that CERN's researches into the particles that may connect the extremities of the universe with the Earth, us and our pets, are conducted, troglodyte fashion, deep underground. A visitor to CERN might expect some gleaming ultra-modern tower or spire to mark the centre of this intriguing world. But, no, this wonder of the modern world, so unlike the Great Pyramid of Cheops, Chartres cathedral or the Forth Railway Bridge, is utterly modest, almost as invisible as the protons that, soon enough, will be whizzing around CERN's magical cavern in search of a particle of matter as momentous as it is minuscule.

Pure energy: a computer-processed photograph of the tracks of sub-atomic particles produced in a proton–anti-proton collision at a total energy of 900 GeV, recorded in the UA5 detector at CERN

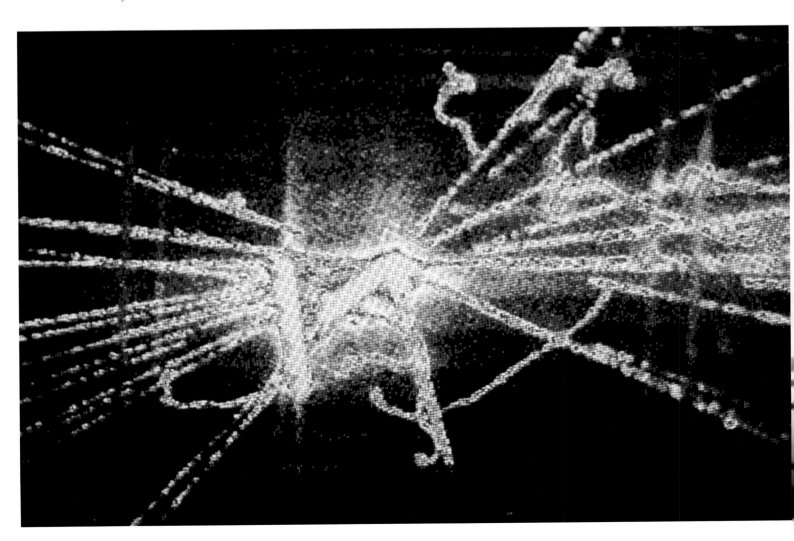

EPILOGUE

Jonathan Glancey

ALL THAT'S SOLID melts into air,' wrote Karl Marx and Friedrich Engels in *The Communist Manifesto* (1848). They were writing about what they saw as capitalism's dance of creative destruction, the great meltdown of place and history in which all previously fixed relationships, of family, community, faith and work were dissolved into a splintered, competitive mess driven by the bourgeois profit motive.

For better or worse, and perhaps a bit of both, an old world of ordered certainty was indeed broken up by the financial forces that drove the great cogwheels, flywheels, cranks and pistons of the Industrial Revolution. The early days of that world-changing revolution resulted, as my essays in the final chapter of this book hope to show, in nevertheless glorious structures and machines that might surely be classed as wonders of the world. And yet Marx was right in the sense that the material world, at least, was dissolving. Not, of course, in the sense that we and all substantial creation were about to vanish, but in the sense that the big solid world of man-made wonders, of cathedrals, of steam locomotives, of heroic industrial machines, were on their way to being reduced in stature in our consciousness – even if they were not to vanish altogether.

What, after all, are the wonders of the contemporary world, and what are the wonders to come? Today, many of the latest wondrous achievements are all but insubstantial. The World Wide Web is one. A plague for those of us inundated with email – much of it 'spam' or junk perhaps, yet a marvel that, though it had been anticipated and predicted over many decades, was unrealisable until very recently. Yet even when realised, there seems to be so little reality to it: here is a microscopic wonder, a thing of electronic pulses and signals that only makes any sense at all to us because its seemingly ineffable workings finally come together on the glowing screens of computers and multi-purpose mobile phones.

Other contemporary wonders come from the world of medicine, physics and genetics. Again, these are tiny wonders in the physical sense, and clearly no match for an Egyptian pyramid or Concorde, yet many have, or have had, the power to affect the lives of every being on our planet. Will wonders of the world, then, cease? Cease, that is, in terms of great, awe-inspiring artefacts made by human hands? I don't think so. I am happy to think that such wonders will continue to enchant and inspire us even in future ages, when those who come after us might well live in a world run by ever tinier machines and infinitely smaller, even if greater, inventions, discoveries and revelations. Why? Because, at least for the foreseeable future, we are not just sentient, but sensual creatures:

> Thou mastering me
> God! giver of breath and bread;
> World's strand, sway of the sea;
> Lord of living and dead;
> Thou hast bound bones and veins in me, fastened me flesh . . .

This is how the Victorian poet and Jesuit priest Gerard Manley Hopkins expressed this fact and feeling. You do not have to share his religion to share his sense of the might and magnificence of creation and the creative spirit, and our reaction to it as creatures of flesh and blood. Just as we will always be drawn to the beauty of the natural world, whether to the flight of a bird, a mackerel-clouded sky, a numinous sunset, shadows cast along a snow-laced valley, the sway of the sea, so we will continue to marvel at the bravest and boldest of our physical creations even as the scientific, technological, electronic and medical minutiae of our world appear, increasingly, to melt into the air.

ILLUSTRATIONS

294

299

INDEX

Numbers in italics refer to pages with illustrations.